MENSA
QUIZ
BOOK

Cover answers

The answers to the questions on the back of this book's cover are:

Nitrogen is the major constituent of ordinary air.
Shogi is a Japanese board game resembling chess.
Sirimavo Bandaranaike of Sri Lanka was the world's first woman prime minister.
Sheherazade by Rimsky-Korsakov is based on *A Thousand and One Nights*.

This edition published by Barnes & Noble Inc.,
by arrangement with Carlton Books Limited

1997 Barnes & Noble Books

0-7607-0431-7

Printed and bound in Great Britain

MENSA

QUIZ

BOOK

ROBERT ALLEN

BARNES
&NOBLE
BOOKS
NEW YORK

Contents

How to use this book...........6

Introduction........................7

Easy quizzes

Medium quizzes

Tough quizzes

How to use this book

Each quiz has exactly 50 questions. Many are themed, and some are completely random – the "Pot Luck" quizzes. They have been categorized according to how difficult they are (of course you may disagree!):

Easy – for children   **Medium** – for teenagers and young adults   **Tough** – for adults

There are 36 quizzes in each level. All the easy quizzes appear in the first section of the book, the medium quizzes in the central section, followed by the tough quizzes toward the end. All the answers are at the back of the book, following the same order as the quizzes.

You may want to answer questions from a whole quiz each, or two or more of you may want to play the same quiz against each other. So that no-one can be accused of picking out the hardest questions to ask his or her opponent, a random grid has been provided on each quiz to divide the questions fairly.

Enjoy yourself... and you may even learn something!

Introduction

It is strange that at a time when quizzes have never been more popular, general knowledge seems to be in decline, especially among children. Go into many bars and you will see a notice advertising quiz night. Ask a school kid for the capital of Poland and you will probably be met with a blank stare. Schools tell us that there is just not time to fit general knowledge in as a subject.

There is also a convenient but wholly reprehensible theory that it is useless to carry information in your head that you could just as well look up in a library. This is nonsense! Without a sound base of general knowledge it is not possible even to be aware of the extent of your own ignorance.

What use, we are asked, are a bunch of disconnected, half-remembered facts? The answer is simple. If you have known something, even though you have long since forgotten the details, you will, when the occasion arises, be able to dredge up that vital bit of information. If you never knew it in the first place, your chances of finding what you want will be slim at best.

Adults have discovered that general knowledge is fun. They run quiz nights for each other and meet to play general knowlege-based board games. Why do they assume that children should not enjoy it too? This book aims to restore a neglected subject to the family agenda and to teach a new generation of kids that knowing things is not a bore.

If you like this book you will like Mensa – a society that exists entirely for people who like to use their brains. If you would like to take the Mensa test and meet people of like mind, then write to us at British Mensa Limited, Mensa House, St John's Square, Wolverhampton, WV2 4AH, England (tel: 01902 772771), or contact Mensa International, 15 The Ivories, 628 Northampton Street, London, N1 2NY, England (tel: 0171 226 6891).

I should like to thank all those who helped with this book, including my wife Doris and my long-suffering editor Liz Wheeler. Facts can be tricky things and, though we have tried to check every answer, there is always the chance that someone has better information. If you want to suggest improvements for a future edition, please write to me at the Mensa address.

Robert Allen
Editorial Director,
Mensa Publications.

History

Answers to this quiz are on page 224

EASY 😊 **EASY**

Player 1	Player 2
12	20
33	24
07	03
46	45
01	28
21	02
23	25
04	32
35	39
14	50
31	08
48	17
11	40
27	43
15	29
06	41
10	30
47	34
26	16
38	05
36	49
13	09
19	18
42	37
44	22

01 How many wives did Henry VIII have?

02 Who was the first president of the USA?

03 The invasion of which country led to the outbreak of World War II: (a) Austria, (b) Poland, (c) France?

04 Which French heroine was burned at the stake having been tried for witchcraft?

05 Cleopatra ruled which country: (a) Egypt, (b) Italy, (c) Turkey?

06 What led to the sinking of the Titanic in 1912?

07 Which French statesman crowned himself emperor in 1804?

08 Which English admiral won the battle of Trafalgar?

09 Who was Spain's dictator until his death in 1975?

10 Which admiral organized the German navy of World War I?

11 Which African–American civil rights leader was shot dead in Memphis in 1968?

12 In which army was Moshe Dayan an important figure?

13 What were the Russian heads of state called before the Revolution in 1917?

14 Who was American president at the start of World War II: (a) Truman, (b) Roosevelt, (c) Jefferson?

15 Who succeeded Bloody Mary as queen of England: (a) Elizabeth I, (b) Victoria, (c) Mary II?

16 When Columbus discovered America in 1492, where did he think he had landed?

17 The Battle of the Somme took place during which war: (a) World War I, (b) Word War II, (c) First Napoleonic War?

18 Which American president became famous for abolishing slavery?

8

19 Who was leader of Germany during the Third Reich?

20 Which judge presided over the Bloody Assize?

21 Where did the Incas originate: (a) Brazil, (b) China, (c) Peru?

22 In which battle did Sitting Bull defeat General Custer: (a) Little Bighorn, (b) Wounded Knee, (c) Bull Run?

23 Which aviator made the first non-stop flight across the Atlantic: (a) Amelia Earhart, (b) Orville Wright, (c) Charles Lindbergh?

24 What started in Pudding Lane on September 2, 1666?

25 Which city was divided into four sectors at the end of World War II?

26 Who was responsible for the assassination of Julius Caesar: (a) Nero, (b) Brutus, (c) Octavian?

27 In which city was Archduke Franz Ferdinand assassinated, causing the start of World War I: (a) Vienna, (b) Munich, (c) Sarajevo?

28 The Battle of Bosworth Field took place during which war: (a) English Civil War, (b) Wars of the Roses, (c) The Hundred Years' War?

29 What was Baron Manfred von Richthofen popularly known as?

30 What was Ferdinand, Graf von Zeppelin famous for?

31 Which civilization did the Norsemen belong to: (a) Vikings, (b) Anglo-Saxons, (c) Franks?

32 What was discovered in California in 1848?

33 When was the American Declaration of Independence: (a) 1776, (b) 1800, (c) 1865?

34 Which state succeeded the Roman Empire: (a) the Carthaginian Empire, (b) the Ottoman Empire, (c) the Byzantine Empire?

35 The Hundred Years' War was between which two countries?

36 In which American state did the English first settle in 1607: (a) Florida, (b) Virginia, (c) Philadelphia?

37 From which French town were more than 330,000 Allied Troops evacuated in 1940: (a) Cannes, (b) Boulogne, (c) Dunkirk?

38 In which country did the Industrial Revolution start?

39 What was the Great War: (a) World War I, (b) World War II, (c) The Hundred Years' War?

40 What, in the 16th century, were the conquistadores?

41 Who was the Russian monk who reputedly could treat the czarevich's haemophilia?

42 Which event triggered the Great Depression?

43 Which army were known for their black-shirted uniforms?

44 Which American gangster was also known as Scarface?

45 Which treaty ended World War I: (a) Treaty of Versailles, (b) Treaty of Brest-Litovsk, (c) Treaty of Washington?

46 What was the Japanese warrior class that rose to power in the 11th century?

47 What is the town of Auschwitz associated with?

48 The tomb of which king was found almost completely intact: (a) Ikhnaton, (b) Tutankhamen, (c) Nefertiti?

49 During which war was the tank first used?

50 William the Conqueror was duke of which French province?

9

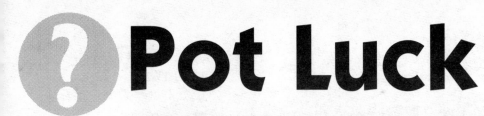

Pot Luck

Answers to this quiz are on page 224

EASY 😊

	Player 1	Player 2
	12	20
	33	24
	07	03
	46	45
	01	28
	21	02
	23	25
	04	32
	35	39
	14	50
	31	08
	48	17
	11	40
	27	43
	15	29
	06	41
	10	30
	47	34
	26	16
	38	05
	36	49
	13	09
	19	18
	42	37
	44	22

01 What is another name for the constellation known as the Big Dipper?

02 What was the name of Robin Hood's girlfriend?

03 Who owned a sword called Excalibur?

04 How many grams are there in a kilogram?

05 What colours would you mix to make purple?

06 Is a north wind coming from or going to the north?

07 What drink is Brazil famous for?

08 Of which country is Stockholm the capital?

09 Which of these Native American tribes did not live on the great plains: (a) Sioux, (b) Apache, (c) Cheyenne?

10 Mohammed was the founder of which religion?

11 Which city is the capital of France?

12 What is titanium: a) animal, b) vegetable, c) mineral?

13 What, according to the proverb, do birds of a feather do?

14 What forms the main diet of the heron?

15 What is a Colt .45?

16 For what purpose were dachshunds originally bred?

17 Which famous outlaw partnered Butch Cassidy?

18 In which criminal act did Bonnie and Clyde specialize?

19 Which planet is so large it could contain all the others?

20 Theoretically, how many bodies the size of the Earth could fit into the Sun?

21 What is the name of the imaginary line of latitude around the middle of Earth?

22 In which story would you find the 'Lost Boys'?

23 Which famous book is divided into two testaments?

24 Who wrote the play *Romeo and Juliet*?

25 What is measured on the Beaufort scale?

26 Who was the infamous captain of The Bounty?

27 What spare-time career did the Hardy Boys follow?

28 Which country did Ivan the Terrible rule?

29 In which country would you find Mandalay?

30 Name Charlie Brown's dog in the *Peanuts* cartoons?

31 Who lives at 10 Downing Street?

32 Who occupies the Oval Office?

33 What sort of plane was a Spitfire?

34 With which festival do you associate Good Friday?

35 To which domestic animal is the tiger related?

36 For what purpose is the husky used?

37 Venison is the meat of which animal?

38 Maco, tiger, and hammer head are all varieties of which creature?

39 In which story does the ghost of Jacob Marley appear?

40 What is another name for the aubergine?

41 Can you eat green tomatoes?

42 According to tradition, what happens to people who pick dandelions?

43 Which American hero was noted for his coonskin cap?

44 Who had a horse called Black Bess?

45 What ancient monuments, all looking similar, is Egypt famous for?

46 What sort of person would live in an igloo?

47 From what was paper traditionally made?

48 From what is glass made?

49 What is Big Ben?

50 What unit is used for measuring the height of horses?

11

The Spectrum

Answers to this quiz are on pages 224-225

EASY :-)

Player 1	Player 2
12	20
33	24
07	03
46	45
01	28
21	02
23	25
04	32
35	39
14	50
31	08
48	17
11	40
27	43
15	29
06	41
10	30
47	34
26	16
38	05
36	49
13	09
19	18
42	37
44	22

01 In war, what does a white flag indicate?

02 Which colour is associated with communism?

03 What does piebald mean?

04 What colour is associated with melancholy music?

05 What colour is the flag flown on a ship where disease has broken out?

06 What are the colours of the rainbow?

07 Name the colours at either end of the spectrum that are invisible to human eyes.

08 What colour is amethyst?

09 What colour do you associate with Ireland?

10 The American, British, and French flags have something in common. What is it?

11 What colour is the heart of an evil person supposed to be?

12 Members of the aristocracy are said to have what colour blood?

13 Which sort of evening sky is an omen of good weather tomorrow?

14 What was produced from the woad plant?

15 What colour dye comes from onions?

16 A blue flame indicates the presence of what metal?

17 What are inexperienced or naive people sometimes called?

18 Cowardly people are supposed to have what sort of streak?

19 What did the giving of a white feather denote?

20 A red sky in the morning is supposed to herald what sort of weather?

21 What is the fast-flowing water that is found near rapids called?

22 Which birch tree is likened to a precious metal?

23 What colour is rosé wine?

24 Where would you find blue grass country?

25 Under which flag did Russians opposed to communism fight?

26 What colour is saffron?

27 What sort of bear is white?

28 Name a colourful heroine associated with *Gone with the Wind.*

29 Squirrels can have fur of several colours. Which of the following is not possible: (a) red, (b) black, (c) white, (d) grey?

30 What substance is, according to superstition, found at the end of a rainbow?

31 Prose of what colour denotes over-descriptive and emotional writing?

32 In poetic language, what colour is the moon said to be?

33 What colours are the Swiss flag?

34 Robert Louis Stevenson wrote a book based on Robin Hood called *The ... Arrow.* The missing word is a colour. What is it?

35 If you are rich and privileged you are said to have been born with 'a ... spoon in your mouth'. What is the missing word?

36 What sort of cat is considered lucky in some countries and an evil omen in others?

37 What are the colours of the Irish flag?

38 What colour were the magic shoes that Dorothy wore in *The Wizard of Oz?*

39 What colour uniforms did the opposing sides wear in the American Civil War?

40 What colour is the River Danube sometimes said to be?

41 Where would you find the Yellow River?

42 What name was given to British soldiers in the days before camouflage uniforms were invented?

43 What name is given to the dull greenish–brown colour used in camouflage?

44 The 0° line of longitude runs through a place with a colour in its name. The same name describes part of New York. What is it?

45 What was the Soviet Army called?

46 What name is given to a dying star as it gets bigger and weaker?

47 What romantic and colourful term was used for the screen in a cinema?

48 What is the name given to the colourful patterns used on Scottish kilts?

49 What colour was the Beatles' submarine?

50 What round citrus fruit is also a colour?

13

Transport

Answers to this quiz are on page 225

EASY 😊 EASY

Player 1	Player 2
12	20
33	24
07	03
46	45
01	28
21	02
23	25
04	32
35	39
14	50
31	08
48	17
11	40
27	43
15	29
06	41
10	30
47	34
26	16
38	05
36	49
13	09
19	18
42	37
44	22

14

01 What is a one-wheeled bicycle called?

02 What is a bicycle for two people called?

03 What was the full name for what we now call a bus?

04 What type of vehicle floats on a cushion of air?

05 What is a catamaran?

06 How would a galleon be powered?

07 On which American vehicles would you have found a cow-catcher?

08 Where on an American freight train would you find the caboose?

09 What three forms of power have been used to drive trains?

10 What sort of car was the Sinclair C5?

11 What is known as 'the ship of the desert'?

12 What are the toothed cogs called that transmit the power of a car's engine to the wheels?

13 What are in-line skates more popularly called?

14 What name is given to a group of camels used for transport?

15 What sort of vessel was a trireme?

16 What sort of vehicles would you have met on the Oregon Trail?

17 What command is given to make a ship go forward as fast as possible?

18 In nautical language what does it mean if you are told to 'belay' something?

19 In the last century which vessel is was popularly associated with the Mississippi river?

20 Why is avoiding work known as 'swinging the lead'?

21 Why was a stage coach so called?

22 What was a landau?

23 What name was given to Viking ships?

24 Which of the folowing makes of car could also be a girl's name: (a) Mercedes, (b) Chevrolet, (c) Renault?

25 What connection is there between the county of Surrey, England, and horse-drawn transport?

26 What is the pillion on a motorcycle?

27 What sort of vehicles did William Harley and Arthur Davidson produce?

28 Which of the following cars contains the German word for Bavaria in its name: (a) VW, (b) Mercedes, (c) BMW?

29 In which sport would you come across the expression 'Formula 1'?

30 What name, other than BMX, is given to a bicycle intended for off-road use?

31 What was a prairie schooner?

32 What was a Zeppelin?

33 What sort of vehicle was the Flying Scot?

34 What was strange about the ship known as the Flying Dutchman?

35 What was odd about the ship named the Mary Celeste?

36 What is the US railway passenger service called?

37 What was a sedan chair?

38 What was the business of Wells, Fargo & Co?

39 What sort of boat is a punt?

40 What sort of vehicle was a penny-farthing?

41 What does the expression BMX stand for?

42 What name is given to a lightweight motorized bicycle that can be pedalled as well as driven by a small engine?

43 What is a wheelie?

44 Which sort of naval vessel fires torpedoes?

45 What is different about the take-off of the so-called Harrier jump jet?

46 What name is given to a boat that carries passengers, vehicles, or goods back and forth across the same route?

47 What name would you give to a wheeled or flying vehicle that carries passengers, vehicles, or goods back and forth across the same route?

48 Henry Ford made the world's first mass-produced car. What was it called?

49 You could buy the Model T in only one colour. What was it?

50 What happened to the German airship Hindenburg in New Jersey in 1937?

? Pot Luck

Answers to this quiz are on page 225

EASY 😊 EASY

Player 1	Player 2
12	20
33	24
07	03
46	45
01	28
21	02
23	25
04	32
35	39
14	50
31	08
48	17
11	40
27	43
15	29
06	41
10	30
47	34
26	16
38	05
36	49
13	09
19	18
42	37
44	22

16

01 Which is world's the most valuable type of gem stone?

02 Is papyrus: a) animal, b) vegetable, or c) mineral?

03 What is a coracle?

04 What is the approximate distance in miles from the Earth to the Sun?

05 What do we call trees that lose their leaves in winter?

06 Which continent, according to legend, mysteriously sank beneath the waves?

07 What was Cambodia called between 1970 and 1975?

08 What fate befell Icarus?

09 Which is the only country in South America where Portuguese is spoken?

10 Which of the following would you not find in Africa: (a) lions, (b) crocodiles, (c) tigers?

11 Name the four gospels of the New Testament.

12 What is a wat in SE Asia?

13 In which town was William Shakespeare born?

14 Which fictional hero shot an apple from his son's head with a crossbow?

15 What is the name which describes all the species of pine tree?

16 Whose nose grew longer every time he told a lie?

17 What path did Dorothy have to follow in The Wizard of Oz?

18 Who, according to the Bible, was swallowed by a whale?

19 Which Dickens character was beaten for asking for more gruel?

20 Which city, according to the well-known proverb, was not built in a day?

21 What is unusual about the way an owl can turn its head?

22 What do we call animals that carry their young in a pouch?

23 What is lace?

24 Who used the code name 007?

25 What do we call it when animals go to sleep during the winter months?

26 Who was Sherlock Holmes' faithful companion?

27 Snoopy, in the *Peanuts* cartoons, fantasized about fighting a German World War I flying ace. Who was he?

28 What, originally, did the word POG stand for?

29 A statue of which fairy-tale character guards Copenhagen harbour?

30 Water is a mixture of which two gases?

31 Which gas do spiders breathe?

32 When are nocturnal animals most active?

33 Which mythical creature is used to represent the constellation of Sagittarius?

34 Which mythological creature, half man and half bull, lived in a labyrinth?

35 Which people fought a famous war against the Trojans?

36 In which continent would you find Zulus?

37 What is the name for a long journey made by Australian Aboriginals?

38 In which city would you find the Louvre?

39 Which country is known for growing tulips?

40 Size for size, spider silk is stronger than steel. True or false?

41 What drink is flavoured with hops?

42 What is produced from fermented grape juice?

43 In the northern hemisphere which is the shortest day?

44 What are the two tropics called?

45 What sport does Magic Johnson play?

46 What role does the Mikado play in Japanese life?

47 Which of these is not a martial art: (a) ikebana, (b) kung fu, (c) judo?

48 Which of these is not a form of pasta: (a) canelloni, (b) paparazzi, (c) penne?

49 Does tea contain caffeine?

50 How many is a gross?

17

Films

Answers to this quiz are on page 225

EASY EASY

	Player 1	Player 2
	12	20
	33	24
	07	03
	46	45
	01	28
	21	02
	23	25
	04	32
	35	39
	14	50
	31	08
	48	17
	11	40
	27	43
	15	29
	06	41
	10	30
	47	34
	26	16
	38	05
	36	49
	13	09
	19	18
	42	37
	44	22

18

01 Walt Disney made a cartoon featuring dalmatians. How many were there in the title?

02 In *Aladdin*, what was the name of the Sultan's evil adviser?

03 Complete the title, *Lady and the ...*

04 Who played Tinkerbell in the film *Hook*?

05 Who played Captain Hook in the film *Hook*?

06 What object had the name Chitty Chitty Bang Bang?

07 In which film would you come across the word supercalifragilisticexpialidotious?

08 In which Disney film does a lion cub called Simba sing, 'I just can't wait to be king'?

09 Who was the villain of *The Lion King*?

10 Name the warthog and meercat who became Simba's friends in *The Lion King*.

11 What was the name of the princess in Disney's *Aladdin*?

12 Who was the female villain of *101 Dalmatians*?

13 What was the name of the Sea Lord in *The Little Mermaid*?

14 Which prince does the little mermaid rescue from the sea?

15 Name the seawitch from *The Little Mermaid*.

16 What was the name of Jodie Foster's son in *Little Man Tate*?

17 What nickname did Fred Tate call his mother by in *Little Man Tate*?

18 Who was the baby elephant with big ears who starred in a Disney cartoon feature?

19 To what use does Dumbo put his big ears?

20 Name Dorothy's dog in *The Wizard of Oz*.

21 Who played the part of Dorothy in the film of *The Wizard of Oz*?

22 What was the song from *The Wizard of Oz* that made Judy Garland famous?

23 Who were the rival gang leaders in *Bugsy Malone*?

24 Who was Bugsy Malone's girlfriend?

25 What was Macaulay Culkin's character called in *Home Alone*?

26 In *Home Alone*, where have Kevin's family gone?

27 In *Home Alone*, why can't Kevin's family phone him to find out if he's all right?

28 What are the names of the villains in *Home Alone*?

29 What was the subtitle of *Home Alone 2*?

30 Where have Kevin's family gone in *Home Alone 2*?

31 In *Home Alone 2*, how does Kevin manage to check into an expensive hotel?

32 In the film *Benji*, what type of creature was the main character?

33 What type of dog was Beethoven in the film of that name?

34 What was the profession of the main villain in *Beethoven*?

35 What was the name of Macaulay Culkin's screen girlfriend in *My Girl*?

36 In *My Girl*, what does Vada's dad do for a living?

37 *My Girl* was actually filmed in Florida, but where was the action supposed to take place?

38 In which country did the film *Buster's World* take place?

39 In *Buster's World*, what is Buster's hobby?

40 In *Buster's World*, how does Buster earn pocket money?

41 Who were Donald Duck's nephews?

42 Name the puppies in *Beethoven 2*.

43 In *Beethoven 2*, who is Beethoven's girlfiend?

44 In *Beethoven 2*, who is Missy's evil owner?

45 In *The Sound of Music*, what was Maria's occupation before she became a governess?

46 What was the name of the family for which Maria worked in *The Sound of Music*?

47 Which prehistoric family, familiar to viewers of TV cartoons, made their own movie?

48 In the film *Babe*, what is the young pig's revolutionary approach to herding sheep?

49 Complete the title, *Honey, I Shrunk the ...*

50 In which film would you find a giant that eats rocks, a boy who hunts purple buffalo, and a child-like empress?

19

Odd One Out

Answers to this quiz are on pages 225-226

EASY 😀 **EASY**

Player 1	Player 2
12	20
33	24
07	03
46	45
01	28
21	02
23	25
04	32
35	39
14	50
31	08
48	17
11	40
27	43
15	29
06	41
10	30
47	34
26	16
38	05
36	49
13	09
19	18
42	37
44	22

20

01 Which bird is the odd one out: (a) eagle, (b) vulture, (c) crow, (d) falcon?

02 Which film is the odd one out: (a) *Licence to Kill*, (b) *The Spy Who Loved Me*, (c) *GoldenEye*, (d) *Back to the Future*?

03 Which language is the odd one out: (a) Chinese, (b) English, (c) French, (d) Spanish?

04 Which personality is the odd one out: (a) Margaret Thatcher, (b) Bill Clinton, (c) Nelson Mandela, (d) Princess Diana?

05 Which fruit is the odd one out: (a) raisin, (b) currant, (c) fig, (d) sultana?

06 Which animal is the odd one out: (a) salamander, (b) crab, c) lobster, (d) shrimp ?

07 Which country is the odd one out: (a) Taiwan, (b) Hong Kong, (c) Russia, (d) China?

08 Which is the odd tree out: (a) cypress, (b) willow, (c) oak, (d) silver birch?

09 Who is the odd one out: (a) Enid Blyton, (b) Roald Dahl, (c) Leonard Bernstein, (d) Mark Twain?

10 Which form of transport is the odd one out: (a) canoe, (b) moped, (c) tandem, (d) glider?

11 Which musical instrument is the odd one out: (a) trumpet, (b) oboe, (c) clarinet, (d) flute?

12 What is the odd device out: (a) tape, (b) record, (c) compact disc, (d) film cartridge?

13 Which of these bird is the odd one out: (a) cuckoo, (b) penguin, (c) emu, (d) ostrich?

14 Which is the odd one out: (a) clog, (b) sarong, (c) pump, (d) moccasin?

15 Who is the odd one out: (a) Nero, (b) Augustus, (c) Claudius I, (d) Alexander the Great?

16 Which is the odd one out: (a) water lily, (b) sea urchin, (c) coral, (d) sea anemone?

17 Which is the odd one out: (a) Scandinavia, (b) Iberian Peninsula, (c) West Indies, (d) Italy?

18 Which musical instrument is the odd one out: (a) grand piano, (b) harpsichord, (c) harp, (d) organ?

19 Which is the odd one out: (a) polka, (b) symphony, (c) waltz, (d) mazurka?

20 Which animal is the odd one out: (a) marmoset, (b) orang-utan, (c) gorilla, (d) gibbon?

21 Which building is the odd one out: (a) Empire State Building, (b) Sears Tower, (c) Westminster Abbey, (d) Capitol Building?

22 Which fruit is the odd one out: (a) damson, (b) greengage, (c) prune, (d) pear?

23 Which personality is the odd one out: (a) Frédéric Chopin, (b) Peter Tchaikovsky, (c) George Frederick Handel, (d) Jean Baptiste Molière?

24 Which is the odd one out: (a) ornithologist, (b) geologist, (c) botanist, (d) zoologist?

25 Which is the odd number out: (a) 11, (b) 8, (c) 9, (d) 15?

26 Which drink is the odd one out: (a) milk, (b) tea, (c) coffee, (d) cocoa?

27 Which animal is the odd one out: (a) shark, (b) piranha, (c) dolphin, (d) sturgeon?

28 Which is the odd one out: (a) *West Side Story*, (b) *Phantom of the Opera*, (c) *Showboat*, (d) *The Magic Flute*?

29 Which is the odd one out: (a) acne, (b) eczema, (c) bronchitis, (d) hives?

30 Which dish is the odd one out: (a) pilaf, (b) risotto, (c) paella, (d) cannelloni?

31 Which person is the odd one out: (a) Peter Tchaikovsky, (b) Peter the Great, (c) John F. Kennedy, (d) Boris Yeltzin?

32 Which animal is the odd one out: (a) badger, (b) mole, (c) raccoon, (d) hedgehog?

33 Which product is the odd one out: (a) leather, (b) fur, (c) cotton, (d) wool?

34 Which is the odd one out: (a) opera, (b) concerto, (c) musical, (d) operetta?

35 Which device is the odd one out: (a) rain gauge, (b) sun dial, (c) sand glass, (d) cuckoo clock?

36 Which is the odd one out: (a) retina, (b) iris, (c) auricle, (d) sclera?

37 Which is the odd one out: (a) baritone, (b) soprano, (c) bass, (d) cantata?

38 Which dish is the odd one out: (a) pie, (b) quiche, (c) pizza, (d) omelette?

39 Who is the odd one out: (a) Isaac Newton, (b) Terry Pratchett, (c) A. A. Milne, (d) E. Nesbitt?

40 Who is the odd one out: (a) J. R. R. Tolkien, (b) Agatha Christie, (c) Alfred Hitchcock, (d) Georges Simenon?

41 Which fruit is the odd one out: (a) plum, (b) peach, (c) apricot, (d) banana?

42 Which work is the odd one out: (a) *The Barber of Seville*, (b) *A Midsummer Night's Dream*, (c) *Aida*, (d) *Madame Butterfly*?

43 Which is the odd one out: (a) femur, (b) pelvis, (c) hamstring, (d) ankle?

44 Which piece of clothing is the odd one out: (a) gaiter, (b) bowler, (c) baseball cap, (d) turban?

45 Which dish is the odd one out: (a) omelette, (b) soufflé, (c) risotto (d) quiche?

46 Which place is the odd one out: (a) Florida, (b) Cuba, (c) Alaska, (d) Hawaii?

47 Which is the odd one out: (a) flotilla, (b) armada, (c) squadron, (d) cavalry?

48 Which is the odd one out: (a) catamaran, (b) yacht, (c) autogyro, (d) schooner?

49 Which is the odd one out: (a) molar, (b) trachea, (c) incisor, (d) canine?

50 What type of food is the odd one out: (a) gruyère, (b) frankfurter, (c) pepperoni, (d) black pudding?

? Pot Luck

Answers to this quiz are on page 226

EASY **EASY**

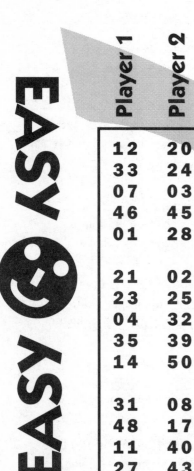

Player 1	Player 2
12	20
33	24
07	03
46	45
01	28
21	02
23	25
04	32
35	39
14	50
31	08
48	17
11	40
27	43
15	29
06	41
10	30
47	34
26	16
38	05
36	49
13	09
19	18
42	37
44	22

01 Who invented the ball-point pen?

02 Is a gorilla a monkey?

03 Would a sculptor be most likely to work in (a) marble, (b) granite, (c) chalk?

04 Which people wrote on sheets of papyrus?

05 In which country do people not normally eat with chopsticks: (a) China, (b) Japan, (c) Thailand?

06 Brittany is part of which country?

07 The expression 'alternating current' refers to which form of energy?

08 What is coal?

09 Cox, Granny Smith, and Golden Delicious are all varieties of which fruit?

10 Which bird is known for laying its eggs in other birds' nests?

11 What did Sir Alexander Fleming discover?

12 From which country would a Magyar come?

13 Which of these snakes is not venomous: (a) rattlesnake, (b) boa constrictor, (c) viper?

14 Which plant, used as a Christmas decoration, was regarded as sacred by the Druids?

15 What is a rickshaw powered by?

16 What purpose is Stonehenge thought to have served?

17 In which country would you pay in baht?

18 How long does it take light to reach Earth from the Sun?

19 'Adios' means 'goodbye' in: (a) French, (b) Italian, (c) Spanish?

20 What is the difference between a meteor and a meteorite?

22

21 In badminton, what do you use instead of a ball?

22 What is the highest number that has a name?

23 Which comes first, thunder or lightning?

24 What character fault is known as the green-eyed monster?

25 What is unusual about sandalwood?

26 A grasshopper has its ears in its legs. True or false?

27 According to the Bible who were the sons of Adam and Eve?

28 In which tale is Morgan le Fay a wicked sorceress?

29 What is a zombie?

30 In which country would you be most likely to eat sauerkraut?

31 Which whip-wielding film hero is named after a US state?

32 In modern terms, what nationality were the Spartans?

33 Who was the Maid of Orleans?

34 The word 'shalom' means 'peace' in (a) Hebrew, (b) Arabic, (c) Japanese?

35 Which of these airports would you find in Japan: (a) O'Hare, (b) Haneda, (c) Ben Gurion?

36 Which German car is named after a bug?

37 What is the name for an elephant's long tooth?

38 Who was the fairy who accompanied Peter Pan?

39 Which are the two major political parties of the USA?

40 What was the coin called a sovereign made of?

41 In SE Asia, what is a stupa?

42 What is brine?

43 The ostrich sticks its head in the sand to avoid danger. True or false?

44 What function did Mercury perform in Greek legend?

45 Where did Norse warriors hope to go when they died?

46 What is a dromedary?

47 We say 'as blind as a bat', but is a bat really blind?

48 How would you get a hen's egg into a bottle without breaking the shell?

49 Who was assassinated on the Ides of March?

50 How many are there in a score?

23

People

Answers to this quiz are on pages 226-227

EASY 😊 **EASY**

Player 1	Player 2
12	20
33	24
07	03
46	45
01	28
21	02
23	25
04	32
35	39
14	50
31	08
48	17
11	40
27	43
15	29
06	41
10	30
47	34
26	16
38	05
36	49
13	09
19	18
42	37
44	22

01 Who was the wizard at King Arthur's court?

02 Name Robin Hood's fat friend.

03 Who was the boy who vowed he would never grow up?

04 Name the boy who befriended Pooh, Piglet, and Eeyore.

05 Which American president supposedly chopped down his father's cherry tree?

06 Which mythical Greek hero performed 12 labours?

07 Which lady guards Upper New York Bay?

08 Name an Italian lady, painted by da Vinci, who is famous for her enigmatic smile.

09 Which king supposedly ordered the waves to turn back?

10 Which English king was executed on the orders of Oliver Cromwell?

11 The three graces are Faith, and who else?

12 Name the hero of *The Hobbit*.

13 Who was principally responsible for the rise of National Socialism in Germany?

14 Name the medical man involved in the *Gunfight at the OK Corral*.

15 Name the British king who supposedly lost his jewels in The Wash.

16 Roald Dahl wrote of a man who owned a fantastic chocolate factory. What was his name?

17 Name the communist leader of Cuba.

18 Who was the first man in space?

19 Who was the first human being to walk on the moon?

20 Which crusading king was known as The Lionheart?

21 What profession did Dick Turpin follow?

22 Who, according to the Bible, was the brother of Cain?

23 Name an Egyptian queen who was the lover of Mark Antony.

24 Who was king of the Greek gods?

25 Name the queen who tells the stories of *One Thousand and One Nights*.

26 Name a legendary Arabian sailor.

27 For what was Dr Crippen hanged?

28 Against which Iraqi dictator was the Gulf War fought?

29 Who was shot at the playhouse by John Wilkes Booth?

30 Which fictional character is famous for the line: 'Frankly, my dear, I don't give a damn'?

31 Name the Chinese leader of the Communist Revolution.

32 Which Frenchman crowned himself Emperor?

33 Which complex character in Greek legend killed his father and married his mother?

34 To what sticky end did Anne Boleyn come?

35 Who, according to Shakespeare, is supposed to have cried: 'A horse, a horse, my kingdom for a horse!'?

36 What was Richard III's nickname?

37 Which boy, whose adventures were created by Mark Twain, later starred as a detective in another novel?

38 What nationality was Goethe?

39 Who was Calamity Jane?

40 What sport is played by Steffi Graf?

41 In which revolution was Emiliano Zapata an important figure?

42 Which British saint is famous for slaying a dragon?

43 Which American President is famous for the line: 'Ich bin ein Berliner'?

44 Which American inventor produced the Kodak camera?

45 Who, according to the fairy tale, had problems with a wolf whilst visiting a sick relative?

46 What was unusual about Gog and Magog?

47 To which king's court did Sir Lancelot belong?

48 Who was the heroine of The Wizard of Oz?

49 Who, according to the Bible, was the brother of Jacob?

50 Which Roman emperor is supposed to have said, 'I came, I saw, I conquered'?

The Earth

Answers to this quiz are on page 227

EASY

EASY

Player 1	Player 2
12	20
33	24
07	03
46	45
01	28
21	02
23	25
04	32
35	39
14	50
31	08
48	17
11	40
27	43
15	29
06	41
10	30
47	34
26	16
38	05
36	49
13	09
19	18
42	37
44	22

01 What is the name given to the Earth's hard outer shell?

02 Which science studies the history, structure, and composition of the Earth?

03 Images of ancient living creatures are sometimes found trapped in rock. What are these called?

04 What is the study of the Earth's surface called?

05 Is the Earth a perfect sphere?

06 What do we call the metallic center of the Earth?

07 How much of the Earth's surface is covered by water?

08 What is the name of the continent which contains the South Pole?

09 What do we call a gap in the Earth's crust through which molten rock escapes onto the Earth's surface?

10 What do we call a shallow depression at the top of a volcanic cone?

11 What is a geyser?

12 What name is given to the sudden emergence of hot material from the Earth's interior?

13 What does the Richter scale measure?

14 What name is sometimes given to the tidal wave set off by an undersea earthquake?

15 What do we call a hill over 2,000 ft (600 m) high?

16 What do we call the imaginary lines that divide the Earth from north to south?

17 What do we call the imaginary lines that divide the Earth from east to west?

18 What is the process by which rock is worn down by weather?

19 What is the name given to the heaps of rock debris formed by frost shattering?

20 Does a stalagmite grow up or down?

21 What is the name for a place where a stream disappears underground in limestone scenery?

22 What is glaciation?

23 What is a glacier?

24 What is an ice age?

25 What is the Norwegian word for a long, deep sea inlet gouged out by a glacier?

26 What is a moraine?

27 What is permafrost?

28 What is a peninsula?

29 What do we call a band of sand, shingle, or pebbles at the edge of the sea?

30 What is strange about the Mediterranean Sea?

31 What is the name for an underwater ridge created by the coral polyp?

32 What is the name for an area of land surrounded by water?

33 What do we call the twice daily rise and fall of the oceans?

34 What is a spring tide?

35 What do we call the thin layer of gases surrounding the Earth?

36 What is the commonest gas in the atmosphere?

37 What is the greenhouse effect?

38 What is a barometer?

39 What is a thermometer?

40 What do we call a stream of air moving from one place to another?

41 Complete the following sentence: An isobar is a line on a map that links points of equal atmospheric...

42 What do we call a dense cloud of water droplets close to the ground?

43 What is humidity?

44 The Beaufort scale describes the effects of various wind speeds. What is the highest speed called?

45 According to the Beaufort scale, is a storm stronger than a gale?

46 What is oil?

47 What is coal?

48 What is so-called 'natural gas' mainly made of?

49 What colour are emeralds?

50 Which are the three rare metals often used in jewellery?

Pot Luck

Answers to this quiz are on page 227

EASY

Player 1	Player 2
12	20
33	24
07	03
46	45
01	28
21	02
23	25
04	32
35	39
14	50
31	08
48	17
11	40
27	43
15	29
06	41
10	30
47	34
26	16
38	05
36	49
13	09
19	18
42	37
44	22

01 Is there more or less water now than when the seas were first formed?

02 Spider, horseshoe, and hermit are all varieties of which sea creature?

03 Which of the following is not a sign of the zodiac: (a) Libra, (b) Aquarius, (c) Ceres, (d) Capricorn?

04 What name is given to a white animal with pink eyes (eg, mouse or rabbit)?

05 What sort of game is Yahtzee?

06 Which of the following is not a gambling game: (a) poker, (b) roulette, (c) backgammon, (d) patience?

07 The leaves of which water plant are called pads?

08 John Constable was: (a) a doctor, (b) a painter, (c) an explorer, (d) a president of the USA?

09 Carmen is: (a) an opera, (b) a car, (c) a game of chance?

10 Which large aircraft has a name that reminds you of an elephant?

11 Which of the following is not a make of car: (a) Rolls Royce, (b) Boeing, (c) Chevrolet, (d) Peugeot?

12 Would a ship called a brigantine be equipped with sails or an engine?

13 Who was the King of Rock 'n' Roll: (a) Cliff Richard, (b) Mick Jagger, (c) Elvis Presley, (d) Paul McCartney?

14 In the northern hemisphere, which wind would you expect to be colder– the north or the south?

15 Which is further north, Turkey or Switzerland?

16 Which city is smaller, São Paulo or Washington DC?

28

17 In which country would you not drive on the left: (a) Thailand, (b) UK, (c) Sweden?

18 What game do the Chicago Bulls play?

19 What do children have in common with young goats?

20 What are young swans called?

21 What are young geese called?

22 What is Esperanto?

23 By what other name is the Religious Society of Friends sometimes known?

24 Which animals are thought to commit mass suicide by hurling themselves into the sea?

25 Which of the following is not a citrus fruit: (a) lemon, (b) rhubarb, (c) orange, (d) grapefruit.

26 Bats' wings are really modified hands. True or false?

27 Is a Portugese Man o' War: (a) a ship, (b) a warrior, (c) a jellyfish, (d) a car?

28 In which country was golf invented: (a) USA, (b) Zaire, (c) Denmark, (d) Scotland?

29 What sort of creature is a Bombay duck?

30 Where would you find the Everglades?

31 By what name did Westerners formerly know Beijing?

32 In which of these places is Chinese not the native language: (a) Taiwan, (b) Hong Kong, (c) Korea?

33 Which religious leader lives in the Vatican?

34 Where in a house would you expect to find the eaves?

35 What is a ravine?

36 Why can't you see around corners?

37 If you flip a coin, what are the chances of it coming down heads?

38 In which country would you find the Sinai Desert?

39 How many years is three score and ten?

40 What is Blue John?

41 What causes hay fever?

42 Which country sent rhubarb to the West?

43 According to the Bible, what was used to feed the five thousand?

44 Which country is the home of the classical guitar?

45 What sort of creature could be described as a thoroughbred, a Shetland, an Arab, or a Mustang?

46 What name is given to ancient Egyptian writing?

47 What is azure?

48 What is serendipity?

49 What is the difference between astrology and astronomy?

50 What other name is given to the constellation of Ursa Major?

Synonyms

Answers to this quiz are on page 227

EASY 😊

Player 1	Player 2
12	20
33	24
07	03
46	45
01	28
21	02
23	25
04	32
35	39
14	50
31	08
48	17
11	40
27	43
15	29
06	41
10	30
47	34
26	16
38	05
36	49
13	09
19	18
42	37
44	22

01 Alive is the same as: (a) animated, (b) busy, (c) exciting.

02 Bleak is the same as: (a) cold, (b) gloomy, (c) hard.

03 Create is the same as: (a) make, (b) excite, (c) grow.

04 Drudge is the same as: (a) dull, (b) toil, (c) brown.

05 Eager is the same as: (a) keen, (b) excited, (c) quick.

06 Fraternal is the same as: (a) kindly, (b) wise, (c) brotherly.

07 Grotesque is the same as: (a) funny, (b) bizarre, (c) obvious.

08 Liberal is the same as: (a) free, (b) generous, (c) socialist.

09 Keepsake is the same as: (a) memento, (b) gift, (c) bribe.

10 Ideal is the same as: (a) cheap, (b) flawless, (c) useful.

11 Jocular is the same as: (a) witty, (b) silly, (c) helpful.

12 Lucid is the same as: (a) clean, (b) understandable, (c) tall.

13 Arcane is the same as: (a) geometrical, (b) mysterious, (c) pretty.

14 Murky is the same as: (a) dark, (b) dangerous, (c) insane.

15 Nimble is the same as: (a) handy, (b) bright, (c) clever.

16 Oral is the same as: (a) verbal, (b) spoken, (c) loud.

17 Plural is the same as: (a) several, (b) deceptive, (c) generous.

18 Robust is the same as: (a) red, (b) rough, (c) strong.

19 Refined is the same as: (a) delicate, (b) snobbish, (c) precious.

30

20 Satisfied is the same as: (a) pleased, (b) contented, (c) proud.

21 Trapped is the same as: (a) killed, (b) caught, (c) closed.

22 Unlikely is the same as: (a) unfortunate, (b) improbable, (c) difficult.

23 Valour is the same as: (a) bravery, (b) virtue, (c) sincerity.

24 Want is the same as: (a) have, (b) require, (c) hunger.

25 Alter is the same as: (a) change, (b) enlarge, (c) sustain.

26 Break is the same as: (a) stop, (b) crack, (c) reform.

27 Caress is the same as: (a) whisper, (b) sing, (c) stroke.

28 Demand is the same as: (a) ask, (b) leave, (c) endanger.

29 Element is the same as: (a) ring, (b) delete, (c) part.

30 Manufacture is the same as: (a) industry, (b) make, (c) business.

31 Noble is the same as: (a) wealthy, (b) honorable, (c) charitable.

32 Organize is the same as: (a) arrange, (b) support, (c) lead.

33 Perpetual is the same as: (a) infinite, (b) occasional, (c) continual.

34 Quantity is the same as: (a) amount, (b) some, (c) enough.

35 Research is the same as: (a) prosecute, (b) colleague, (c) inquiry.

36 Sample is the same as: (a) specimen, (b) determine, (c) contents.

37 Treachery is the same as: (a) cowardice, (b) disloyalty, (c) avarice.

38 Ungrateful is the same as: (a) offensive, (b) bragging, (c) thankless.

39 Whip is the same as: (a) beat, (b) swipe, (c) deflate.

40 Yearn is the same as: (a) vomit, (b) crave, (c) delay.

41 Absolute is the same as: (a) perfect, (b) summit, (c) greatness.

42 Brutish is the same as: (a) dirty, (b) beastly, (c) concerned.

43 Concentrate is the same as: (a) condense, (b) testify, (c) gratify.

44 Dangle is the same as: (a) decorate, (b) hang, (c) destroy.

45 Earn is the same as: (a) behave, (b) acquire, (c) have.

46 Frequent is the same as: (a) sometimes, (b) constantly, (c) often.

47 Grapple is the same as: (a) handle, (b) wrestle, (c) frame.

48 Harken is the same as: (a) listen, (b) wait, (c) entertain.

49 Begrudge is the same as: (a) envy, (b) dislike, (c) greed.

50 Leave is the same as: (a) depart, (b) escape, (c) engross.

Nature

Answers to this quiz are on pages 227-228

EASY 😊 EASY

Player 1	Player 2
12	20
33	24
07	03
46	45
01	28
21	02
23	25
04	32
35	39
14	50
31	08
48	17
11	40
27	43
15	29
06	41
10	30
47	34
26	16
38	05
36	49
13	09
19	18
42	37
44	22

01 What is the difference between a moth and a butterfly?

02 **What is the difference between a frog and a toad?**

03 To what family do lions, tigers, and cheetahs belong?

04 **What domestic animal is the closest relative of the wolf?**

05 Where are penguins found?

06 **Where are polar bears found?**

07 Which common vegetable did Sir Walter Raleigh bring back from the Americas?

08 **Which birds are collectively known as a 'murder'?**

09 What is the largest species of shark?

10 **What is taxonomy?**

11 What is the difference between frog spawn and toad spawn?

12 **Which bird is notorious for laying its eggs in another bird's nest?**

13 What is a dingo?

14 **What is a feral animal?**

15 What is the name for the Australian bird rather like an ostrich?

16 **What domestic animal did the Egyptians worship as a god?**

17 Do birds sing for pleasure?

18 **Does a fish normally have lungs?**

19 Is the cheetah the world's fastest running animal?

20 **Is a sponge a plant?**

21 Is a lizard warm or cold blooded?

22 **Is it true that some birds can use tools?**

23 To what family do spiders and scorpions belong?

24 To what family do crabs and lobsters belong?

25 What is the purpose of a rattlesnake's rattle?

26 Do male or female lions do the hunting?

27 What sort of creature is a koi?

28 Which blackbird is not black?

29 Which two animals were responsible for the spread of the Black Death?

30 Is a tomato a fruit or a vegetable?

31 In northern latitudes what are swallows famous for doing in autumn?

32 Is it true that the sight of seagulls inland means there are storms at sea?

33 Is the owl really wise?

34 Which animal defends itself by spraying enemies with an evil-smelling fluid?

35 Which creature is known as a glutton?

36 What do satsumas, clementines, and mandarins have in common?

37 What is another name for a Daddy Longlegs?

38 From which flower is opium produced?

39 What is lichen?

40 Which scavenging animal is famous for its laugh?

41 Where would you find alligators?

42 Are giant pandas herbivores?

43 What is a young swan called?

44 What is a young eel called?

45 What is another name for a dung beetle?

46 Does a frog have ears?

47 Oxeye is a variety of which common wild flower?

48 Girls called Erica are named after which wild flower?

49 What sort of creature is a stickleback?

50 What is the common name for fishes of the family *Diodontidae*, which have strong, sharp spines on the body and are capable of inflating themselves when attacked?

Pot Luck

Answers to this quiz are on page 228

EASY ☺ EASY

Player 1	Player 2
12	20
33	24
07	03
46	45
01	28
21	02
23	25
04	32
35	39
14	50
31	08
48	17
11	40
27	43
15	29
06	41
10	30
47	34
26	16
38	05
36	49
13	09
19	18
42	37
44	22

01 Which film studio made *Lady and the Tramp*, *Dumbo*, and *Pocahontas*?

02 Which family group did Michael Jackson sing with when he was a boy?

03 Of which country is Warsaw the capital city?

04 Which is referred to as the 'near side' of a car?

05 Which famous black South African leader spent many years in prison before becoming president of his country?

06 Of which country was Abraham Lincoln president?

07 Which sign of the Zodiac is represented by a crab?

08 What are Tarot cards used for?

09 What is the first letter of the Greek alphabet?

10 What type of shellfish produce pearls?

11 Is it true that a singer can shatter a wine glass simply by hitting a high note?

12 By what name were the National Socialist Party better known?

13 What have Auschwitz, Dachau, and Treblinka in common?

14 Which national American organization is devoted to fighting crime?

15 Which is the USA's intelligence gathering organization?

16 Which country has a security organization called MI5?

17 What do pilgrims expect to receive at Lourdes?

18 In which country did the Khmer Rouge carry out mass murder?

19 What sport is Andre Agassi famous for?

20 What is NASA known for?

21 Which country is the home of the game of boules?

22 What is a so-called fairy ring?

23 To which country does the island of Crete belong?

24 Which two countries dispute ownership of Cyprus?

25 How much of the human body is composed of oxygen?

26 What was Rip van Winkle noted for?

27 In which country did the film *You Only Live Twice* mainly take place?

28 Where would you expect to meet Hawk, Nitro, Jet, Warrior, and Dynamite?

29 In *The Lion, the Witch and the Wardrobe*, what was the first thing Lucy found in Narnia?

30 How many feet make one fathom?

31 Which of the Walton children ran his own newspaper?

32 In *The Cosby Show*, what is Mrs Huxtable's profession?

33 Which is the first book of the Bible?

34 Which is the odd one out: (a) Daisy, (b) Poppy, (c) Geranium, (d) Althea?

35 Julius Caesar's horse was supposed to have unusual feet. What was strange about them?

36 Why were some Romans called Postumus?

37 Who would have used wampum?

38 Apart from the animal of that name, what is a white elephant?

39 What does a squirrel live in?

40 Who lives in an igloo?

41 In Thailand, houses were traditionally built on stilts. Why?

42 What name is given to Estonia, Latvia and Lithuania?

43 Where did Robin Hood live?

44 On which coast of the USA would you find Oregon?

45 What other name is given to a harmonica?

46 Which boy's name, made popular by a great conqueror, means 'defender of men'?

47 How do you judge the age of a tree which has been felled?

48 On the internet, what is a URL?

49 By what name is Southern Rhodesia now known?

50 Lucifer, Beelzebub, and Baphomet are all names for what?

Opposites

Answers to this quiz are on page 228

EASY 😊 **EASY**

Player 1	Player 2
12	20
33	24
07	03
46	45
01	28
21	02
23	25
04	32
35	39
14	50
31	08
48	17
11	40
27	43
15	29
06	41
10	30
47	34
26	16
38	05
36	49
13	09
19	18
42	37
44	22

36

01 The opposite of eager is: (a) slovenly, (b) lethargic, (c) disinterested.

02 The opposite of grateful is: (a) thankless, (b) euphoric, (c) ingratiating.

03 The opposite of generous is: (a) mean, (b) rich, (c) spiteful.

04 The opposite of captive is: (a) escape, (b) free, (c) release.

05 The opposite of profound is: (a) abysmal, (b) superficial, (c) recondite.

06 The opposite of lazy is: (a) busy, (b) keen, (c) industrious.

07 The opposite of real is: (a) imaginary, (b) dream, (c) strange.

08 The opposite of tense is (a) happy, (b) relaxed, (c) sleepy.

09 The opposite of defunct is: (a) extant, (b) extinct, (c) bygone.

10 The opposite of increase is: (a) poverty, (b) less, (c) decrease.

11 The opposite of frivolous is: (a) flighty, (b) jejune, (c) earnest.

12 The opposite of total is: (a) some, (b) most, (c) partial.

13 The opposite of grief is: (a) parsimony, (b) delectation, (c) rectitude.

14 The opposite of crowded is: (a) replete, (b) vacuous, (c) sordid.

15 The opposite of jejune is: (a) mediocre, (b) insipid, (c) fascinating.

16 The opposite of gravid is: (a) barren, (b) light, (c) hilarious.

17 The opposite of sell is: (a) invest, (b) purchase, (c) haggle.

18 The opposite of energetic is: (a) drowsy, (b) listless, (c) asleep.

19 The opposite of retreat is: (a) flee, (b) advance, (c) fight.

20 The opposite of sharp is: (a) dull, (b) cloudy, (c) witty.

21 The opposite of quiescent is: a) frolicsome, b) noisy, c) gradual?

22 The opposite of glum is: (a) morose, (b) laughter, (c) cheerful.

23 The opposite of conflate is: a) deflate, b) overlook, c) disperse,

24 The opposite of stupid is: (a) learned, (b) clever, (c) knowledgeable.

25 The opposite of degrade is: a) promote, b) grow, c) fertilize.

26 The opposite of sweet is: (a) acid, (b) piquant, (c) sour.

27 The opposite of catch is: (a) escape, (b) free, (c) deport.

28 The opposite of climb is: (a) fall, (b) abseil, (c) descend.

29 The opposite of barbarous is: a) kind, b) civilized, c) polite.

30 The opposite of contempt: a) esteem, b) perdition, c) contumely.

31 The opposite of preserve is: a) encapsulate, b) discreate, c) render.

32 The opposite of optimistic is: (a) worried, (b) pessimistic, (c) unhappy.

33 The opposite of proponent is: a) ally, b) antagonist, c) advocate.

34 The opposite of euphony is: a) dissonance, b) symphony, c) criticism.

35 The opposite of create is: a) establish, b) dismantle, c) reduce.

36 The opposite of satiety is: a) glut, b) starve, c) dearth.

37 The opposite of intrinsic is: a) extraneous, b) excluded, c) inculcated.

38 The opposite of hostile is: (a) surrender, (b) friendly, (c) malicious.

39 The opposite of tactful is: (a) blunt, (b) lying, (c) rude.

40 The opposite of gregarious is: a) lonely, b) withdrawn, c) solitary.

41 The opposite of grow is: (a) decay, (b) shrink, (c) fall.

42 The opposite of convenient is: (a) handy, (b) awkward, (c) distant.

43 The opposite of flammable is: (a) inflammable, (b) combustible, (c) flameproof.

44 The opposite of diminutive is: (a) big, (b) global, (c) prolific.

45 The opposite of minuscule is: (a) microscopic, (b) huge, (c) enlarged.

46 The opposite of chaos is: (a) order, (b) conformity, (c) universe.

47 The opposite of arid is: (a) fertile, (b) wet, (c) marshy.

48 The opposite of hungry is: (a) greedy, (b) sick, (c) fed.

49 The opposite of bizarre is: a) outlandish, b) traditional, c) grotesque.

50 The opposite of tasty is: (a) bland, (b) spicy, (c) disgusting.

Classical Music

Answers to this quiz are on pages 228-229

EASY EASY

Player 1	Player 2
12	20
33	24
07	03
46	45
01	28
21	02
23	25
04	32
35	39
14	50
31	08
48	17
11	40
27	43
15	29
06	41
10	30
47	34
26	16
38	05
36	49
13	09
19	18
42	37
44	22

01 Which composer wrote the opera *The Magic Flute*?

02 How many symphonies did Beethoven write?

03 In which opera can you find the 'Triumphal March'?

04 What nationality was Antonín Dvořák?

05 Who wrote the "Royal Fireworks Music"?

06 In which tempo should a piece of music annotated with the term presto be played?

07 How many movements does a classical symphony usually have?

08 Herbert von Karajan was the conductor of which orchestra?

09 Who wrote the '1812 Overture'?

10 How many operas did Beethoven write?

11 What type of instrument is a clarinet?

12 What kind of musical work is *Swan Lake*?

13 Who wrote the *Peer Gynt* suites?

14 In which country was Frédéric Chopin born?

15 How should music described as *adagio* be played?

16 Of which major work is *Götterdämmerung* a part?

17 What is the text of an opera correctly termed?

18 In which voice does Luciano Pavarotti sing?

19 Who wrote *The Barber of Seville*?

20 What does the term *pizzicato* mean?

21 What type of instrument is a trombone?

22 What is the name of Prokofiev's symphonic fairy tale?

23 Who wrote the *Brandenburg Concertos*?

24 What is peculiar about Schubert's *Symphony No. 8*?

25 Mstislav Rostropovich is an artist on which instrument?

26 What nationality was Jean Sibelius?

27 Who wrote the 'Moonlight Sonata'?

28 By what other name is a cembalo also known?

29 During which musical era was Bach's music written?

30 Who is a concerto usually written for?

31 What type of musical work is *Die schöne Mullerin*?

32 Who wrote the opera *Carmen*?

33 What type of instrument is a saxophone?

34 Who was the leading English composer of the Baroque era?

35 Which instrument was *Pictures at an Exhibition* written for?

36 Which opera contains the aria 'La ci darem la mano'?

37 Who wrote *Bolero*?

38 Who lived earlier – Haydn or Schubert?

39 What did Beethoven suffer from in his later years?

40 What is the name of Mozart's last symphony?

41 Pinchas Zukerman was an artist on which instrument?

42 Who wrote *The Four Seasons*?

43 What type of music is a *minuet*?

44 Which nationality was composer Gustav Mahler?

45 How many strings does a guitar usually have?

46 What does the term *crescendo* mean?

47 In which suite can you find the 'Dance of the Sugar Plum Fairy'?

48 Daniel Barenboim is an artist on which instrument?

49 Who wrote *From the New World*?

50 In which tempo should a movement described as *largo* be played?

Pot Luck

Answers to this quiz are on page 229

EASY ☺

Player 1	Player 2
12	20
33	24
07	03
46	45
01	28
21	02
23	25
04	32
35	39
14	50
31	08
48	17
11	40
27	43
15	29
06	41
10	30
47	34
26	16
38	05
36	49
13	09
19	18
42	37
44	22

01 Which female detective partners Fox Mulder in *The X-Files*?

02 **Which detective did Clint Eastwood play?**

03 Which fictional 19th-century detective was killed by his creator but resurrected by popular demand?

04 **Where is Dixie?**

05 What is a pecan?

06 **Which nut is named after a South American country?**

07 Which popular children's entertainment features a crocodile, a baby, a policeman, and a string of sausages?

08 **In which country is a country home called a *dacha*?**

09 What would you do with a glockenspiel?

10 What are timpani?

11 With which sport do you associate the NBA?

12 **With which sport do you associate the MCC?**

13 What sort of illness does a paediatrician treat?

14 **What does a taxidermist do?**

15 Which language very nearly became the official language of the USA?

16 **Is the Suez Canal longer than the Panama Canal?**

17 Which metal provides fuel for nuclear power stations?

18 **Hum the opening bars of Beethoven's *Fifth Symphony*.**

19 What caused the Titanic to sink?

20 **In which long-running TV show did Lisa Bonet appear as a teenage daughter?**

21 Which American actress played the part of a gangster's girlfriend when she was only 12 years old?

22 Which American sitcom is named after a flower?

23 Which of Charlie Brown's friends plays Beethoven on a toy piano?

24 Name the dirty child in the *Peanuts* cartoons.

25 Who was the Native American princess in *Peter Pan*?

26 What American plant sends horses mad if they eat it?

27 What does the Spanish phrase Hasta la vista mean?

28 What do German and Jewish people say when you sneeze?

29 What is a begel?

30 Which country is the home of sukiyaki?

31 What have currants, raisins, and sultanas got in common?

32 What does the Spanish word *corrida* mean?

33 In which country would you find the Dordogne?

34 Who played the film role of *Mary Poppins*?

35 Who played the male lead in *Mary Poppins*?

36 What is the connection between LaToya, Janet and Michael?

37 Which country is the home of tacos?

38 What is tequila?

39 What is a chihuahua?

40 What would you do with a stethoscope?

41 Name the giant tortoise in *The Never-ending Story*?

42 What do the stripes on the American flag represent?

43 What is supposed to happen in the Bermuda Triangle?

44 What do the Australians call the uncultivated parts of their country?

45 What are grissini?

46 In which country is Tangiers?

47 What is the main constituent of risotto?

48 Shinto is the national religion of which country?

49 Which country uses roubles as currency?

50 Where would you pay in shekels?

41

Nature

Answers to this quiz are on page 229

EASY 😊 EASY

Player 1	Player 2
12	20
33	24
07	03
46	45
01	28
21	02
23	25
04	32
35	39
14	50
31	08
48	17
11	40
27	43
15	29
06	41
10	30
47	34
26	16
38	05
36	49
13	09
19	18
42	37
44	22

42

01 A mule is a cross between which two animals?

02 Which position does a hedgehog take on to protect himself?

03 Which animal is known for being able to change his colour?

04 Why are the tusks of elephants so much valued?

05 What makes the larch different from other pine trees?

06 On which continent do koalas live?

07 What is the most obvious difference between a female lion and a male one?

08 Which is the tallest animal?

09 How many humps does a llama have?

10 What do bees gather in order to make honey?

11 Which limb of a tadpole disappears when it turns into a frog?

12 What is the name given to a young horse?

13 What do you call the fruit of an oak tree?

14 What type of animal is a squirrel?

15 How many legs are there on a spider?

16 Which organ do fish breathe with?

17 Which is the largest mammal?

18 What do you call the larva of a butterfly?

19 Which organ do snakes hear with?

20 In what way does the appearance of the fur of a leopard differ from that of a tiger?

21 What does a kangaroo carry in its pouch?

22 The cry of which animal resembles laughter?

23 What colour are the flowers of the gorse shrub?

24 Is the guinea pig related to the pig?

25 What do you call dogs of mixed race?

26 What sort of animal is a terrapin?

27 What distinguishes the bat from other mammals?

28 What do you call a male non-working bee?

29 What do you call a female fox?

30 What do vultures mainly feed on?

31 Why do woodpeckers peck holes in trees?

32 What substance can octopuses eject when disturbed?

33 Where do badgers make their homes?

34 What type of animal is a lizard?

35 What sort of plant is a death cap?

36 What is a cobra able to do to its neck?

37 What do female mosquitos feed on?

38 What do you call an adult male chicken?

39 Which is the largest bird?

40 What does the giant panda mainly feed on?

41 What do you call the groups wolves make up?

42 What is the most obvious difference between a slug and a snail?

43 What animal class does a spider belong to?

44 Where do beavers make their habitat?

45 Where are kippers caught?

46 What do you call a female dog?

47 How do hippopotamuses spend most of their day?

48 How does a hedgehog spend the winter?

49 What is a piranha?

50 What type of animal is a frog?

43

Odd One Out

Answers to this quiz are on page 229

EASY 😀

EASY

Player 1	Player 2
12	20
33	24
07	03
46	45
01	28
21	02
23	25
04	32
35	39
14	50
31	08
48	17
11	40
27	43
15	29
06	41
10	30
47	34
26	16
38	05
36	49
13	09
19	18
42	37
44	22

01 Who is the odd one out: (a) Magic Johnson, (b) Liam Neeson, (c) Sylvester Stallone, (d) Mel Gibson?

02 Who is the odd one out: (a) Tolstoy, (b) Yeltsin, (c) Chekov, (d) Pasternak?

03 Which of these singers is the odd one out: (a) Luciano Pavarotti, (b) Placido Domingo, (c) Maria Callas, (d) Barbra Streisand?

04 Which of the Marx Brothers is the odd one out: (a) Groucho, (b) Karl, (c) Chico, (d) Harpo?

05 Which of these are not famous brothers: (a) Grimm, (b) Wright, (c) Karamazov, (d) Chaplin?

06 Which is not a form of pasta: (a) spaghetti, (b) grissini, (c) tagliatelli, (d) lasagne?

07 Which of these fish is the odd one out: (a) cod, (b) stickleback, (c) halibut, (d) coley?

08 Which of these languages is the odd one out: (a) Romanian, (b) Spanish, (c) Hungarian, (d) Italian?

09 Which of these drinks is not derived from grapes: (a) sherry, (b) whisky, (c) port, (d) wine?

10 Which of these wild animals is the odd one out: (a) lion, (b) dingo, (c) wolf, (d) mastiff?

11 Which of these precious metals is the odd one out: (a) gold, (b) uranium, (c) silver, (d) platinum?

12 Which of these trees is the odd one out: (a) oak, (b) ash, (c) willow, (d) cedar?

13 Which of these cats is the odd one out: (a) Siamese, (b) Tabby, (c) Burmese, (d) Russian Blue?

14 Which country is the odd one out: (a) Denmark, (b) Sweden, (c) Estonia, (d) Norway?

15 Which of these flags is the odd one out: (a) British, (b) American, (c) German, (d) French?

16 Which does not have a Celtic culture: (a) Ireland, (b) England, (c) Scotland, (d) Wales?

17 Which of these is not a language: (a) Serbo-Croat, (b) Basque, (c) Urdu, (d) Grimaldi?

18 Which of these is the odd one out: (a) Africa, (b) Asia, (c) Atlantis, (d) Europe?

19 Which of these groups of animals is the odd one out: (a) giggle, (b) swarm, (c) herd, (d) flock?

20 Which of these is not a cheese: (a) camembert, (b) parmesan, (c) garibaldi, (d) stilton?

21 Which ship is the odd one out: (a) The Mayflower, (b) The Golden Hind, (c) QE2, (d) The Victory

22 Which is the odd one out: (a) Crete, (b) Sicily, (c) Madagascar, (d) Luxembourg?

23 Which leader is the odd one out: (a) Roosevelt, (b) Gladstone, (c) Truman, (d) Kennedy?

24 Who is the odd one out: (a) Queen Victoria, (b) Kaiser Wilhelm, (c) Charlemagne, (d) Czar Nicholas II?

25 Which of these languages is not written in the Roman alphabet: (a) French, (b) Russian, (c) Spanish, (d) Finnish?

26 Which card is the odd one out: (a) nine of diamonds, (b) queen of clubs, (c) king of hearts, (d) jack of spades?

27 Which of these is not a culinary herb: (a) thyme, (b) arabica, (c) sage, (d) fennel?

28 Which of these is not an aid to sight: (a) monocle, (b) speculum, (c) telescope, (d) bifocals?

29 Which is not a type of footwear: (a) pattens, (b) moccasins, (c) clogs, (d) bloomers?

30 Which is the odd one out? (a) Blue Mountain, (b) Lapsang Souchong, (c) Darjeeling, (d) Earl Grey?

31 Which of these famous people is not French: (a) Brigitte Bardot, (b) Gabriela Sabatini, (c) Maurice Chevalier, (d) Cyrano de Bergerac?

32 Which is not made from carbon: (a) fibreglass, (b) soot, (c) diamond, (d) pencil lead?

33 Which of these is the odd one out: (a) kayak, (b) coracle, (c) binnacle, (d) canoe?

34 Which of these is not a dwelling: (a) topi, (b) bungalow, (c) tepee, (d) igloo?

35 Which of these is the odd one out: (a) jeans, (b) plus-fours, (c) chinos, (d) long johns?

36 Which of these is not a mollusc: (a) snail, (b) crab, (c) abalone, (d) periwinkle?

37 Which of these is not a mammal: (a) barracuda, (b) dolphin, (c) whale, (d) dormouse?

38 Which of these is not a rodent: (a) gerbil, (b) porcupine, (c) squirrel, (d) fruit bat?

39 Which of the following is not a bone of the human body: (a) tibia, (b) vertebra, (c) avuncular, (d) fibula?

40 Which is not a cloud formation: (a) tumulus, (b) cumulus, (c) cirrus, (d) nimbus?

41 Which of the following is not a flower: (a) geranium, (b) aster, (c) lucifer, (d) daisy?

42 Which of these is not a rock: (a) quartz, (b) diamond, (c) incunabula, (d) granite?

43 Which of the following museums would you find in Spain: (a) Prado, (b) Louvre, (c) Victoria and Albert, (d) Guggenheim?

44 Which of the following places would you not find in London: (a) Buckingham Palace, (b) Piccadilly, (c) Greenwich Village, (d) Soho?

45 Which of the following places would you not find in New York: (a) Harlem, (b) Leicester Square, (c) Queens, (d) Little Italy?

46 Which country is not in Africa: (a) Zaire, (b) Rwanda, (c) Ethiopia, (d) Ecuador?

47 Which of these was not a writer: (a) Laurie Lee, (b) George Orwell, (c) Marcel Proust, (d) Leon Trotsky?

48 Which of these is not a musical term: (a) piano, (b) lepidoptera, (c) concerto, (d) symphony?

49 Which of these is not a language: (a) Gaelic, (b) Hindi, (c) Catalan, (d) Jewish?

50 Which of these is a prime number: (a) 13, (b) 27, (c) 50, (d) 126?

45

Pot Luck

Answers to this quiz are on page 230

EASY 😊 **EASY**

Player 1	Player 2
12	20
33	24
07	03
46	45
01	28
21	02
23	25
04	32
35	39
14	50
31	08
48	17
11	40
27	43
15	29
06	41
10	30
47	34
26	16
38	05
36	49
13	09
19	18
42	37
44	22

01 What do you call the fortified section of an Ancient Greek city?

02 What type of plant is known as a sapling?

03 What distinguishes a nectarine from a peach?

04 Which is the largest planet?

05 What do caterpillars feed on?

06 What do you call the control panel of a car?

07 What do you call the process by which birds fly to warmer regions in winter?

08 Which singer is known as the 'King' of Rock 'n' Roll?

09 What do you call that part of the skin that contains the root of the hair?

10 Which sign of the Zodiac represents twins?

11 Who was the drummer with the Beatles?

12 What type of crystal is used in electronic watches?

13 In which part of the Americas did the Aztecs live?

14 What do you call the material Egyptians used to write on?

15 What do you call a young lion?

16 In which country would you find Florence?

17 What do the letters of the film *E.T.* stand for?

18 What do you call the meat produced from deer?

19 In which US city would you find Wall Street?

20 Which pop album has sold the most copies?

21 Who played the leading role in the film *Mrs Doubtfire*?

22 From which country does the flamenco dance originate?

23 In which part of the world is Laos?

24 What do you call trees that shed their leaves in the autumn, or fall?

25 What is the name of the molten rock which comes out of an erupting volcano?

26 Who uses Braille?

27 What type of vegetable is used for making sauerkraut?

28 Which animal's diet consists solely of eucalyptus leaves?

29 A horn belongs to which class of musical instruments?

30 What do the letters VIP stand for?

31 Which female singer released the album *Foreign Affair*?

32 What sort of animals are dolphins?

33 What type of medicine would you take to fight off bacteria?

34 What do you call a dog that descends from several species?

35 What are the colours of the Japanese flag?

36 What implement did farmers use to cut their crops by hand?

37 Which is the hottest planet?

38 What type of animal is a jackal?

39 Mick Jagger is the lead singer of which group?

40 The weight of which precious metal is measured in carats?

41 What type of writing was used in Ancient Egypt?

42 In Greek mythology, who was Icarus's father?

43 What do you call paintings on plaster which are found in old palaces and churches?

44 Which period of history means 'rebirth'?

45 What do you call a five-sided figure?

46 What do you call a thousand years?

47 Which awards are given out anually in Hollywood for achievements in movies?

48 What do you call the arms of an octopus?

49 What people used a tepee as a dwelling?

50 How did the Ancient Egyptians preserve the bodies of their kings?

Books

Answers to this quiz are on page 231

EASY 😊 EASY

Player 1	Player 2
12	20
33	24
07	03
46	45
01	28
21	02
23	25
04	32
35	39
14	50
31	08
48	17
11	40
27	43
15	29
06	41
10	30
47	34
26	16
38	05
36	49
13	09
19	18
42	37
44	22

01 Who wrote *Little Women*?

02 **Name the little creatures in the *Moomin* books who were attracted by thunder storms?**

03 In which book would you find Mayella Ewell?

04 **Who wrote *Jane Eyre*?**

05 In which series of books would you find the fortress of Salamandastron?

06 **In which William Golding book did a party of schoolboys turn cannibal?**

07 Which Astrid Lindgren character has a propeller protruding from his back?

08 **In which book would you meet Vermicious Knids?**

09 Where did Mr Badger live in *The Wind in the Willows*?

10 **Who was the author of *Farmer Giles of Ham*?**

11 Which creatures lived in Arnold Bros (est. 1905)?

12 **In which Terry Pratchett novel do we find the Nomes living in a quarry?**

13 In which novel was a toad taken in hand by a mole, a rat, and a badger?

14 **In which Conan Doyle novel did explorers find live dinosaurs?**

15 In which novel do we meet Gagool the witch-finder?

16 **What finally killed the invading aliens in *War of the Worlds*?**

17 What is the connection between birds, mythical female warriors, and an Arthur Ransom novel?

18 **In which Raymond Briggs book did a boy have a cold companion?**

19 In the book *Five Children and It* what was 'It's' proper name?

48

20 C.S Lewis's *Narnia* novels had a religious significance. Who did the lion represent?

21 In which novel was it 'always winter but never Christmas'?

22 Why do hobbits never need shoes?

23 What was the name of the devilish cat in Robin Jarvis's *Deptford Mice* novels?

24 What dire threat did Violet regularly make in the *William* series of books?

25 What was Dorothy's dog called in *The Wizard of Oz*?

26 Who was the villain of *The Adventures of Tom Sawyer*?

27 Who maintained law and order in Noddy's Toyland?

28 Who wrote *The Indian in the Cupboard*?

29 Which girl had a cannibal king for a father and lived with a horse and a monkey?

30 In the book *The Once and Future King*, who was the king?

31 In what situation might you need the help of Nancy Drew?

32 After the conclusion of *The Adventures of Tom Sawyer*, Tom and Huck meet up in another story and make a long journey. What sort of transport do they use?

33 What were the names of the Hardy Boys?

34 Which Dickens novel takes place during the French Revolution?

35 Which fictional hero, named after a flower, helped people to escape the guillotine?

36 Which Rosemary Sutcliffe novel concerned a Roman legion?

37 Who wrote *Three Men in a Boat*?

38 Who found himself in Lilliput?

39 Who wrote *Dido and Pa*?

40 Who is the main character in *The Red-Headed League*, *The Sign of Four*, and *The Speckled Band*?

41 Who wrote *The Call of the Wild*?

42 The hero of a Rudyard Kipling novel played a game which was supposed to improve his memory. Children still play the game at parties. What is it called?

43 Which small children's hero was, at the end of the original story, eaten by a spider (though later versions avoid this episode)?

44 Which pirate cook was eventually handed the black spot in *Treasure Island*?

45 What sort of creature was Tarka?

46 Where does the action of *Lorna Doone* take place?

47 In which novel would you find Heathcliff and Catherine Earnshaw?

48 What is the connection between E. Nesbitt and railways?

49 In which country is the action of War and Peace set?

50 In the early 19th century two German brothers wrote a collection of fairy tales. Who were they?

49

Places

Answers to this quiz are on page 231

EASY 😊 **EASY**

Player 1	Player 2
12	20
33	24
07	03
46	45
01	28
21	02
23	25
04	32
35	39
14	50
31	08
48	17
11	40
27	43
15	29
06	41
10	30
47	34
26	16
38	05
36	49
13	09
19	18
42	37
44	22

01 Which waterway separates Africa from Asia?

02 What is the capital city of Australia?

03 What is the city of Constantinople now called?

04 Which country does Greenland belong to?

05 Which city is further north – Paris or New York?

06 Which two countries does Norway have borders with?

07 Which is the second largest country in the world?

08 What do you call the narrow coastal inlets in Scandinavia?

09 Which are the two official languages of South Africa?

10 In which city would you find the Parthenon?

11 Which is the highest peak in the Alps?

12 Which country has the largest supplies of gold?

13 What is the capital of Massachusetts?

14 Which is the most southerly point of South America?

15 Which is the longest river in North America?

16 In which US city would you find the Sears Tower?

17 Which two languages are spoken in Belgium?

18 If you are at Orly Airport which city would you be in?

19 Which country has about 40% of its land situated below sea level?

20 In which Italian city would you find the Bridge of Sighs?

21 Which two countries make up the Iberian Peninsula?

22 In which country would you pay in drachmas?

23 Which volcano is situated on the island of Sicily?

24 Which country does Corsica belong to?

25 Which of these countries does the Equator not go through:
a) Zaire, b) Indonesia,
c) Argentina, d) Kenya, e) Brazil?

26 In which continent is Lake Victoria?

27 Which city does the Sugar Loaf Mountain overlook?

28 Which country does Iceland belong to?

29 In which city is the church Sacre Coeur situated?

30 What language is spoken in Syria?

31 Which is the largest state of the USA?

32 Which country is Helsinki the capital of?

33 Which religious community has its headquarters in Salt Lake City?

34 Which is the largest country in South America?

35 In which city would you find the Brandenburg Gate?

36 Which is the highest mountain peak in Africa?

37 What is the name of the island state situated south of the Malay Peninsula?

38 On which river is Paris situated?

39 To which group of islands does Lanzarote belong?

40 On which lake is Chicago situated?

41 Under what name was Thailand formerly known?

42 What is the name of the Italian island to the South of Corsica?

43 Where are the Atlas Mountains?

44 Where is the seat of the International Red Cross?

45 What is the capital of Argentina?

46 Which is the largest of the Greek islands?

47 What language is spoken in Brazil?

48 What is Leningrad now called?

49 In which country would you pay with guilders?

50 Before Kenya gained independence, which country had been its governor?

51

Pot Luck

Answers to this quiz are on pages 230-231

EASY 😊 **EASY**

Player 1	Player 2
12	20
33	24
07	03
46	45
01	28
21	02
23	25
04	32
35	39
14	50
31	08
48	17
11	40
27	43
15	29
06	41
10	30
47	34
26	16
38	05
36	49
13	09
19	18
42	37
44	22

01 What was the prehistoric predecessor of the elephant?

02 Which sign of the Zodiac represents a pair of scales?

03 What is the main difference between a guitar and a violin?

04 Who was the lead singer of the group Queen?

05 What type of entertainment was Fred Astaire famous for?

06 How many minutes does a soccer match last?

07 What type of instrument would you use to view a distant star?

08 Which people built longships?

09 During a period of high pressure, would you expect sunny or changeable weather?

10 Which was Walt Disney's first full-length animated cartoon?

11 Which title was given to the kings of Ancient Egypt?

12 In which period of American history does the film *Gone with the Wind* take place?

13 What is the name of the layer that protects the Earth from the ultraviolet rays of the Sun?

14 In which country was paper invented?

15 From which European country does the paella originate?

16 What does a flag at half mast indicate?

17 In which Steven Spielberg film would you find dinosaurs living in modern times?

18 Which group of animals form a shoal?

19 What type of stories did Hans Christian Andersen write?

52

20 What is special about the Dog Star (Canis Major)?

21 What does a skunk do to ward off predators?

22 In which country is Krakow situated?

23 In which country would you find the river Seine?

24 What is the name of the professional fighters in Ancient Rome who engaged in public performances?

25 What distinguishes a British stamp from all other stamps in the world?

26 Which country is also referred to as Eire?

27 What do you call a person that studies the stars?

28 A silkworm feeds on the leaves of which tree?

29 In which country did people first have a Christmas tree?

30 In which European city would you find Euro Disney?

31 What are the colours of the German flag?

32 *The Marseillaise* is the national anthem of which country?

33 In Greek mythology, what was the most prominent feature of a Cyclops?

34 Where is Robin Hood supposed to have lived?

35 What does supersonic mean?

36 Which of the following is not a measurement of length: (a) meter, (b) cubic feet, (c) inch, (d) yard, or (e) mile?

37 In a soccer team, who is the only player who can pick up a ball with his hands?

38 What is a gaucho?

39 Which of the following countries are not monarchies: (a) The Netherlands, (b) Sweden, (c) Italy?

40 What do you call a flesh-eating animal?

41 What do you call a person who prepares weather forecasts?

42 What do you call the figure written below the line in a fraction?

43 What do you call the process by which gas or vapour turns liquid?

44 What do you call the place a rabbit lives in?

45 Which Greek goddess is believed to have emerged from the sea?

46 Which country would a cosmonaut come from?

47 What do you call it when the Moon moves in front of the Sun and blocks out all the light?

48 What sort of animal is a gibbon?

49 In a soccer match, what does a player have to do if he is shown a red card?

50 What do you call a group of lions?

53

Synonyms

Answers to this quiz are on page 231

EASY EASY

54

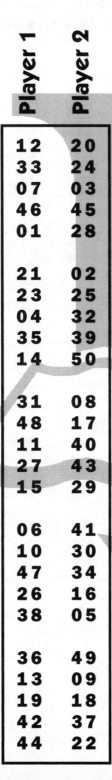

Player 1	Player 2
12	20
33	24
07	03
46	45
01	28
21	02
23	25
04	32
35	39
14	50
31	08
48	17
11	40
27	43
15	29
06	41
10	30
47	34
26	16
38	05
36	49
13	09
19	18
42	37
44	22

01 Honest is the same as: (a) right, (b) honorable, (c) clever.

02 Scared is the same as: (a) frightened, (b) awful, (c) cowardly.

03 Fat is the same as: (a) big, (b) heavy, (c) obese.

04 Glad is the same as: (a) happy, (b) relieved, (c) encouraged.

05 False is the same as: (a) obscure, (b) untrue, (c) debased.

06 Hygienic is the same as: (a) moral, (b) new, (c) healthy.

07 Greedy is the same as: (a) hungry, (b) grasping, (c) rude.

08 Infantile is the same as: (a) silly, (b) stupid, (c) childish.

09 Indelicate is the same as: (a) indecent, (b) clumsy, (c) careless.

10 Gratitude is the same as: (a) pleasure, (b) thanks, (c) friendship.

11 Civil is the same as: (a) polite, (b) public, (c) sneaky.

12 Confront is the same as: (a) fight, (b) encounter, (c) reject.

13 Eliminate is the same as: (a) exclude, (b) include, (c) prejudice.

14 Surmount is the same as: (a) ride, (b) settle, (c) overcome.

15 Plead is the same as: (a) excuse, (b) beg, (c) grant.

16 Advance is the same as: (a) overtake, (b) progress, (c) consult.

17 Suppose is the same as: (a) believe, (b) suspect, (c) guess.

18 Debate is the same as: (a) quarrel, (b) return, (c) argue.

19 Relieve is the same as: (a) ease, (b) copy, (c) weigh.

20 Derange is the same as: (a) destroy, (b) upset, (c) break.

21 Profit is the same as: (a) reward, (b) gain, (c) grow.

22 Pursue is the same as: (a) catch, (b) entrap, (c) follow.

23 Graceful is the same as: (a) elegant, (b) kind, (c) supple.

24 Fierce is the same as: (a) wild, (b) strong, (c) ferocious.

25 Hazardous is the same as: (a) risky, (b) evil, (c) impolite.

26 Faint is the same as: (a) ill, (b) fuzzy, (c) fall.

27 Morose is the same as: (a) gloomy, (b) secret, (c) angry.

28 Nimble is the same as: (a) quick, (b) clever, (c) agile.

29 Glorious is the same as: (a) marvellous, (b) quaint, (c) expensive.

30 Savage is the same as: (a) native, (b) vicious, (c) gross.

31 Belated is the same as: (a) overdue, (b) crowded, (c) shouted.

32 Complete is the same as: (a) final, (b) perfect, (c) absolute.

33 Confidence is the same as: (a) happiness, (b) sureness, (c) popularity.

34 Vivacious is the same as: (a) lively, (b) pretty, (c) rich.

35 Elucidate is the same as: (a) terminate, (b) explain, (c) affront.

36 Rotate is the same as: (a) turn, (b) rumble, (c) ascend.

37 Divine is the same as: (a) spooky, (b) holy, (c) tasty.

38 Glamour is the same as: (a) luck, (b) charm, (c) heroism.

39 Grief is the same as: (a) sadness, (b) misfortune, (c) loss.

40 Trivial is the same as: (a) poor, (b) petty, (c) unlucky.

41 Jovial is the same as: (a) ruddy, (b) sweaty, (c) merry.

42 Lament is the same as: (a) sing, (b) moan, (c) dream.

43 Youthful is the same as: (a) juvenile, (b) inexperienced, (c) silly.

44 Clamorous is the same as: (a) attractive, (b) loudmouthed, (c) crowded.

45 Ornate is the same as: (a) flamboyant, (b) antique, (c) detailed.

46 Basic is the same as: (a) flat, (b) elementary, (c) straight.

47 Outlandish is the same as: (a) fashionable, (b) bizarre, (c) foreign.

48 Horrid is the same as: (a) grim, (b) fierce, (c) ugly.

49 Fortunate is the same as: (a) lucky, (b) sincere, (c) wealthy.

50 Normal is the same as: (a) boring, (b) usual, (c) safe.

Books

Answers to this quiz are on page 232

EASY EASY

Player 1	Player 2
12	20
33	24
07	03
46	45
01	28
21	02
23	25
04	32
35	39
14	50
31	08
48	17
11	40
27	43
15	29
06	41
10	30
47	34
26	16
38	05
36	49
13	09
19	18
42	37
44	22

01 In *Alice in Wonderland*, was it the bottled drink or the cake which made Alice smaller?

02 What sort of hat did the Mad Hatter wear?

03 Who faded away until only his grin was left?

04 Which comic book heroes lived in a sewer and enjoyed martial arts?

05 Who had the code number 007?

06 Which comic–book hero had a girlfriend called Dale Arden?

07 In the New Testament, which John was beheaded for the sake of a dance?

08 Which French army is featured in the novel *Beau Geste*?

09 Which Rider Haggard character found the secret of eternal youth?

10 Who lost his trousers in *King Solomon's Mines*?

11 Who was Jeeves?

12 Which series of children's stories was written by the Duchess of York of England?

13 In which novel do we first meet Zaphod Beeblebrox?

14 Who invented Disc World?

15 Which Dickens character never recovered from her wedding?

16 In *Great Expectations*, what trade did Pip's brother-in-law and guardian follow?

17 Which villain in *Oliver Twist* owned a dog?

18 Which novel opens with the words, 'Marley was dead, to begin with'?

19 What was Scrooge's first name?

20 Which comic-strip detective would you find in the company of Captain Haddock and the Thompson twins?

21 What was the name of Tin Tin's dog?

22 In which novels are you likely to find a Fillyjonk?

23 Which Moomin character freezes the ground on which it sits?

24 Which Moomin character rides a black panther?

25 Which important person did the BFG meet?

26 In which book would you find Uncas and Chingachgook?

27 In which book did Scout go to a school pageant dressed as a ham?

28 Complete the title *The Thirty-nine...*

29 Complete the title *The Red Badge of...*

30 Complete the title *The Man in the Iron...*

31 Complete the title *Anne of ... Gables.*

32 Which vampire was defeated by Professor van Helsing?

33 For what sort of books is John Wyndham famous?

34 Which jungle hero was created by Edgar Rice Burroughs?

35 What was the sequel to *What Katy Did?*

36 Complete the title *The Little House on the...*

37 Complete the title *The Restaurant at the End of the...*

38 Who wrote *Sense and Sensibility?*

39 Who wrote *2001: A Space Odyssey?*

40 What was a Triffid?

41 Where, according to John Wyndham, did the Kraken live?

42 In which John Wyndham book did children develop telepathy after a nuclear war?

43 What sort of stories would you find in the *Goosebumps* series?

44 Complete the title *The Count of Monte...*

45 In which country does Tolstoy's *War and Peace* take place?

46 Which boy, according to Roald Dahl, was 'Champion of the World'?

47 Why did Roald Dahl's *Enormous Crocodile* think he would be successful in catching a child for lunch?

48 What happened to Roald Dahl's enormous crocodile?

49 What is unusual about the book *The Hungry Caterpillar?*

50 Who created *The Cat in the Hat?*

Pot Luck

Answers to this quiz are on page 231

EASY 😊 **EASY**

Player 1	Player 2
12	20
33	24
07	03
46	45
01	28
21	02
23	25
04	32
35	39
14	50
31	08
48	17
11	40
27	43
15	29
06	41
10	30
47	34
26	16
38	05
36	49
13	09
19	18
42	37
44	22

58

01 What is the British flag commonly known as?

02 Which are the two main political parties in the USA?

03 In which city would you find the cathedral of Notre Dame?

04 Is the average temperature on Mars higher or lower than that on Earth?

05 What type of musical instrument is a trumpet?

06 Which instrument would you use if you want to know which direction to go when travelling?

07 In information storage terms what does CD stand for?

08 What type of sport is sumo?

09 What was the first type of air travel?

10 What is the name given to our galaxy?

11 Which of the following materials is not produced naturally: (a) polyester, (b) cotton, (c) silk?

12 Where would you find stalagmites and stalactites?

13 Which of the planets is referred to as the red planet?

14 What would you call a mass of slow-moving ice?

15 What is the main character in the film *Babe*?

16 How long does it take for the Earth to travel round the Sun?

17 Who plays the lead in the film *Home Alone*?

18 Which member of the Beatles was shot dead in 1980?

19 What is the largest stringed instrument?

20 In which country would you find the Dordogne?

21 What is a prime number?

22 What do you call an artist that makes columns and statues by carving materials such as stone and marble?

23 Which part of a plant causes hayfever?

24 What would you call a flat, curved implement that, when thrown, always comes back to the thrower?

25 Which was the first of the *Indiana Jones* films?

26 In the game of Badminton, what do you call the thing you hit with your racket?

27 Which people would use a tomahawk as a weapon?

28 What does VE Day stand for?

29 The farther south you go the warmer the climate usually gets. Is this statement true?

30 What is the American flag commonly known as?

31 How long does it take for the Earth to make one complete revolution on its axis?

32 Who is the main character in the film *Licence to Kill*?

33 Which is the hardest naturally occurring substance found?

34 Which major sporting event originated in Ancient Greece?

35 With which country do you associate Sadam Hussein?

36 Which of the following is not a measurement of weight: (a) ounce, (b) kilogram, (c) ton, (d) litre, (e) pound?

37 What shape is an amphitheatre?

38 For which invention is Samuel Morse best known?

39 In Greek mythology, a Minotaur is a cross between what?

40 What would you call a figure with six sides?

41 How many is half a dozen?

42 Which film's main attraction is a St Bernard puppy?

43 From which country do noodles originate?

44 Where is the centre of the US film industry?

45 What is the name of the German tennis player who first won Wimbledon in 1985 at the age of 17?

46 With which game do you associate knights, bishops, and queens?

47 In information technology what does PC stand for?

48 From what material are jeans made?

49 What type of vessel travels on a cushion of air?

50 What do you call a ditch around a castle?

59

Places

Answers to this quiz are on page 233

01 Which country is associated with bullfighting?

02 **In which European city would you find Westminster Abbey?**

03 Which is the largest country in South America?

04 **In which European country, apart from Germany, is German the only official language?**

05 Which is the smallest continent?

06 **In which country would you find the pyramids?**

07 What region are Denmark, Sweden, Norway, and Finland known as?

08 **On which continent is Israel situated?**

09 What is the capital of Japan?

10 **Which canal links the Atlantic and Pacific Oceans in Central America?**

11 In which country would you find Cape Town?

12 **In which European city would you find the Colosseum?**

13 In which city would you find the Kremlin?

14 **On which ocean is San Francisco situated?**

15 Which is the highest mountain range in the world?

16 **Which language is spoken in Mexico?**

17 What do the stars on the American flag stand for?

18 **Which is the most famous building in Pisa?**

19 What is the capital of Germany?

EASY 😊 EASY

Player 1	Player 2
12	20
33	24
07	03
46	45
01	28
21	02
23	25
04	32
35	39
14	50
31	08
48	17
11	40
27	43
15	29
06	41
10	30
47	34
26	16
38	05
36	49
13	09
19	18
42	37
44	22

20 Which island state lies to the south-east of Australia?

21 What is the Serengeti known for?

22 What is the Sahara?

23 Which is the most northerly state in the USA?

24 In which continent would you find the country of Zaire?

25 What religion are the majority of the people of India?

26 Which city is further north – New York or Moscow?

27 Which country would you go through in order to travel by land from France to Portugal?

28 Which island state lies to the west of Great Britain?

29 Which continents do the Ural Mountains separate?

30 In which US city would you find the Golden Gate Bridge?

31 With which countries does Iceland border?

32 What is the capital of Egypt?

33 Which is the largest mountain range in Europe?

34 In which European city would you find the Parthenon?

35 Rio de Janeiro is situated in which country?

36 What type of fish can you find in the Dead Sea?

37 Which inhabited continent is entirely in the Southern Hemisphere?

38 Which ocean would you have to cross to travel from London to New York?

39 In which city would you find the Hermitage Museum?

40 In which island group would you find Honolulu?

41 Ottawa is the capital of which country?

42 In which city would you find the Empire State Building?

43 Which of these cities is the odd one out: Calcutta, Bombay, New Delhi, Bangkok, Madras?

44 The Bloody Tower is part of which English castle?

45 The island of Sicily belongs to which country?

46 What is the capital of China?

47 Which island state lies to the South of Florida?

48 In which European city would you find the Eiffel Tower?

49 Which is the main language spoken in Israel?

50 On which continent is Sydney situated?

63

Pot Luck

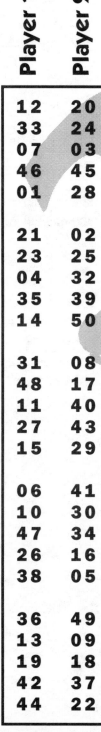

EASY 😀 **EASY**

Player 1	Player 2
12	20
33	24
07	03
46	45
01	28
21	02
23	25
04	32
35	39
14	50
31	08
48	17
11	40
27	43
15	29
06	41
10	30
47	34
26	16
38	05
36	49
13	09
19	18
42	37
44	22

01 What sort of animal was Shere Khan?

02 Which sort of tree produces acorns?

03 What is important about the years 1939 to 1945?

04 Which English king was beheaded?

05 What is the capital of Egypt?

06 How many bits are there in one byte?

07 What is the chemical symbol for water?

08 Watts, volts, and amperes are all associated with which form of power?

09 Which planet of our solar system is farthest from the Sun?

10 What sort of things do weather forecasters mean when they talk about 'precipitation'?

11 The Chinese call a man-powered cart *ren li che*. What is the English name?

12 What is a durian?

13 Is the fruit of the horse chestnut tree edible by humans?

14 What were fathoms traditionally used to measure?

15 Bosnia and Croatia used to be part of which Country?

16 Which country was once ruled by General Franco?

17 What is the Japanese name for the art of paper folding?

18 On which continent would you find Algeria?

19 Are flying fish capable of powered flight?

20 The Chinese used tea as money. True or false?

21 Can gold be any colour other than yellow?

22 Are white elephants really white?

23 How many is a score?

24 How many is a baker's dozen?

25 Which mammal is widely regarded as the ugliest on Earth?

26 In the works of J.R.R. Tolkien what were Ents?

27 Which is the odd one out: (a) Sahara, (b) Gobi, (c) Camargue?

28 Why do unsupported objects fall to Earth?

29 Which of these is the hardest: (a) granite, (b) sandstone, (c) chalk?

30 Which of the following is the odd one out: (a) Chopin, (b) Tolstoy, (c) Beethoven?

31 In which kind of year does February have 29 days?

32 Which dog is known for having a purple tongue?

33 Snoopy, in the *Peanuts* cartoons, is what breed of dog?

34 Gdansk is part of which country?

35 What is the difference between frog spawn and toad spawn?

36 Which comic book hero features in a song by Queen?

37 What was the name of Mickey Mouse's dog?

38 If you saw 'escargots' on a menu what would you expect to get?

39 How many soldiers would a centurion have commanded?

40 What is the collective name for several machine guns?

41 What is a guppy?

42 What sort of insect transmits the disease malaria?

43 What disease caused the Black Death?

44 If you cut an earthworm in half, what happens to it?

45 What do herbivores eat?

46 What do 'Mach' speeds represent?

47 What is the fastest traveling thing we know?

48 Where would a troglodyte live?

49 What is agoraphobia?

50 Siamese, Russian Blue, and Manx are all varieties of what?

Pop Music

Answers to this quiz are on pages 232-233

EASY 😊

Player 1	Player 2
12	20
33	24
07	03
46	45
01	28
21	02
23	25
04	32
35	39
14	50
31	08
48	17
11	40
27	43
15	29
06	41
10	30
47	34
26	16
38	05
36	49
13	09
19	18
42	37
44	22

01 Which group released the album *Definitely Maybe*?

02 Which nationality is the singer Björk?

03 With which group do you associate Ali Campbell?

04 What is the title of the *Best of Bryan Adams* album?

05 Which Roxette song appears in the film *Pretty Woman*?

06 On which R.E.M. album would you find the song 'Everybody Hurts'?

07 In 1996 Take That had a hit with 'How Deep is Your Love'. Which group recorded the song originally?

08 Who is the lead singer of Simply Red?

09 Which group did Deborah Harry front?

10 Which group released the album *Jollification*?

11 What is the title of the greatest hits compilation of Simple Minds?

12 Which nationality is the singer Celine Dion?

13 On which Genesis album would you find the song 'No Son of Mine'?

14 What is the name of the album Pink Floyd brought out in 1994?

15 Which British group revived the 70s disco hit 'Don't Leave Me This Way' in 1986?

16 Which group released the album *The Great Escape*?

17 Which was Whitney Houston's first No. 1 hit?

18 Which of Madonna's hits dealt with a teenage pregnancy?

19 Who was the lead singer of the Pretenders?

20 Bob Geldof gained international recognition for the organization of which musical event?

21 Which was Dire Straits' first Top Ten hit?

22 Roger Taylor was the drummer of which rock group?

23 Which female group released the album *Power of a Woman*?

24 What is the name of the greatest hits compilation of Bon Jovi?

25 On which Sting album would you find the songs 'Fields of Gold' and 'If I Ever Lose My Faith in You'?

26 On which Michael Jackson album would you find 'The Way You Make Me Feel'?

27 With which group do you associate Jarvis Cocker?

28 Who is Annie Mae Bullock better known as?

29 With which group was Boy George associated?

30 Which female singer released the album *Tuesday Night Music Club*?

31 What is the title of the greatest hits compilation of Deacon Blue?

32 On which Meatloaf album would you find 'I'd Do Anything For Love'?

33 In 1982 Phil Collins had a hit with 'You Can't Hurry Love'. Who recorded the original version of the song?

34 Which singer wrote the UB40's hit 'Red, Red Wine'?

35 Damon Albarn is the lead singer of which group?

36 Which group recorded the album *Bizarre Fruit*?

37 With whom did George Michael team up with to form the duo Wham! in 1982?

38 With which group would you associate Boon and Phil Gould?

39 Richie Wermerling is the lead singer of which band?

40 Which group had hits in 1995 with 'Tell Me When' and 'One Man in My Heart'?

41 Which group brought out the album No Need to Argue ?

42 With which group(s) would you associate Vince Clarke?

43 Which female singer recorded the album *Medusa*?

44 Peter Buck is guitarist of which group?

45 What is the title of *The Best of the Beautiful South* album?

46 With which group do you associate Shane McGowan?

47 Which group revived the old 'Love Me For a Reason' in 1995?

48 Who wrote the Eric Clapton hit 'I Shot the Sheriff'?

49 Which group released the album *Unplugged in New York*?

50 Which group performed the title song to the James Bond film *View to a Kill*?

67

Science

Answers to this quiz are on page 233

EASY 😊

	Player 1	Player 2
	12	20
	33	24
	07	03
	46	45
	01	28
	21	02
	23	25
	04	32
	35	39
	14	50
	31	08
	48	17
	11	40
	27	43
	15	29
	06	41
	10	30
	47	34
	26	16
	38	05
	36	49
	13	09
	19	18
	42	37
	44	22

68

01 What happens to objects in zero gravity?

02 **What do you call the thin coil of wire inside a light bulb?**

03 Why do water pipes often burst in freezing weather?

04 **What happens if you push a north pole of one magnet towards a north pole of another magnet?**

05 Which are the primary colours?

06 **Which instrument would you use to measure air pressure?**

07 Why would a balloon filled with hot air fly better on a cold day than on a warm day?

08 **What do vibrations in the air produce?**

09 What do you call a material that can carry electricity?

10 **What would you test with litmus paper?**

11 What is electric current measured in?

12 **What is the so-called 'greenhouse effect'?**

13 Which two metals does bronze mainly consist of?

14 **Which theory is express by the equation $E = mc^2$?**

15 Which of the following was not a scientist: (a) Copernicus, (b) Gogol, or (c) Pasteur?

16 **What is the process by which seeds produce roots and shoots?**

17 What is the process by which iron rusts?

18 **Water can fall below freezing point without turning to ice. True or false?**

19 Some parts of the Sun are cooler and darker than others. What are these called?

20 If a creature is described as 'saurian' what is it like?

21 What do botanists study?

22 Do heavy objects fall faster than light ones?

23 In the northern hemisphere, in which direction would the winds of a low pressure system circulate?

24 There is a theory that the continents once fitted together like pieces of a jigsaw puzzle but have since moved apart. What is this movement called?

25 What is the hottest part of a candle flame?

26 What force makes objects fall to earth?

27 What is meant by the 'escape velocity' of a rocket leaving the earth?

28 Which type of carbon is used both as a lubricant and as the 'lead' in pencils?

29 Iron pyrites has a golden colour. What is its nickname?

30 Which very precious stone is made from heavily compressed carbon?

31 Which strong metal is composed mainly of iron and carbon?

32 If at least 10% chromium is added to steel to prevent corrosion, what is the resulting metal called?

33 Where in the garden would you expect to find humus?

34 What useful function does the Earth's ozone layer perform?

35 What is a common name for the Aurora Borealis?

36 What is the storage capacity of a floppy disk measured in?

37 What is the full name for the 'tube' of a television?

38 Does water ice exist on Mars?

39 The planet Uranus is orbited by at least 15 moons. What other objects surround the planet?

40 If something is called 'vitreous', what does this mean?

41 What is the difference between flammable and inflammable?

42 What gas is found in marshes (marsh gas) and down coal mines (fire damp)?

43 Where would you expect to find gluten?

44 Neon signs contain the gas neon, of course, but what other gas is also commonly used?

45 With the development of what weapon is J. Robert Oppenheimer associated?

46 In computers what does BIOS stand for?

47 What does CD-ROM stand for?

48 What is solid carbon dioxide called?

49 Apart from freezing water vapour, what else is necessary for a snow flake to form?

50 The air mixture breathed by divers contains oxygen mixed with what other gas?

69

Pot Luck

EASY 😊 **EASY**

Player 1	Player 2
12	20
33	24
07	03
46	45
01	28
21	02
23	25
04	32
35	39
14	50
31	08
48	17
11	40
27	43
15	29
06	41
10	30
47	34
26	16
38	05
36	49
13	09
19	18
42	37
44	22

70

01 In Greek mythology, who slew the Minotaur?

02 Lufthansa is the national airline of which country?

03 A muslim is a follower of which religion?

04 What do you call a plant-eating animal?

05 What do you call a group of stars?

06 Which painter created the *Mona Lisa*?

07 What does a philatelist collect?

08 Which instrument would a doctor use to listen to your chest?

09 From which material is a xylophone made?

10 Which prize is awarded annually in Norway for outstanding achievements in promoting world peace?

11 Christopher Reeve became famous for his portrayal of which comic book character?

12 Which country's flag is referred to as 'Tricolor'?

13 What do you call a person who studies the history, structure and, origin of the Earth?

14 Which sign of the zodiac represents a goat?

15 Which title does a Jewish religious leader carry?

16 What are teeth used for cutting called?

17 In which country would you hear Flemish being spoken?

18 On which islands do people dance the Hula Hula?

19 In which state does the Pope live?

20 Who played James Bond in the film *The Spy Who Loved Me*?

21 What treasure is kept in Fort Knox?

22 In which building does the president of the USA live?

23 What is a person with arachnophobia frightened of?

24 What kind of animals were Lady and the Tramp?

25 Which actor played Kojak on television?

26 Which direction does the needle on a compass always point to?

27 Which European city does the Greenwich Meridian go through?

28 What do you call the wind that accompanies the wet season in India and South-east Asia?

29 What was the sequel to *Star Wars*?

30 How many degrees does a right angle have?

31 What would you find in the Louvre?

32 What is the capital of Belgium?

33 What sort of animal is a gerbil?

34 What would somebody perform an autopsy on?

35 Who directed the film *Jaws*?

36 Which character's nose grew longer when he told a lie?

37 What system do the brain and spinal cord form?

38 In which country would you find Adelaide and Brisbane?

39 What is the name for a river that flows into a larger river?

40 What suits are there in a pack of cards?

41 Which film features the song 'Take My Breath Away'?

42 If it is lunchtime in London, what time of day would it be in New York?

43 What are 100 acres called?

44 Which country does Edam cheese come from?

45 Which country has the largest population?

46 A person with the most common form of colour blindness cannot distinguish between which two colours?

47 What do you call animals with a pouch?

48 In which country is the Black Forest situated?

49 In which part of the body are the vertebrae?

50 Which country would you have to cross to travel from Alaska to the rest of the USA?

Places

Answers to this quiz are on pages 233-234

EASY

Player 1	Player 2
12	20
33	24
07	03
46	45
01	28
21	02
23	25
04	32
35	39
14	50
31	08
48	17
11	40
27	43
15	29
06	41
10	30
47	34
26	16
38	05
36	49
13	09
19	18
42	37
44	22

01 What is the capital of Italy?

02 **Which ocean would you have to cross to travel from North America to Japan?**

03 In which European city do canals replace roads and people travel around by gondolas and boats?

04 **Which is the main language spoken in Egypt?**

05 On which sea are Italy, Greece, and the south of France situated?

06 **In which country would you pay in Deutschmarks?**

07 On which continent is Mexico situated?

08 **What is the capital of the USA?**

09 Which city is further north – London or Los Angeles?

10 **Which is the highest mountain in the world?**

11 With which of these countries does France not border: (a) Germany, (b) Spain, (c) Russia?

12 **In which country would you find the Rocky Mountains?**

13 If you are travelling to Heathrow Airport, which country would be your destination?

14 **Which city is the odd one out: (a) New York, (b) Washington, (c) San Francisco, (d) Paris, (e) New Orleans?**

15 Which waterway must you cross to travel from England to France?

16 **Los Angeles, San Francisco and San Diego are all in which US state?**

17 On which continent is Spain situated?

18 **Which are the only two continents that are joined together?**

19 Which is the odd country out: (a) Great Britain, (b) Ireland, (c) Greenland, (d) New Zealand, (e) Germany?

72

20 What is the capital of Russia?

21 Does Canada lie north or south of the Equator?

22 Which country lies to the north of England?

23 In which city is Red Square situated: (a) New York, (b) Moscow, (c) Athens?

24 If you travelled to Australia in July, what season would it be?

25 In which European city would you find Big Ben?

26 Which is the largest city in the Netherlands?

27 On which ocean is New York situated?

28 In which country would you find Barcelona, Madrid and Malaga?

29 Which two languages are spoken in Wales?

30 Which is the odd country out: (a) USA, (b) France, (c) Australia, (d) Ireland, (e) Great Britain?

31 In which city would you find Manhattan, Ellis Island and Central Park?

32 Which country would you need to cross to travel from Canada to Mexico?

33 What is the capital of Israel?

34 Which pole is New Zealand nearest to?

35 With which country does China not form a border: (a) Russia, (b) Mongolia, (c) Israel?

36 Which US state is further west, Texas or Florida?

37 What type of mountain is Fujiyama?

38 Athens is the capital of which country: (a) Greece, (b) Egypt, (c) Denmark?

39 Apart from France, which other country uses Francs: (a) Italy, (b) Switzerland, (c) Russia?

40 Which of the following cities is not situated at the coast: (a) Boston, (b) Copenhagen, (c) Moscow?

41 In which US state is Disneyland situated: (a) California, (b) Texas, (c) Oregon?

42 In which European city would you find the Champs Elysées and the Arc de Triomphe?

43 In which of the following countries would you not find any Inuit: (a) Canada, (b) Mexico, (c) Greenland?

44 In which country would you most likely find a mosque as a country's main place of worship: (a) China, (b) Australia, (c) Saudi Arabia?

45 In which African state is Johannesburg situated: (a) South Africa, (b) Egypt, (c) Kenya?

46 Which European country has the shape of a boot?

47 Which continent is situated south of Europe?

48 Which of the following countries does not border the Atlantic: (a) France, (b) USA, (c) China?

49 Where would the climate be warmer – Norway or Portugal?

50 Which is the odd one out: (a) Paris, (b) Oxford, (c) Rome, (d) Tokyo, (e) Moscow?

73

Pot Luck

Answers to this quiz are on page 234

EASY 😊 **EASY**

Player 1	Player 2
12	20
33	24
07	03
46	45
01	28
21	02
23	25
04	32
35	39
14	50
31	08
48	17
11	40
27	43
15	29
06	41
10	30
47	34
26	16
38	05
36	49
13	09
19	18
42	37
44	22

74

01 Do stalactites grow up or down?

02 **What is another name for the constellation Orion?**

03 Lakota, Dakota, and Arapaho are all what sort of people?

04 **What are clouds usually made of?**

05 Who was imprisoned and executed at Fotheringay?

06 **Do daffodils grow from (a) seeds, (b) bulbs, or (c) corms?**

07 'Bald', 'golden', and 'sea' are all varieties of what sort of bird?

08 **What completely harmless creature is sometimes called a devilfish because of its horned head?**

09 What sort of creature is a flying fox?

10 **Vampire bats exist only in stories. True or false?**

11 What weather phenomenon was the Norse god Thor thought to control?

12 **What was strange about the appearance of a cyclops?**

13 Which constellation can be seen in Australia but not in the Northern Hemisphere?

14 **What does a snake do to aid its growing process?**

15 Which soldiers were known as 'iron sides'?

16 **Narcissus stared at his reflection in a pond for so long that something unfortunate happened to him. What was it?**

17 What causes the phenomena known as shooting stars?

18 **By what other name is the Yeti known?**

19 Of which community is the Dalai Lama the spiritual head?

20 Of which country was Lenin the leader?

21 What number is meant by a 'gross'?

22 Which town lost its children to the Pied Piper?

23 What was the name of the uncouth savages in *Gulliver's Travels*?

24 What is the difference between pianoforte and forte-piano?

25 Antonio Stradivari was a famous maker of musical instruments. In what did he specialize?

26 On which side of a tree would you expect to see lichen growing?

27 In which country does most of Siberia lie?

28 Which so-called sea is actually the world's largest lake?

29 Where would you find the Sea of Tranquillity?

30 Which lake in north-central Scotland is reputed to contain a monster?

31 What is a kumquat?

32 What is meant by the expressions 'in the land of Nod' and 'in the arms of Morpheus'?

33 How many bits make one byte?

34 What mysterious event took place at Belshazzar's feast?

35 Which building is occupied by the US Defense Department?

36 What does 1760 yards make?

37 Is a tomato a vegetable?

38 What is a prickly pear?

39 What is another name for eggplant?

40 What wood was frequently used for making longbows?

41 What wood did the British Navy use to build its ships?

42 How was Hamlet's father murdered?

43 Who wore an ass's head in *A Midsummer Night's Dream*?

44 Who was the villain in *Tom Brown's Schooldays*?

45 How often does Halley's comet return to the vicinity of Earth?

46 How did the Invisible Man cover up his problem?

47 Which H.G. Wells story showed horrific visions of the future?

48 Which character in ancient mythology had a sword suspended over his head, held by a single hair?

49 Who turned his daughter to gold with a kiss?

50 What supposedly happens to trolls caught in the daylight?

The Human Body

Answers to this quiz are on page 234

Player 1	Player 2
12	20
33	24
07	03
46	45
01	28
21	02
23	25
04	32
35	39
14	50
31	08
48	17
11	40
27	43
15	29
06	41
10	30
47	34
26	16
38	05
36	49
13	09
19	18
42	37
44	22

EASY 😀 **EASY**

76

01 What name is more usually given to the epidermis?

02 What do we call the collection of bones that supports the body?

03 What part of your body has auricles and ventricles?

04 What is a more common name for the patella?

05 Your hair and nails continue to grow after you are dead. True or false?

06 What part of the mouth is affected by periodontitis?

07 How many milk (first) teeth do we have?

08 What are the bones of the spine called?

09 In which body organ would you find a retina?

10 The body has two intestines; what are they called?

11 Men have a lump clearly visible at the front of the throat. What is the common name for it?

12 Is it true that men and women have different numbers of ribs?

13 What is the common name for the oesophagus?

14 What is the hard substance just under the white enamel of your teeth?

15 What is the average pulse rate for an adult at rest?

16 We have much more liver than we actually need. True or false?

17 Which human organ, shaped rather like a small sack, can become full of stones?

18 What is the technical name for the vertical bone that runs down the middle of the chest?

19 Where would you find the ulna and radius?

20 What is the technical name for the liquid waste which is collected in the bladder?

21 The skin is covered with millions of tiny holes. What are these called?

22 What effect does the diasease haemophilia have on the blood?

23 What is the name given to the large chewing teeth at the back of the mouth?

24 What is the pigment that gives some people brown skin?

25 Where in the body would you find saliva?

26 What is dandruff?

27 What is the disease in which the body's joints wear out?

28 Which are the smallest blood vessels: (a) arteries, (b) capillaries or (c) veins?

29 What is myopia?

30 Where would you find the tibia and fibula?

31 What is the name for the two spongy organs with which we breathe?

32 Which of these is not a body organ: (a) eulogy, (b) spleen, or (c) pancreas?

33 What organs transmit messages from parts of the body to the brain?

34 By what other name are the front cutting teeth known?

35 In what part of the body would you find a drum?

36 What is the mat of muscle that makes the lungs move?

37 What is inside the eyeball?

38 In which organ of the body would you find the pituitary gland?

39 What is the bone to which the legs are attached?

40 What is the main purpose of sweating?

41 In which part of the body would you find biceps and triceps?

42 Which part of the body is attacked by the disease meningitis?

43 Which childhood disease causes the salivary glands in the jaw to swell dramatically?

44 Which of these is not part of the body: (a) coccyx, (b) occiput, or (c) pachyderm?

45 What is the process called by which food is broken down and nutrition extracted?

46 What is the technical name for breathing?

47 Where would you find the gluteus maximus muscles?

48 Which part of the inner ear controls our sense of balance?

49 What is the condition in which a small part of the stomach lining is attacked and inflamed by gastric juices?

50 Which substance, associated with animal fat, is responsible for the narrowing of arteries?

Pot Luck

Answers to this quiz are on page 234

EASY

Player 1	Player 2
12	20
33	24
07	03
46	45
01	28
21	02
23	25
04	32
35	39
14	50
31	08
48	17
11	40
27	43
15	29
06	41
10	30
47	34
26	16
38	05
36	49
13	09
19	18
42	37
44	22

01 In Greek mythology, who married Eurydice?

02 Through which film did Paul Hogan come to fame?

03 Which country does the island of Crete belong to?

04 In which of the following countries are you most likely to come across a synagogue: (a) Egypt, (b) China, (c) Israel?

05 In computer language, what does MB stand for?

06 What do you call an optical instrument through which you look at pieces of coloured glass that form numerous symmetrical patterns when rotated?

07 In which country are you most likely to hear the bagpipes being played?

08 What does a seismograph record?

09 What type of organism is a sea anemone?

10 What do you call the tall posts, carved and painted by Native Americans?

11 According to legend, by which animal were Romulus and Remus nourished?

12 Which of the following languages is not written from left to right: (a) Arabic, (b) Russian, (c) Greek?

13 What do you call a pupa of a butterfly, enclosed in a cocoon?

14 What type of stories is Aesop famous for?

15 What is a facsimile machine commonly known as?

16 Which machine preceded the record player?

17 Which is the largest ape?

18 What could you do with a magic lantern?

19 What do you call a device in which two small telescopes are joined together and looked through simultaneously with both eyes?

20 What does a flint do when struck with a piece of steel?

21 In which country would you buy a stamp with the word Hellas on it?

22 In which country is the Sea of Galilee?

23 What would you make on a spinning wheel?

24 What is the title of the last Indiana Jones film?

25 What were catacombs used as?

26 What do fleas live on?

27 Which Greek philosopher lived in a tub?

28 What is measured on the Beaufort scale?

29 In which country is The Hague situated?

30 Which group brought out the album *Invisible Touch*?

31 What do you call the part of a river where it meets the sea?

32 With which organ do fish breathe?

33 Which part of a ship is the stern?

34 What name is given to troops that fight on horseback?

35 In computer terms, what does VDU stand for?

36 How many squares are there on a chessboard?

37 What is a loom used for?

38 Can you name the three kinds of honeybee?

39 What do you call a person who studies plants scientifically?

40 A quintet is made up of how many musicians?

41 In which European city would you find Tower Bridge?

42 A sphinx has a body of what animal?

43 Can you name the four oceans?

44 What do you call a shape whose two halves are mirror images of each other?

45 With which TV series do you associate Mr Spock?

46 Which nationality was Peter the Great?

47 Which street in New York is famous for its theatres?

48 What do you call a person who dies for his religious beliefs?

49 Which country does Camembert cheese come from?

50 Which animal is associated with being lazy?

79

History

Answers to this quiz are on page 235

MEDIUM 😊 **MEDIUM**

	Player 1	Player 2
	12	20
	33	24
	07	03
	46	45
	01	28
	21	02
	23	25
	04	32
	35	39
	14	50
	31	08
	48	17
	11	40
	27	43
	15	29
	06	41
	10	30
	47	34
	26	16
	38	05
	36	49
	13	09
	19	18
	42	37
	44	22

80

01 Who was the first Roman emperor?

02 **Where did the last battle of the Napoleonic Wars take place, resulting in a defeat for the French army?**

03 Who was beaten in the Battle at Gettysburg?

04 **What was the name of the British ship sunk by a German submarine on May 7, 1915?**

05 What was the name of the wars between Rome and Carthage, leading to Roman supremacy?

06 **What does Hadrian's Wall mark?**

07 Where was Joan of Arc burned?

08 **Who discovered Botany Bay in Australia?**

09 Who was Charles I fighting against in the English Civil War?

10 **Who succeeded Peter the Great as czar?**

11 Who was president of the Weimar Republic?

12 **Which two countries sided with Franco's Nationalists in the Spanish Civil War?**

13 Which empire did Hammurabi found?

14 **Mount Vernon is the estate of which American president?**

15 Who sailed to the USA on the Mayflower?

16 **What was the name of the people of the Bronze Age civilization on the island of Crete?**

17 Who was the leader of the Jacobins in the French Revolution?

18 **Where did the Black Death first strike?**

19 Who was the last czar of Russia?

20 **Who published the Communist Manifesto?**

21 Which country was the Spanish Armada set to invade?

22 From which area did the Mayan tribes originate?

23 Who was the first Englishman to sail around the world?

24 The peoples of which civilization invented the alphabet?

25 Which animals did Hannibal take with him for the invasion of Italy?

26 Which North American state did the Americans purchase from Napoleon in 1803?

27 Who was the longest-reigning British monarch?

28 Who was crowned emperor by the Pope in AD 800?

29 Which French Monarch was known as the Sun King?

30 What was the purpose of the Crusades?

31 Who was fighting the Peloponnesian War?

32 Which Roman emperor was regarded as the founder of the Christian Empire?

33 What was the name of Lenin's party during the Russian Revolution?

34 Who was American president at the start of the Great Depression?

35 Which important British document was issued in AD 1215?

36 During the reign of which king did the French Revolution start?

37 Which countries formed the Central Powers at the outbreak of World War I?

38 What was the name of the international conference held in order to redraw the map of Europe after Napoleon's downfall?

39 What did Martin Luther post on the church door at Wittenberg?

40 Who was Stalin's main opponent as Lenin's successor?

41 Which important waterway was opened in 1914?

42 What was the name of the French protestants during the 16th and 17th centuries?

43 Which incident started the Thirty Years' War?

44 Who was Henry VIII's first wife?

45 Which country did Frederick the Great rule?

46 Which Royal Family ruled England from 1485 to 1603?

47 In which year did William the Conqueror invade England?

48 Who was the wife of Louis XVI who was later tried by a Revolutionary Tribunal and guillotined?

49 Where was Napoleon exiled in 1815?

50 What was the name of the German king and emperor who led the Third Crusade?

Technology

Answers to this quiz are on page 235

MEDIUM ☻ MEDIUM MEDIUM

Player 1	Player 2
12	20
33	24
07	03
46	45
01	28
21	02
23	25
04	32
35	39
14	50
31	08
48	17
11	40
27	43
15	29
06	41
10	30
47	34
26	16
38	05
36	49
13	09
19	18
42	37
44	22

82

01 What is the difference between a mixture and a compound?

02 **What are the three methods by which heat travels?**

03 What force does a car have to overcome when it starts moving?

04 **What do we call the point about which a lever turns?**

05 Oil is used in machines to reduce what?

06 **What is an abacus?**

07 What are the two ways by which nuclear energy is produced?

08 **Centrifugal force pushes things outwards. What do we call the force that pulls objects inwards?**

09 Why do streamlined vehicles use less fuel?

10 **What simple machines are often used to change the direction of a force?**

11 In the Middle Ages what use did candles have apart from illumination?

12 **What was unusual about the Heinkel He 178?**

13 What was notable about the Focke-Wulf 61?

14 **Which time-keeping device had the most moving parts?**

15 Which time-keeping device had no moving parts?

16 **What is the cause of the apparent bending of a stick when it is thrust into water?**

17 If three light bulbs were wired in parallel and three identical ones were wired in series, which would be the brighter?

18 **If you wire up a small torch bulb in an electrical circuit containing a fresh lemon, the bulb will light. True or false?**

19 Nutcrackers are an example of what sort of mechanical device?

20 Why are drainage inspection covers usually round?

21 What device, which made use of phosphorus, was patented by shoemaker Alonzo D. Phillips in 1836 and was to become a familiar object in every household?

22 What improvement did John B. Dunlop make to the bicycle?

23 In 1849 Walter Hunt reinvented a device that had been used by ancient peoples for fastening clothes. What was it?

24 What oar-propelled craft did Dutchman Cornelius van Drebbel invent and demonstrate in the London reaches of the Thames in 1615?

25 What invention did Sir John Harrington bring back to the court of Queen Elizabeth I from a trip to Italy in 1595?

26 What device, still in common use, was invented by Alessandro Volta?

27 In which part of the world was the wheel invented?

28 Which city built the world's second underground railway?

29 What is the connection between Leonardo da Vinci and the bicycle?

30 Who was Laika?

31 Elisha Greaves Otis demonstrated his newly invented lift by stepping into it and asking a spectator to cut the cable. What happened?

32 Which household device originated in observations of the way in which ether evaporates?

33 What does the cochineal beetle have in common with gastropods of the Murex family?

34 Who invented the mercury thermometer?

35 Which was invented first, the screw or the screwdriver?

36 In which country was the mechanical clock first devised?

37 Salvino degli Armati was far-sighted enough to invent this common device in about 1280. What was it?

38 What device did Jethro Tull invent to improve agriculture?

39 In the 1930s Chester Carlson carried out research on a device which, by the 1950s, became common in many offices. What was it?

40 Nicolas Appert, a Paris confectioner and baker, won a prize of 12,000 francs for his invention. Napoleon had offered the prize because this invention would be of immense benefit to his armies. What was it?

41 The Remington company produced only guns until Christopher Latham Sholes sold them his invention. What was it?

42 Outside which famous building were the first traffic signals erected?

43 The zip fastener was invented by Henrik Zipper. True or false?

44 The safety razor was invented by a king. True or false?

45 What did Guglielmo Marconi invent in his parents' attic?

46 How were the earliest glass windows made?

47 What was Parkesine?

48 What items, initially made from ivory, were replaced by ones of celluloid?

49 What was a Bissell Grand Rapids?

50 In 1882 Henry W. Seeley, a New York inventor, came up with idea that smoothed the way for many a housewife or husband. What was it?

83

Food & Drink

Answers to this quiz are on pages 235-236

MEDIUM 😐 😵 **MEDIUM**

Player 1	Player 2
12	20
33	24
07	03
46	45
01	28
21	02
23	25
04	32
35	39
14	50
31	08
48	17
11	40
27	43
15	29
06	41
10	30
47	34
26	16
38	05
36	49
13	09
19	18
42	37
44	22

84

01 Which vegetable is used for making tzatziki?

02 From which French region does Muscadet originate?

03 What type of meat is used for osso buco?

04 Which is the main spice found in goulash?

05 What type of stew is a bouillabaisse?

06 Which country does Tokaj wine come from?

07 What is the name of a Greek dish with layers of minced lamb or beef and aubergines (eggplant), topped with a cheese sauce?

08 Which vegetable does the dish choucroute contain?

09 What type of meat is haggis made of?

10 What type of cheese is used for tiramisú?

11 What is couscous made of?

12 What is borscht?

13 What is a crêpe?

14 What type of meat is used for making ratatouille?

15 What type of cheese is gorgonzola?

16 What is ouzo flavoured with?

17 What does kedgeree consist of?

18 What do you call nut kernels (frequently almonds), cooked in boiling sugar syrup until crisp and brown?

19 In crème fraîche, what has the crème been thickened with?

20 What is the type of brandy which is made in north-western France from apples?

21 In dolmades, what type of leaf is stuffed with meat and other ingredients?

22 What do you call the spicy sauce eaten with Mexican food, especially tortillas, that is made of tomatoes, chilli, and onions?

23 What type of meat is used for châteaubriand?

24 What is wan tun?

25 What sort of fruit is shiraz?

26 What is claret?

27 What gives a bloody Mary its spicy flavour?

28 What are calamari?

29 With what is kirschwasser flavoured?

30 What sort of ice-cream is Neopolitan?

31 What is special about a glass of sambuca?

32 What is the Angler fish often called when served as a food?

33 Amazonian Indians eat the giant tarantula baked. True or false?

34 What sort of meat would you expect to find in kleftico?

35 What does the word 'spaghetti' literally mean?

36 What do anthropophagi eat?

37 What fungus is associated with the production of alcohol?

38 From what is taramasalata made?

39 What do you call the type of ribbon noodles that are about a third as thick as spaghetti?

40 What sort of dish is mulligatawny?

41 What is baklava?

42 What is zabaglione made of?

43 What part of the cow is a T-bone steak taken from?

44 What is the name of the soft, white, Italian cheese which is similar to cottage cheese?

45 Which family does the caraway seed come from?

46 What is turnip cabbage also called?

47 What sort of dish is julienne?

48 What is the name for a confection which consists of jelly-like cubes dusted in icing sugar?

49 What is minestrone?

50 What are gnocchi?

85

History

Answers to this quiz are on page 236

MEDIUM **MEDIUM** **MEDIUM**

Player 1	Player 2
12	20
33	24
07	03
46	45
01	28
21	02
23	25
04	32
35	39
14	50
31	08
48	17
11	40
27	43
15	29
06	41
10	30
47	34
26	16
38	05
36	49
13	09
19	18
42	37
44	22

86

01 Which admiral organized the German navy of World War I?

02 What was the name of the book in which William the Conqueror listed all British lands and landowners?

03 In which war did Wellington drive the French out of Spain?

04 What culinary disaster befell King Alfred?

05 What culinary delight did Henry IV of France promise each of his subjects?

06 Who conquered most of the known world before dying at the age of 33?

07 Who became first president of the Indonesian republic in 1945?

08 Name all the US presidents who have been assassinated.

09 When told the people had no bread she is reputed (probably unjustly) to have said, 'Let them eat cake.' Who was she?

10 By what name was Thailand known prior to 1949?

11 By what name is southern Rhodesia now known?

12 The flower Sweet William was named after the Duke of Cumberland. What do the Scots, who have a very different opinion of the Duke, call it?

13 In which country did shoguns wield political and military power?

14 In which year did the Confederate army fire on Fort Sumter?

15 On December 29 1890, nearly 200 Native Americans were killed by US troops in a creek in southwest Dakota. By what name is the place popularly known?

16 In 1520, Henry VIII of England and Francis I of France met near Calais. By what name was this site later known?

17 In 1879 140 British soldiers held off an army of 4,000 Zulus. Name the place.

18 Of which country was Brian Boru king?

19 Name the artefact whose discovery allowed Egyptian hieroglyphs to be translated.

20 What event took place in England in the years 1642–51?

21 Clausewitz was an acknowledged authority on what subject?

22 Which line of Egyptian kings began with one of Alexander the Great's generals?

23 What was cuneiform?

24 In which country was there a Cultural Revolution in 1966–8?

25 Name the French literary character who is chiefly famous for his enormous nose.

26 What important historical documents were discovered by accident in caves near Qumran?

27 Vlad IV The Impaler was a 15th-century Walachian prince. What fictional character did he inspire?

28 Who were the murderous followers of the goddess Kali suppressed by the British in the early 19th century?

29 Whose early experiments with electricity included flying a kite during a thunderstorm.

30 What calendar was used in England until 1752?

31 What Georgian city is famous for being burned by General Sherman during the American Civil War?

32 In which country was Ned Kelly noted as an outlaw?

33 What do we call books printed before 1500?

34 Name the Italian whose writings describe China under the rule of Kublai Khan.

35 What sect was founded by George Fox in the 1640s as the Religious Society of Friends?

36 For which enterprise was Baron Paul von Reuter famous?

37 Who famously rode to warn the people of Massachusetts that the British were coming?

38 Who was the first woman to fly solo across the Atlantic and Pacific Oceans?

39 Who founded the Society of Jesus in 1540?

40 What institution was charged with the task of fighting heresy in the early Church?

41 What would you expect to find in the caves of Lascaux?

42 Who was 'The Welsh Wizard' who led Britain in the First World War?

43 Who was the wife of the Emperor Claudius notorious for her promiscuity?

44 The atom bomb was used only twice in warfare. Where was it dropped?

45 On what paper-like substance did the ancient Egyptians write?

46 Of which country was Ngo Dinh Diem president?

47 What name did the victorious North Vietnamese call Saigon?

48 Which leader of the French Revolution was called 'The Incorruptible'?

49 Who headed Hitler's infamous Gestapo?

50 Who was the first English sea captain to sail around the world?

87

Sport

Answers to this quiz are on page 236

MEDIUM 😖 **MEDIUM** 😖 **MEDIUM**

Player 1	Player 2
12	20
33	24
07	03
46	45
01	28
21	02
23	25
04	32
35	39
14	50
31	08
48	17
11	40
27	43
15	29
06	41
10	30
47	34
26	16
38	05
36	49
13	09
19	18
42	37
44	22

01 Which countries played in the in the 1990 Football World Cup final?

02 Who won the ladies' singles tennis championship at Wimbledon in 1978?

03 What is the name of the American swimmer who won seven gold medals in the 1972 Olympics?

04 In which discipline was Ben Johnson stripped of his gold medal in the 1988 Olympics?

05 What is the name of the British ice dancing couple who won gold at the 1984 Winter Olympics?

06 The Rugby Union Players from which country are referred to as the All Blacks?

07 Who won the Masters Golf Tournament in 1988?

08 Which American athlete set a new record in the 100 meters in 1991?

09 How many holes does a golf course consist of?

10 How many consecutive Wimbledon titles did Bjorn Borg win?

11 In which sport would you use a foil, épée, and sabre?

12 With which sport do you associate the American Charles Daniels?

13 How many players are there in a cricket team?

14 Which Soviet gymnast won three gold medals in the 1972 Olympics in Munich?

15 The Corbillon Cup is associated with which sport?

16 With which sport is Pete Rose associated?

17 Which female American sprinter won three gold medals at the 1988 Olympics?

18 Which American boxer won the world heavyweight title in 1964, 1974, and 1978?

19 Which country did West Germany defeat in the final of the 1974 Football World Cup?

20 Which black American athlete won four gold medals in the 1936 Olympics in Berlin?

21 Who won the 1988 men's singles tennis championship at Wimbledon?

22 In which sport could you win a Drysdale Cup as an award?

23 Which American swimmer won five gold medals at the 1988 Olympics?

24 With which sport is Byron Nelson associated?

25 Which American long jumper set a new world record in the 1968 Olympics?

26 With which sport is Jack Dempsey associated?

27 Who became the ladies' French Open Singles Champion from 1990 to 1992?

28 How many players are there in a hockey team?

29 Who won the Masters Golf Tournament in 1993?

30 With which sport do you associate the Calcutta Cup?

31 Who became the youngest ever heavyweight champion in 1986?

32 Which country won the Football World Cup in 1970?

33 In which city did the first modern Olympic Games take place?

34 Which Romanian gymnast won six medals in the 1976 Olympics and four in the 1980 Olympics?

35 Which male tennis player won the US Open Championship in 1994?

36 With with sport is the Ryder Cup associated?

37 What was unusual about the 1980 Olympic Games held at Moscow?

38 A world famous event, the Indianapolis 500, is held in the city each year. What is it?

39 What popular name was given to the American boxer Joe Louis?

40 How many players are there in a handball team?

41 Who came first in the Tour de France for the fourth consecutive year in 1994?

42 Who beat Bjorn Borg in the men's singles tennis championships at Wimbledon in 1981?

43 Which golf player won the British Open in 1987, 1990, and 1992?

44 What name is given to the umpire in American football?

45 With which sport is the Davis Cup associated?

46 What was the location of the Summer Oympics in 1988?

47 If you score two points in a billiard game, what do you get?

48 Which American tennis player won the Women's Singles at Wimbledon in 1974, 1976, and 1981?

49 What do the symbols on the Olympic flag stand for?

50 In the Olympics, which five events make up the modern pentathlon?

89

The Arts

Answers to this quiz are on page 236

MEDIUM MEDIUM

Player 1	Player 2
12	20
33	24
07	03
46	45
01	28
21	02
23	25
04	32
35	39
14	50
31	08
48	17
11	40
27	43
15	29
06	41
10	30
47	34
26	16
38	05
36	49
13	09
19	18
42	37
44	22

01 What was unusual about the gangster movie *Bugsy Malone*?

02 On which book by George Bernard Shaw was the musical *My Fair Lady* based?

03 What was the name of Leonard Bernstein's musical based on Shakespeare's *Romeo and Juliet*?

04 In which film did Gregory Peck play the part of Atticus Finch?

05 Apart from John, Paul, George, and Ringo, name two other Beatles.

06 Who made the film *Fantasia*?

07 Which detective story became the UK's longest-running stage play?

08 By what name did Harry Webb find fame?

09 Which film actor sounded less scary by his real name of William Henry Pratt?

10 Which film, directed by David Lynch, concerned a hideously deformed Victorian man?

11 Which film, starring Richard Attenborough, told the story of the murderer John Christie?

12 Which three Beatles singles reached No. 1 in the UK charts in 1963?

13 Which Canadian singer wrote the novel *Beautiful Losers*?

14 Who said, 'Extraordinary how potent cheap music is'?

15 With which group was Sid Vicious associated?

16 Who made the album *Sweet Baby James*?

17 Which British guitarist of the 1950s had a phenomenal success with his *Play in a Day* guitar manual?

18 Who played the female lead in the 1976 version of *A Star is Born*?

19 Who directed the 1956 version of *The Ten Commandments*?

20 Which classic John Ford western of 1939 was remade in 1966?

21 Who played Zorba the Greek in the 1964 film?

22 Who wrote the play *The Importance of Being Earnest*?

23 In which Edward Albee play did Virginia Woolf feature?

24 Who wrote the poem 'If ' in a volume entitled *Barrack-Room Ballads*?

25 In which film did Charlotte Rampling and Dirk Bogarde resurrect a relationship that began in a concentration camp?

26 Who was the first actor to talk in the film *The Jazz Singer*?

27 Which Shakespeare play is considered unlucky to mention by name?

28 Why did Gore Vidal fall out with Charlton Heston over the film *Ben Hur* years after it was made?

29 Who painted *The Sun of Venice Going to Sea*?

30 Which US state starred in a Rodgers and Hammerstein musical?

31 Who composed 'Rhapsody in Blue'?

32 Who wrote 'Take Five'?

33 Who wrote the music for the 1986 musical *Phantom of the Opera*?

34 Who played the part of Eliza Doolittle in the 1964 film *My Fair Lady*?

35 Which Margaret Mitchell novel became one of the greatest movies of all time?

36 Which poem by Tennyson contains the lines: 'Theirs not to reason why, Theirs but to do and die'?

37 Who painted *The Laughing Cavalier*?

38 What name connects Phil Collins with a book of the Bible?

39 By what name is Cherilyn Sarkasian LaPierre better known?

40 Which singer, famed for his large nose, sang 'The Man Who Found the Lost Chord'?

41 Which song was Norman Greenbaum's only real claim to fame?

42 Where did the band Men at Work come from?

43 Who was best known for her rendering of 'There's No Business Like Show Business'?

44 Who appeared naked on the cover of the album *Unfinished Music No 1: Two Virgins*?

45 Which member of the Rolling Stones died in his swimming pool days after leaving the group?

46 The musical *Kismet* was based on the work of which Russian composer?

47 Name the London playhouse where most of Shakespeare's plays were presented.

48 By what nickname was the actress Lillie Langtry known?

49 For what theatrical entertainment was William Cody responsible?

50 What does the word 'opera' mean?

91

Seas

Answers to this quiz are on pages 236-237

MEDIUM MEDIUM MEDIUM

	Player 1	Player 2
	12	20
	33	24
	07	03
	46	45
	01	28
	21	02
	23	25
	04	32
	35	39
	14	50
	31	08
	48	17
	11	40
	27	43
	15	29
	06	41
	10	30
	47	34
	26	16
	38	05
	36	49
	13	09
	19	18
	42	37
	44	22

01 In which ocean would you find Tristan da Cunha?

02 **Where would you find the Weddell Sea?**

03 In which ocean are the Seychelles?

04 **In which ocean would you find the Canary Islands?**

05 Which sea separates Egypt and the Arabian Peninsula?

06 **In which sea would you find the Dardanelles?**

07 Which sea separates the Aegean and the Black Sea?

08 **In which sea would you find Corsica and Sardinia?**

09 What does Mediterranean literally mean?

10 **What name is given to the arm of the Atlantic Ocean that separates Ireland from Great Britain?**

11 What is the French name for the English Channel?

12 **Which stretch of water separates Spain from Africa?**

13 Which sea lies to the west of Korea?

14 **Into which body of water does the River Ganges flow?**

15 Which sea lies east of Kamchatka?

16 **Where would you find Palk Strait?**

17 What body of water separates the Persian Gulf from the Arabian Sea?

18 **Which sea separates Australia and New Zealand?**

19 In which sea do the West Indies lie?

20 **Which is the world's largest ocean?**

21 What is the sea between Java and Borneo called?

22 The sea between New Ireland and New Britain bears the name of a German statesman. What is it?

23 In which sea would you find the Great Barrier Reef?

24 In which sea would you find Christmas Island?

25 What body of water separates Borneo from the Malay Peninsula?

26 To the south of Timor lies the Timor Sea. What lies to the north?

27 What body of water separates Borneo from the Celebes?

28 Which sea is contained within the Philippines?

29 Where would you find the Gulf of Carpentaria?

30 Where would you find the Flores Sea?

31 The two halves of which country are separated by the Cook Strait?

32 The Tasman Sea lies to the west of New Zealand. What lies to the east?

33 Which basin would you find off the west coast of South America?

34 Which basin would you find to the north of the North Sea?

35 Which sea would you find to the north of Norway and Finland?

36 Seas lie to the west and east of the Republic of Georgia. What are they?

37 What gulf lies between North Vietnam and China?

38 Which body of water lies to the west of Cuba?

39 What is the name of the passage south of Cape Horn?

40 What is the large body of water between Quebec and the Northwest Territories?

41 Name two of the large bodies of water surrounding Baffin Island.

42 In which sea would you find the Dogger Bank?

43 What body of water is found to the west of Newfoundland?

44 Near which sea would you find Mecca?

45 Near which body of water, after which a city is named, would you find Brigham City, Utah?

46 Into which body of water does the Mississippi flow?

47 Where, in the Pacific Ocean, would you find the Channel Islands?

48 Which two US cities border the Gulf of Santa Catalina?

49 What water lies between the Gulf of Mexico and the Atlantic Ocean?

50 What body of water separates Long Island from Connecticut?

93

History

MEDIUM **MEDIUM** **MEDIUM**

Player 1	Player 2
12	20
33	24
07	03
46	45
01	28
21	02
23	25
04	32
35	39
14	50
31	08
48	17
11	40
27	43
15	29
06	41
10	30
47	34
26	16
38	05
36	49
13	09
19	18
42	37
44	22

94

01 Which were the two sides in the War of the Roses?

02 Who were the Luddites?

03 What was the name of the war between Russia and the allied powers of Turkey, England, France, and Sardinia between 1853 and 1856?

04 What was the Bastille used as?

05 Which Italian general conquered Naples and Sardinia in 1860 with the aid of 1000 volunteers, which led to the formation of the kingdom of Italy?

06 Which German statesman was known as 'The Iron Chancellor'?

07 Who was Queen Victoria's husband?

08 Henry VIII's divorce from which wife led to his break with the Roman Catholic Church?

09 Nebuchadnezzar was king of which country?

10 Which secret American organization was started with the purpose of terrorizing Blacks into not voting?

11 What was the name of the imaginary line between the 'slave' and the 'free' states before the American Civil War?

12 What was the name of the trials held in 1945 in which Nazi leaders were tried for war crimes?

13 Georgi Malenkov became Soviet leader after the death of which statesman?

14 Which French statesman was known as 'The Little Corporal'?

15 With which war is Marston Moor associated?

16 What was the name of the moderate republicans during the French Revolution?

17 What was the name of the war fought between South Africa and Great Britain from 1899 to 1902?

18 Who wrote the American Declaration of Independence?

19 Who were the Mau Mau?

20 Who were the forty-niners?

21 What were the American Abolitionists concerned with?

22 Which general in the American Civil War was commonly known as 'Stonewall'?

23 Who were the Romanovs?

24 What was the name of the republic that preceded the Third Reich in Germany?

25 Which war is associated with Rorke's Drift?

26 What did the British Empire turn into in 1931?

27 In Greek mythology, which event caused the Trojan War?

28 How long did the Hundred Years' War last?

29 Which Roman gladiator led a slave revolt in 71 BC?

30 Which king was defeated in the English Civil War?

31 What was the name given to the Australian and New Zealand armies during the two world wars?

32 What age preceded the Iron Age?

33 Who was the first Queen of England?

34 Which Roman city was devastated by an eruption of the volcano Vesuvius in AD 79?

35 Which country was devastated by the Great Potato Famine between 1845 and 1849?

36 Which Muslim race invaded Spain in the 8th century and established a civilization in Andalusia?

37 Which event does the Bayeux tapestry depict?

38 Who was the commander of Hitler's Luftwaffe?

39 Where in Australia was the first British settlement?

40 Who was Hitler's propaganda minister?

41 Who, according to legend, founded Rome?

42 Which three heads of state took part in the Yalta Conference in 1945?

43 Who became emperor of Rome after the death of Tiberius?

44 Which Sioux leaders joined Sitting Bull in the Battle of Little Bighorn?

45 What does the Arc de Triomphe in Paris commemorate?

46 What was London first called after being founded by the Romans?

47 Which British naval ship was the scene of a mutiny in 1789 while on a trading voyage in the Pacific?

48 During which war did the Battle of the Coral Sea take place?

49 Which English navigator sailed on the Golden Hind?

50 Who, in Greek mythology, was the leader of the Greeks in the Trojan War?

95

Cities

Answers to this quiz are on page 237

MEDIUM 😖 **MEDIUM**

Player 1	Player 2
12	20
33	24
07	03
46	45
01	28
21	02
23	25
04	32
35	39
14	50
31	08
48	17
11	40
27	43
15	29
06	41
10	30
47	34
26	16
38	05
36	49
13	09
19	18
42	37
44	22

01 Which two cities in the world have the largest populations?

02 Which city in Europe has the largest population?

03 Name the city with the largest population in the USA.

04 What is the capital of Cambodia?

05 Istanbul is the capital of Turkey. True or false?

06 By what name is Baile Atha Cliath better known?

07 Thai people seldom call their capital Bangkok. What is its local name?

08 If you visited the city of Tallinn, which country would you be in?

09 Of which country is Ulan Bator the capital?

10 If you landed at O'Hare airport, which city would you be in?

11 Is Jerusalem or Tel Aviv the capital of Israel?

12 Where would you find Chang Kai Shek airport?

13 Which city, according to Oscar Wilde, is an expensive place to die?

14 'If a man is tired of ... he is tired of life.' Of which city was this said?

15 There are two monuments called Cleopatra's Needle. In which cities are they?

16 Which large Kenyan city lies to the east of Lake Victoria?

17 What is the state capital of Georgia, USA?

18 What is the capital of Florida?

19 Which city, known for its gambling, is found in Nevada?

20 What does the name 'Philadelphia' mean?

21 Which US city is known as Motown?

22 In which state would you find Sioux Falls?

23 Which was the 'rose red city half as old as time'?

24 Which European city relies entirely on its waterways for transport?

25 Which city was often called Blighty by its inhabitants?

26 Which city is called The Big Apple?

27 In which city would you find the cemetery of Père Lachaise?

28 In which city would you find the Paseo del Prado?

29 Tiananmen Square is found in Beijing. What does the name mean?

30 St. Petersburg was known by what name until recently?

31 Why are there two Kansas Cities?

32 Who described London as 'a modern Babylon'?

33 What new name did the British give to the settlement known as New Amsterdam?

34 Which Indian city was infamous for the 'Black Hole' incident?

35 Which city was Japan's capital from AD 794 to 1868?

36 Which city boasted a street called Unter den Linden?

37 In which city was King Wenceslas, of Christmas carol fame, murdered?

38 In which cathedral city did Thomas à Becket meet his death?

39 What do the Cambridges of England and the USA have in common?

40 Where in England would you find one of the largest cathedrals in one of the smallest cities?

41 Which city of ancient Palestine was, according to the Bible, to be the site of the Armageddon?

42 Why was the town of Cairo, Illinois, given its name?

43 In which city would you find the Lido?

44 Which European city is built on a system of semi-circular canals?

45 Which German city lends its name to a smoked sausage?

46 Which city is found beside Botany Bay?

47 Which city gave its name to a doughnut?

48 Which city was known as Auld Reekie?

49 What is the capital of Sweden?

50 Which German city gives its name to a perfume?

97

Events

1960
1961
1962

Answers to this quiz are on pages 237-238

MEDIUM ☺ MEDIUM

Player 1	Player 2
12	20
33	24
07	03
46	45
01	28
21	02
23	25
04	32
35	39
14	50
31	08
48	17
11	40
27	43
15	29
06	41
10	30
47	34
26	16
38	05
36	49
13	09
19	18
42	37
44	22

98

01 In which year did Kenya gain independence from Britain: (a) 1922, (b) 1963, (c)1973?

02 In which year did Britain impose direct rule over Northern Ireland, and Ceylon change its name to Sri Lanka?

03 In which year was the state of Israel founded: (a) 1918, (b) 1945, (c) 1948?

04 In which year did Eisenhower become US president: (a) 1945, (b) 1952, (c) 1955?

05 In which year did Valentina Tereshkova become the first woman in space?

06 In which year did the airship The Hindenburg burst into flames and explode: (a) 1914, (b) 1932, (c) 1937?

07 In which year did Adolf Hitler survive an assassination attempt?

08 Which year saw San Francisco's worst earthquake: (a) 1888, (b) 1900, (c) 1906?

09 In which year was the Wall Street crash?

10 In which year did Robert Mugabe become the first black leader in Zimbabwe after independence: (a) 1980, (b) 1982, (c) 1983?

11 In which year was the Ford Motor Company founded: (a) 1872, (b) 1898, (c) 1903?

12 In which year was Mount Everest is conquered for the first time?

13 In which year did the Falklands War take place: (a) 1982, (b) 1988, (c) 1991?

14 In which year did the Live Aid concert take place: (a) 1980, (b) 1985, (c) 1989?

15 In which year was George Orwell's novel 1984 published: (a) 1902, (b) 1933, (c) 1949?

16 In which year did the American spacecraft Apollo 16 land on the moon?

17 In which year did the Beatles score their first number one hit: (a) 1960, (b) 1962, (c) 1963?

18 In which year did the Suez Canal first open to traffic: (a) 1848, (b) 1869, (c) 1937?

19 In which year did Brazil win the Football World Cup, Salvador Allende become president of Chile, and Jimi Hendrix die of a drug overdose?

20 In which year did the Boxer Rising take place: (a) 1900, (b) 1918, (c) 1944?

21 In which year did George Gershwin write 'Rhapsody in Blue': (a) 1878, (b) 1901, (c) 1924?

22 In which year did Hawaii and Alaska become US states: (a) 1948, (b) 1959, (c) 1963?

23 In which year did the following events take place: Yuri Gagarin becomes the first man in space, Rudolf Nureyev defects to the West, and the Berlin Wall is erected?

24 When was the Six-Day War: (a) 1956, (b) 1967, (c) 1973?

25 In which year did Richard Nixon resign as US president: (a) 1970, (b) 1972, (c) 1974?

26 In which year did Roald Amundsen become the first man to reach the South Pole: (a) 1812, (b) 1864, (c) 1911?

27 In which year did the Titanic sink: (a) 1912, (b) 1917, (c) 1919?

28 In which year did US Vice-President Spiro Agnew resign over tax evasion?

29 In which year did Disneyland open: (a) 1955, (b) 1962, (c) 1974?

30 In which year did Neil Armstrong become the first man on the moon: (a) 1963, (b) 1969, (c) 1971?

31 In which year did the Battle of Britain take place: (a) 1917, (b) 1940, (c) 1945?

32 In which year did the following events take place: Civil rights leader Martin Luther King is assassinated, tanks move into Czechoslovakia, and the rock musical *Hair* opens on Broadway?

33 In which year was the Marshall Plan implemented: (a) 1918, (b) 1945, (c) 1948?

34 In which year was the Hungarian uprising: (a) 1949, (b) 1956, (c) 1968?

35 In which year did Cyprus gain independence: (a) 1960, (b) 1968, (c) 1974?

36 In which year did the following events take place: 176 people are killed after riots in Soweto, Jimmy Carter wins the US presidential election, and the hijacking of a French airliner comes to an end at Entebbe airport in Uganda?

37 In which year did the Sharpeville massacre take place: (a) 1922, (b) 1960, (c) 1974?

38 In which year were Bonnie and Clyde shot by police after having killed 12 people: (a) 1934, (b) 1952, (c) 1967?

39 In which year was *King Kong* released, and Roosevelt inaugurated as US President?

40 In which year was Walt Disney's *Snow White and the Seven Dwarfs* released: (a) 1922, (b) 1938, (c) 1952?

41 In which year was Cambodia overrun by the Khmer Rouge: (a) 1975, (c) 1978, (d) 1983?

42 Which year saw the reign of three popes: (a) 1966, (b) 1970, (c) 1978?

43 In which year was John Lennon shot dead in New York?

44 Which decade is associated with the Jazz Age?

45 Which decade saw the Watergate scandal and the Yom Kippur War?

46 Which year saw the death of Noel Coward and Pablo Picasso: (a) 1973, (b) 1979, (c) 1992?

47 When did Margaret Thatcher resign as prime minister: (a) 1986, (b) 1989, (c) 1990?

48 In which year did the following events take place: Australia celebrates its becentenary, Reagan and Gorbachev sign the INF Treaty, and Ben Johnson is stripped of his gold medal after having tested positive for drugs?

49 Which year saw a devastating famine in Ethiopia: (a) 1978, (b) 1984, (c) 1988?

50 In which year did Eva Peron die: (a) 1952, (b) 1960, (c) 1972?

99

The Arts

Answers to this quiz are on page 238

MEDIUM ☺ MEDIUM

Player 1	Player 2
12	20
33	24
07	03
46	45
01	28
21	02
23	25
04	32
35	39
14	50
31	08
48	17
11	40
27	43
15	29
06	41
10	30
47	34
26	16
38	05
36	49
13	09
19	18
42	37
44	22

01 Which of the duo Laurel and Hardy was British by birth?

02 In which year did *South Pacific* first appear on Broadway?

03 Which American musical comedy actress was noted for her 1946 appearance in *Annie Get Your Gun*?

04 For what catch phrase was Bugs Bunny famous?

05 In which year did Mickey Mouse first appear as a comic figure?

06 Who were the owners of the fictional Fresh-Air Taxicab Company of America?

07 When did *Sergeant Pepper's Lonely Hearts Club Band* appear?

08 Which artist was famous for his portrayal of the music halls and cafés of Montmartre?

09 On which island did Gauguin paint some of his finest works?

10 Which musical celebrated an Argentine president's wife?

11 Who played the female lead in the 1937 musical *One Hundred Men and a Girl*?

12 In which film did Greta Garbo utter the famous line, 'I want to be alone'?

13 Who was the female lead in *Jezebel* in 1938?

14 Who said: 'If Mr Vincent Price were to be co-starred with Miss Bette Davis in a story by Mr Edgar Allan Poe directed by Mr Roger Corman, it could not fully express the pent-up violence and depravity of a single day in the life of the average family'?

15 Which British actor made his name playing villains such as Dracula and Dr Fu Manchu?

16 Who is often regarded as the national poet of Scotland?

17 By what fictional name do TV and film viewers recognize Leonard Nimoy?

18 Who wrote *Under Milk Wood*?

19 Which 60s youth hero and singer said: 'I'm glad I'm not me'?

20 What was the name of the Music and Art Fair held in the Catskill Mountains at Bethel, N.Y. in 1969?

21 Which instrument is Yehudin Menuhin famous for playing?

22 Who is reputed to be the greatest maker of violins?

23 Why is a 'jews harp' so called?

24 The defeat of which military leader is celebrated by the 1812 Overture?

25 Who painted Le Déjeuner sur l'Herbe?

26 'April is the cruellest month, breeding lilac out of the dead land...' From which poem does this come?

27 Who wrote: 'Do not go gentle into that good night... Rage, rage, against the dying of the light'?

28 Which author wrote the Gormenghast novels?

29 In which book was the future said to be like 'a boot stamping on a human face – for ever'?

30 Who said, 'The only end of writing is to enable the readers better to enjoy life, or better to endure it'?

31 Who wrote The Red Badge of Courage?

32 Who played the lead role in The Bridge on the River Kwai?

33 Which film, starring Hugh Grant, concerned rites of passage?

34 Daniel Day Lewis starred in which film based on a book by James Fennimore Cooper?

35 Who played the young female lead in A Room With a View?

36 Which creatures, invented by Tove Jansson, featured in her series of children's novels?

37 Who was the wizard, created by J.R.R. Tolkien, who befriended dwarves and hobbits?

38 What was the name of the evil lord in Lord of the Rings?

39 Name two boys whose evidence saved Muff Potter from the hangman?

40 Gulliver visited a land of giants. What was it called?

41 What novel of the future by Anthony Burgess featured Alex and his droogs?

42 In the film Bringing up Baby, who was Baby?

43 Who says of his creator: 'There were things which he stretched, but mainly he told the truth'?

44 In which book does a crocodile swallow an alarm clock?

45 Which jungle-dweller appears in the film Greystoke?

46 Which murderous British barber became the subject of a musical?

47 Which heroine of a Swedish children's story is famous for her strength?

48 Which British crime writer was played by Vanessa Redgrave in a film about a mysterious incident in her life?

49 The Osmonds were made up of four brothers and a sister. Who was the sister?

50 What is Meat Loaf's real name?

101

Inventions

Answers to this quiz are on page 238

MEDIUM MEDIUM MEDIUM

Player 1	Player 2
12	20
33	24
07	03
46	45
01	28
21	02
23	25
04	32
35	39
14	50
31	08
48	17
11	40
27	43
15	29
06	41
10	30
47	34
26	16
38	05
36	49
13	09
19	18
42	37
44	22

01 Who invented the telephone?

02 What did John Logie Baird invent?

03 What function did a polygraph have?

04 Who was widely praised for his pocket calculator but ridiculed for inventing the C5 electric car?

05 By what name was the John Gabel Entertainer to become better known?

06 What was the purpose of the Archimedes Screw?

07 Who invented the first mechanical calculating machine?

08 What did Elisha Greaves Otis demonstrate in New York in 1853?

09 The Romans invented hypocaust. What did it do?

10 Who invented the sandwich?

11 Who is thought to be the first person to discover the art of reading silently to oneself rather than reading aloud?

12 Who invented the phonograph?

13 In spite of the sophistication of the ancient Egyptians, what piece of basic technology did they fail to invent?

14 Which people invented the first real paper?

15 In which part of the world was the ice-skate invented?

16 In which country did the longbow originate?

17 What invention revolutionized horse riding?

18 Which human invention was the first object to travel faster than the speed of sound?

19 In 1656 a Dutch mathematician and astronomer invented something which was to revolutionize time-keeping. What was it?

20 What mechanical device did people, especially scientists, use to help with their mathematics before the invention of the pocket calculator?

21 In the late 18th century two Frenchmen – Duchateau and De Chemant – invented something that would be a boon to those with a taste for sweets. What was it?

22 Which spinning machine, named after a girl, was invented by James Hargreaves in 1764?

23 What was Sheffield silver?

24 The Chinese discovered the principle, Leonardo da Vinci designed one, but what was it that Louis Lenormand actually tested himself in 1783?

25 What did Benjamin Franklin invent that helped people who wore glasses?

26 Which French brothers demonstrated a working hot air balloon?

27 What did Samuel Harrison do to help people who wrote with quill pens?

28 Which Scots inventor came up with an improved road surface that was to bear his name?

29 With which invention do you associate the name Alan Turing?

30 With what process would you associate the name Daguerre?

31 Lots of people invented sewing machines that were never popular. Who was the first person to come up with one that was a commercial success (and which still bears his name).

32 Who invented the saxophone?

33 Ascanio Sobrero, who is little known, invented something that was improved by Alfred Nobel, who became famous for it. What was the original invention and why did it do Sobrero so little good?

34 What contribution did William Fox Talbot make to photography?

35 Who invented an electric telegraph that transmitted messages in a code of dots and dashes?

36 Charles Pravaz invented a means of administering drugs that did not require them to be swallowed. What was it?

37 What important photographic process did James Clark Maxwell invent in 1861?

38 What did American farmer James Glidden do to improve the production of barbed wire?

39 What was the first stapling machine used for?

40 The Romans invented the hipposandal. What did it do?

41 Thomas Adams took some chicle and added liquorice flavouring and sold it as Black Jack. What had he invented?

42 Which invention was sold as 'the esteemed brain tonic and intellectual beverage'?

43 Waterman is remembered in connection with the fountain pen, but he did not invent it. What is the connection?

44 The principal ingredient of Aspirin was known to the ancient Greeks. From what was it obtained?

45 Scipione Riva-Rocci invented a device to measure blood pressure. It is still used, but what is its name?

46 How did the military tank get its name?

47 In 1921 it was discovered that insulin, a hormone extracted from the pancreas of pigs, could be used to treat which disease?

48 What was the first product to be made of nylon?

49 What did Percy Shaw invent when he saw his headlights reflected in the eyes of a cat crossing the road?

50 What was the world's first synthetic insecticide?

103

Current Affairs

Answers to this quiz are on page 238

MEDIUM ☺ MEDIUM MEDIUM

Player 1	Player 2
12	20
33	24
07	03
46	45
01	28
21	02
23	25
04	32
35	39
14	50
31	08
48	17
11	40
27	43
15	29
06	41
10	30
47	34
26	16
38	05
36	49
13	09
19	18
42	37
44	22

01 What is the name of the leader of the PLO who made a peace agreement with Israel?

02 Who became the first black South African president in 1994?

03 In 1986 was the world's worst nuclear reactor accident. Where?

04 Which Soviet head of state was largely responsible for the break-up of communism in Eastern Europe?

05 What is the popular name given to the barrier between western Europe and the Eastern Block countries after World War II?

06 Which record did Reiner Hege achieve?

07 Which Israeli prime minister was assassinated in November 1995?

08 What is the name of the Irish nationalist organization responsible for many bombings and terrorist attacks in Northern Ireland and Britain since the '70s?

09 Which American president started his career as a film actor and went on to become governor of California?

10 In which year did Nelson Mandela first make a state visit to the UK?

11 Which country won the Six Day War?

12 With which organization do you associate Boutros Boutros-Ghali?

13 Who became the first chancellor of a reunited Germany?

14 What strange meteorological phenomenon struck South Africa in July 1996?

15 Who became the first head of state of the People's Republic of China in 1949?

16 Which western country supported the South Vietnamese forces during the Vietnam War?

104

17 Which city was divided between East and West Germany between the end of World War II and 1989?

18 Which Indian political and religious leader was largely responsible for his country's independence from Britain?

19 Shortly after becoming Israeli prime minister Binyamin Netanyahu caused a storm by sacking his children's nanny. Why?

20 Which of the following countries was the last to join the European Union: (a) France, (b) Great Britain, or (c) Spain?

21 Which European country is associated with having had a succession of short-lived coalition governments since World War II?

22 What distinguished Pope John Paul II from his predecessors of the last 450 years?

23 Who was the last white South African president?

24 In which country is the so-called 'marching season' traditionally a time of sectarian hostility?

25 Which North American city was damaged by an earthquake in 1994?

26 During the war in the former Yugoslavia, Slobodan Milosevic was leader of which state?

27 In which year did Queen Elizabeth II of England come to the throne?

28 Which political party did George Bush campaign for?

29 Who became first president of Russia after the disintegration of the Soviet Union?

30 In 1989 Soviet troops withdrew from which Asian country after a 10-year guerrilla war?

31 Which incident led to the Gulf War?

32 Who was Lee Harvey Oswald alleged to have shot dead?

33 Who stood in the 1992 US presidential election against Bill Clinton?

34 Which island broke away from the People's Republic of China in 1949 and set up its own Nationalist government?

35 Which was the first Eastern European Country to set up a trade union federation in 1980?

36 Which country did the West Bank belong to before Israeli occupation in 1967?

37 What was the name of Indira Gandhi's father?

38 Who was vice president under Ronald Reagan?

39 Which city near Johannesburg was the centre of a student protest that turned into widespread violence and rioting in 1976?

40 Who was US president during the Cuban Missile Crisis?

41 Who became Libya's head of state in 1969 by means of an military coup?

42 Which position did Bill Clinton hold before becoming US president?

43 In which year was the Gulf War?

44 Which hostage drama contributed to Jimmy Carter's defeat in the US presidential election of 1980?

45 King Hussein is ruler of which country?

46 Who succeeded Anwar Sadat as Egyptian president?

47 What is the Common Market also called?

48 Which country did Cyprus belong to before gaining independence in 1960?

49 In which year was the Yom Kippur War?

50 Which scandal cost Richard Nixon his presidency?

People

Answers to this quiz are on pages 238-239

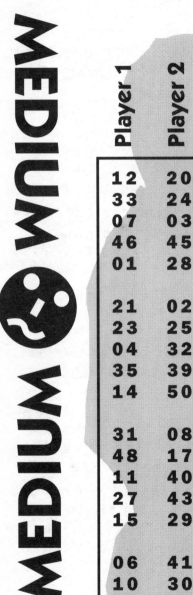

MEDIUM

Player 1	Player 2
12	20
33	24
07	03
46	45
01	28
21	02
23	25
04	32
35	39
14	50
31	08
48	17
11	40
27	43
15	29
06	41
10	30
47	34
26	16
38	05
36	49
13	09
19	18
42	37
44	22

106

01 In which year was John F. Kennedy assassinated?

02 Which movie mogul said: 'That's the trouble with directors. Always biting the hand that lays the golden egg'?

03 Which cartoon character had a girlfriend called Olive Oyl?

04 Whose face reputedly 'launched a thousand ships and burnt the topless towers of Ilium'?

05 Which name connects Woody Allen with Bob Dylan?

06 Who was Russia's 'Mad Monk'?

07 Name a sergeant whose band was made famous by the Beatles.

08 By what name was Marion Morrison better known?

09 Under what name did Samuel Langhorne Clemens find fame?

10 Name the outlaw couple immortalized on film by Faye Dunaway and Warren Beatty.

11 Which Indian political leader was known as 'Mahatma'?

12 Who was the first president of the USA?

13 Which marooned fictional character had a companion called Man Friday?

14 Name the Three Musketeers and their constant companion.

15 Who did Scout, Jem, and Dill want to tempt out of his house?

16 Which Black civil rights leader is famous for the phrase, 'I have a dream'?

17 Which boxer was formerly known as Cassius Clay?

18 Which king died at the Battle of Hastings as a result of being shot through the eye?

19 Which Soviet Russian leader took a name which meant 'steel' in his own language?

20 Which 18th-century British explorer was killed by the natives of Hawaii in 1779?

21 Which famous fictional jungle-dweller was created by Edgar Rice Burroughs?

22 With which security organization was J. Edgar Hoover associated?

23 Who is notorious for plotting to blow up the UK Houses of Parliament with gunpowder?

24 Which Polish–French woman scientist discovered radium?

25 Who was the constant companion of Tom Sawyer?

26 Which American politician was known as LBJ?

27 Which Mexican General did Davy Crockett and Jim Bowie face at the Alamo?

28 What machine was first manufactured by the gunsmith Philo Remington in 1874?

29 What do the intials of O.J. Simpson's name stand for?

30 Who was the leader of the Free French in World War II?

31 Name the Scottish-born American whose detective agency was famous for solving railroad robberies, spying behind Confederate lines, and strike breaking?

32 What was Henry Deringer famous for inventing?

33 Charles Lutwidge Dodgson was a mathematician. For what was he better known?

34 Which film star was famous for the phrase 'You dirty rat!', even though he never used it in any of his films?

35 Which Hunkpapa Sioux leader is given principal credit for defeating General Custer at the Battle of the Little Big Horn?

36 Who was the pirate, Bluebeard or Blackbeard?

37 By what name was William H. Bonney better known?

38 On which vessel would you expect to find William Shatner and Leonard Nimoy?

39 Which British author wrote gloomily about the year 1984?

40 Which fictional heroine lived in a house with green gables?

41 Who was treated as a giant by the Lilliputians?

42 When a lady told him, 'Sir, you smell!' he replied, 'No, Madam, you smell, I stink'. Who was he?

43 Which name links a South African statesman with the Battle of Trafalgar?

44 Which French heroine was burned as a witch by the English?

45 Which Scottish king defeated the English at the Battle of Bannockburn?

46 Which Italian dictator was known as 'Il Duce'?

47 Sir Edmund Hillary climbed Everest in 1953. Who was his Sherpa companion?

48 Which fictional hero came from the planet Krypton?

49 Which outlaw lived with his Merry Men in Sherwood Forest?

50 Which British scientist discovered gravity, supposedly with the help of an apple?

Events

Answers to this quiz are on page 239

MEDIUM 😐 **MEDIUM**

Player 1	Player 2
12	20
33	24
07	03
46	45
01	28
21	02
23	25
04	32
35	39
14	50
31	08
48	17
11	40
27	43
15	29
06	41
10	30
47	34
26	16
38	05
36	49
13	09
19	18
42	37
44	22

108

01 In which year did Turkish troops invade Cyprus resulting in a partition of the country: a) 1960, b) 1966, c) 1974?

02 In which year did the Panama Canal open to traffic: (a) 1900, (b) 1914, (c) 1929?

03 In which year was the Eiffel Tower completed: (a) 1802, (b) 1852, (c) 1889?

04 In which year did Idi Amin gains power in Uganda, and a war break out between India and Pakistan over Bangladesh?

05 In which year did Hitler stage an abortive putsch in a Munich beer-hall? (a) 1923, (b) 1929, (c) 1933?

06 In which year did Algeria gain independence: (a) 1952, (b) 1962, (c) 1971?

07 In which year was the tomb of Tutankhamen discovered: (a) 1812, (b) 1889, (c) 1922?

08 In which year did Elvis Presley have his first hit with 'Heartbreak Hotel'?

09 In which year was the first heart transplant carried out: (a) 1962, (b) 1967, (c) 1970?

10 In which year was the Yom Kippur War: (a) 1948, (b) 1966, (c) 1973?

11 In which year was the uprising of the Warsaw ghetto: (a) 1936, (b) 1940, (c) 1943?

12 In which year did the following events take place: The Greenpeace ship Rainbow Warrior is blown up, Mexico is shaken by an earthquake that claims the lives of up to 20,000 people, and Boris Becker has his first win at Wimbledon?

13 In which year did Tito become president of Yugoslavia: (a) 1948, (b) 1953, (c) 1960?

14 In which year did the Battle of the Somme take place: (a) 1916, (b) 1918, c) 1942?

15 In which year was the Communist Manifesto published: (a) 1798, (b) 1847, (c) 1912?

16 In which year did the following events take place: a Lufthansa plane is highjacked in Mogadishu, Menachem Begin comes to power in Israel, and the film Saturday Night Fever is released?

17 When was the Statue of Liberty erected in New York harbour: (a) 1776, (b) 1865, (c) 1886?

18 In which year did the communists finally rout the South Vietnamese army:

(a) 1971, (b) 1975, (c) 1980?

19 In which year was Ghandi assassinated: (a) 1948, (b) 1949, (c) 1954?

20 **In which year did the following events take place: Brasilia becomes Brazil's new capital, the Moroccan town of Agadir is devastated by an earthquake, and the Olympic Games take place in Rome?**

21 When was the SALT 1 Treaty signed: (a) 1962, (b) 1972, (c) 1978?

22 **When was the United Nations set up: (a) 1945, (b) 1948, (c) 1958?**

23 In which year did the following events take place: the Shah of Iran is exiled, the Salt 2 Treaty is signed, and John Wayne dies?

24 **In which year did Willy Brandt become German chancellor: (a) 1960, (b) 1969, (b) 1973?**

25 In which year did the Bay of Pigs invasion take place: (a) 1959, (b) 1961, (c) 1965?

26 **In which year were the first modern Olympic Games held: (a) 1896, (b) 1900, (c) 1912?**

27 In which year was gold first discovered in California: (a) 1812, (b) 1833,(c) 1848?

28 **In which year did England's footballers win the World Cup?**

29 In which year did the protests in Tiananmen Square take place: (a) 1988, (b) 1989, (c) 1992?

30 **In which year did Czechoslovakia split into two states: (a) 1967, (b) 1986, (c) 1993?**

31 In which year was the wedding between Prince Charles and Lady Diana Spencer: (a) 1981, (b) 1983, (c) 1985?

32 **In which year was the Lockerbie disaster?**

33 In which year did Queen Victoria start her reign: (a) 1801, (b) 1819, (c) 1837?

34 **In which year was NATO established: (a) 1945, (b) 1949, (c) 1955?**

35 In which year was Nelson Mandela sentenced to life imprisonment and Marin Luther King awarded the Nobel Peace Price?

36 **In which year did Iraq invade Kuwait: (a) 1989, (b) 1990, (c) 1991?**

37 In which year was the Treaty of Versailles signed: (a) 1848, (b) 1889, (c) 1919?

38 **In which year was Nelson Mandela released from prison: (a) 1988, (b) 1990, (c) 1992?**

39 In which year did Yitzhak Shamir become premier of Israel?

40 **In which year was Manfred von Richthofen shot down: (a) 1918, (b) 1941, (c) 1945?**

41 In which year did the war in Vietnam come to an end:

(a) 1969, (b) 1973, (c) 1975?

42 **In which year did the Japanese attack Pearl Harbor? (a) 1939, (b) 1941, (c) 1945?**

43 In which year was Manuel Noriega ousted from power in Panama: (a) 1980, (b) 1985, (c) 1989?

44 **In which year did the following events take place: stocks and shares all over the world fall dramatically on one day which becomes known as Black Monday, a 19-year old German pilot lands his light aircraft on the Red Square in Moscow, and hearings take place into the Iran-Contra affair?**

45 In which year was Anwar Sadat assassinated: (a) 1972, (b) 1979, (c) 1981?

46 **In which year did Concorde made its maiden flight: (a) 1965, (b) 1969, (c) 1972?**

47 In which year did Winston Churchill first became leader of Great Britain: (a) 1938, (b) 1940, (c) 1945?

48 **In which year was the world's first test tube baby born?**

49 When was the Golden Gate Bridge in San Francisco opened: (a) 1879, (b) 1900, (c) 1937?

50 **In which year did the Soviet Union withdraw their troops from Afghanistan: (a) 1978, (b) 1985, (c) 1989?**

Nature

Answers to this quiz are on page 239

MEDIUM **MEDIUM** **MEDIUM**

Player 1	Player 2
12	20
33	24
07	03
46	45
01	28
21	02
23	25
04	32
35	39
14	50
31	08
48	17
11	40
27	43
15	29
06	41
10	30
47	34
26	16
38	05
36	49
13	09
19	18
42	37
44	22

01 What is a bilberry also known as?

02 Which family does the honeysuckle belong to?

03 Where does the labrador retriever originate?

04 What is a black leopard better known as?

05 What does the fly agaric look like?

06 What type of plant is a bladderwort?

07 Where do dragonflies lay their eggs?

08 How do lampreys eat their food?

09 What type of animal is a gharial?

10 Under what name is woodbine also known?

11 What age can a parrot live to?

12 What distinguishes the tenrec from the hedgehog in appearance?

13 What types of tree would you find in the tundra?

14 What do the roots of the scammony plant yield?

15 How many pairs of legs does a centipede have on average?

16 Where do walrusses live?

17 In which position do sloths spend the majority of their time?

18 In what type of habitat do gentians grow?

19 What type of animal is an ibex?

20 What do wild pigs use their upturned canines for?

21 Which domesticated animal is the guanaco related to?

22 What sort of animal is the flying fox?

23 How does a chipmunk carry his food?

24 Where do tapirs live?

25 Which is the world's largest land animal after the elephant?

26 What sort of animal is a caribou?

27 What type of vegetation can you find in the taiga?

28 What is a Painted Lady?

29 Which family does the crocus belong to?

30 Which is the largest bird of prey?

31 How does a cheetah bring down its prey?

32 On what type of plant do kiwis grow?

33 What is a syringa also known as?

34 What sort of animal is a marmoset?

35 How does a python kill its prey?

36 Which order does the kangaroo belong to?

37 Where do giraffes live?

38 What sort of animal is a wildebeest?

39 To which family do salamanders belong?

40 What is the name of the insect that transmits malaria?

41 Which type of bear is also called silvertip?

42 The adult male of which monkey has a brightly coloured face and buttocks?

43 Where does the emu live?

44 Which is the largest freshwater fish?

45 What do koalas feed on?

46 What is the name of the insect that transmits sleeping sickness?

47 Do pumas have a spotted skin?

48 Which animal does the okapi resemble?

49 What does a tick feed on?

50 What kind of animal is a chinchilla?

111

Costume

Answers to this quiz are on pages 239-240

MEDIUM 🙂 MEDIUM

Player 1	Player 2
12	20
33	24
07	03
46	45
01	28
21	02
23	25
04	32
35	39
14	50
31	08
48	17
11	40
27	43
15	29
06	41
10	30
47	34
26	16
38	05
36	49
13	09
19	18
42	37
44	22

01 Which people invented the parka?

02 What name is given to the small cap often worn by Jewish men?

03 What is the Mexican name for a blanket with a hole in the centre which is used as a cloak?

04 What is a toupee?

05 Men in India wear a wide length of cotton wrapped around the waist, with the end pulled up and tucked between the legs. What is this called?

06 What is the name of the traditional chequered scarf worn by Palestinians?

07 What is the name of the traditional skirt worn by men and women in Indonesia?

08 Sarongs are often dyed by a process that utilizes hot wax. What is this process called?

09 What is the name of the traditional black robe worn by women in Iran?

10 What colour are the robes of a Buddhist monk in Thailand?

11 What is the traditional costume of Japanese women called?

12 What name is given to the decorative sash worn with a kimono?

13 American cowboys wear protective leather coverings over their trousers. What are they called?

14 Western men wearing evening dress sometimes add a brightly coloured sash around the waist. What is it called?

15 What head covering do Sikh men wear?

16 What is the name given to the furry pocket hung at the front of a kilt?

17 What encouraged women to adopt the wearing of bloomers?

18 What was a bustle?

19 What name is given to the tall bearskin hats worn by members of the British guards regiments?

20 What is the name of the flowing robe worn by Indian women?

21 What is a ballerina's dress called?

22 What was the robe of the ancient Romans called?

23 What was Beau Brummell's connection with clothes?

24 What women's fashion was created by Christian Dior just after the Second World War?

25 What name was given to young British men in the 1950s who wore drape coats, drainpipe trousers, and crêpe-soled shoes?

26 What were the two tunic-like garments worn in ancient Greece?

27 What did the double crown worn by the Pharaohs of ancient Egypt signify?

28 Which garment did the ancient Greeks regard as the infallible mark of a barbarian?

29 On what part of the body is a snood worn?

30 What adornment did the Romans award to those who deserved public praise?

31 What distinguishing mark could Roman patricians add to their toga?

32 The soldiers of which country (excluding Scotland) wear a skirt as part of their ceremonial dress?

33 What leg covering was worn with a doublet?

34 What hat was once regarded as the distinguishing mark of British businessmen?

35 Witches are popularly supposed to have a worn a high, pointed hat. What was it called?

36 What is the name given to an eye glass held in one eye?

37 For what footwear are the Dutch best known?

38 Which British nobleman was credited with the invention of waterproof boots?

39 What metallic addition did Levi Strauss make to blue jeans?

40 In western countries, black clothes are associated with funerals. What colour is widely worn for this purpose in the East?

41 In China, clothes of a certain colour were reserved for the emperor. What was the colour?

42 The coats used for fox hunting appear to be red. What is the official name for this colour?

43 What name is given to the soft leather shoes traditionally worn by Native Americans?

44 What is a bolero?

45 What was a goose-belly?

46 What were the advantages of wigs made from horse hair rather than human hair?

47 Where did the word bikini originate?

48 What sort of jacket would a British Victorian gentleman have worn?

49 What surprising feature did top hats worn for the opera have?

50 Golfers in the 1920s often wore wide knickerbockers. What were they called?

113

Nature

MEDIUM ☺ MEDIUM

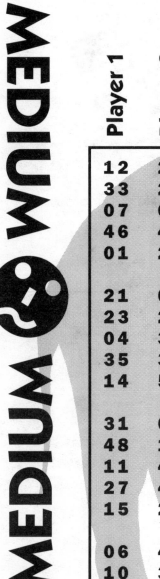

Player 1	Player 2
12	20
33	24
07	03
46	45
01	28
21	02
23	25
04	32
35	39
14	50
31	08
48	17
11	40
27	43
15	29
06	41
10	30
47	34
26	16
38	05
36	49
13	09
19	18
42	37
44	22

114

01 What do you call small insectivorous mammals of the family Erinaceidae, which have their back covered with dense, erectile spines and which characteristically roll into a ball for protection?

02 Is the potato related to the sweet potato?

03 Is rice paper made from rice?

04 What fruit would you expect to get from trees of the genus Quercus?

05 What sort of 'horse' is a hippocampus?

06 On which tree would you expect to find catkins?

07 'Doubtless God could have made a better berry, but doubtless God never did.' Dr Boteler said this of which fruit?

08 What common wild flower is of the genus Papaver?

09 What is the more common name for a hamadryad?

10 Which is the only poisonous snake found in the British Isles?

11 What kind of bird is a helldiver?

12 What is the more common name for plants of the genus Primula?

13 What is unusual about the sundew plant?

14 Which is larger, the hare or the rabbit?

15 Which is the larger species of elephant, the African or Asian?

16 Why is the elephant seal so called?

17 Is the disease elephantiasis caused by contact with elephants?

18 Which deadly disease was pronounced eradicated world-wide in the 1970s?

19 According to the nursery rhyme, which insect is advised urgently to 'fly away home'?

20 John Keats wrote a poem entitled 'Endymion'. What does the word mean?

21 Yerba mate is a herbal drink. What is its other name?

22 What is a silverback?

23 What animal does this describe: an arboreal anthropoid ape of Borneo and Sumatra, having a shaggy reddish-brown coat, very long arms, and no tail.

24 What word describes humans, chimpanzees, gorillas, and monkeys?

25 What name is commonly given to creatures such as pithecanthropus?

26 What animal name is given to the eye-tooth?

27 Which breed of dog is known for its black tongue?

28 By what geographical name is the German Shepherd dog sometimes known?

29 By what name is the Tibetan lion dog better known?

30 Which of these is the slowest: the giant tortoise, the three-toed sloth, or the garden snail?

31 Which lives longer, the hippopotamus or the horse?

32 What is the highest recorded age for a horse?

33 Which has the longer gestation period, the rhinoceros or the elephant?

34 Of what substance is rhinoceros horn made?

35 What does the word 'hippopotamus' mean literally?

36 What name is used to describe animals such as the elephant, rhinoceros, and hippopotamus?

37 Which Hindu god is portrayed as having the head of an elephant?

38 To which flower did the German botanist Leonhard Fuchs give his name?

39 By what other name is belladonna popularly known?

40 Which common or garden bird was once known for its lechery?

41 To what does the word 'hircine' mean?

42 What does the word 'simian' mean?

43 What does the word 'saurian' mean?

44 Of which animals is scrapie a disease?

45 Cattle may suffer from a disease known as BSE. What do the initials stand for?

46 By what other name is hydrophobia known?

47 What unpleasant habit do bats of the family Desmodontidae display?

48 What is a pipistrelle?

49 On what animal did the welfare of the Great Plains Indians mostly depend?

50 What is a beefalo?

115

# Shakespeare

Answers to this quiz are on page 240

Player 1	Player 2
12	20
33	24
07	03
46	45
01	28
21	02
23	25
04	32
35	39
14	50
31	08
48	17
11	40
27	43
15	29
06	41
10	30
47	34
26	16
38	05
36	49
13	09
19	18
42	37
44	22

01 In which play do we find the lines: 'The fault, dear Brutus, is not in our stars, But in ourselves, that we are underlings'?

02 Who died with the words 'Et tu, Brute?'?

03 Which character in Julius Caesar had 'a lean and hungry look'?

04 Who said of Caesar, 'He was my friend, faithful and just to me'?

05 Of which date did the Soothsayer in Julius Caesar warn ?

06 'No grave upon the earth shall clip in it a pair so famous.' Who were they?

07 In which play would you find the lines, 'Blow, blow thou winter wind, Thou art not so unkind as man's ingratitude'?

08 Of which country was Hamlet king?

09 Who said, 'There is nothing either good or bad, but thinking makes it so'?

10 Where was Hamlet's castle?

11 What was Yorick's profession?

12 Hamlet claimed to have loved Ophelia more than how many brothers?

13 Complete the following lines: 'Lay her i' the earth; And from her fair and unpolluted flesh...'

14 Whose 'foul and most unnatural murder' was Hamlet to avenge?

15 Which play begins: 'O! for a Muse of fire, that would ascend, The brightest heaven of invention'?

16 Complete these lines from *Henry V*: 'If we are marked to die, we are enow to do our country loss; and if to live...'

17 On what day was the Battle of Agincourt fought?

18 From which play is the line, 'The prince of darkness is a gentleman'?

19 What was the name of Lear's dutiful daughter?

20 Complete this line from King Lear: 'As flies to wanton boys, are we to the gods...'

21 In which play does a forest appear to walk?

22 Complete the line: 'When shall we three meet again...'

23 Answer the question from *Macbeth*: 'What three things does drink especially provoke?'

24 Complete the line: 'By the pricking of my thumbs...'

25 Who says: 'Out, damned spot! out, I say!'

26 Macbeth was supposed to be invulnerable to anyone born of a woman. Why did this not bother Macduff?

27 Which play has the line, 'It is a wise father that knows his own child'?

28 Who is the villain of *The Merchant of Venice*?

29 Name the woman lawyer who outwits Shylock.

30 Give the line that follows: 'The quality of mercy is not strained...'

31 Give the line that follows: 'How far that little candle throws his beams...'

32 In which play is the phrase, 'the world's mine oyster'?

33 What, according to the Merry Wives of Windsor, is associated with odd numbers?

34 Who claimed to be able to 'put a girdle round about the earth in forty minutes'?

35 Complete the following line: 'Ill met by moonlight...'

36 Complete the line: 'I know a bank whereon...'

37 Add the final line: 'You spotted snake with double tongue, Thorny hedgehogs, be not seen; Newts, and blind-worms, do no wrong...'

38 Who was the villain in *Othello*?

39 Who was Othello's wife?

40 What dreadful act was Othello driven to by jealousy?

41 'From forth the fatal loins of these two foes, A pair of star-crossed lovers take their life.' Who were they?

42 In *Romeo and Juliet*, who tells of Queen Mab, the fairies' midwife?

43 Who did Juliet's father want her to marry?

44 Who are the two rival families in *Romeo and Juliet*?

45 Complete the lines: 'Swear not by the moon, the inconstant moon, That monthly changes in her circled orb...'

46 Who says, 'A plague o' both your houses!'?

47 Who describes himself as 'Fortune's fool'?

48 From which play is the line, 'Kiss me Kate, we will be married o' Sunday'?

49 Who is the heroine of *The Tempest*?

50 The words missing from this quotation became the title of a famous book. What are they? 'How many goodly creatures are there here! How beauteous mankind is! O..., that has such people in't.'

Places

Answers to this quiz are on page 240

MEDIUM MEDIUM MEDIUM

Player 1	Player 2
12	20
33	24
07	03
46	45
01	28
21	02
23	25
04	32
35	39
14	50
31	08
48	17
11	40
27	43
15	29
06	41
10	30
47	34
26	16
38	05
36	49
13	09
19	18
42	37
44	22

01 Which country would you reach if you crossed the Strait of Gibraltar due south from Spain?

02 On which border is Lake Geneva?

03 What is the name of the Australian island south of Victoria?

04 In which US state would you find the Grand Canyon?

05 What was Rock Island used for during the American Civil War?

06 Which country has the world's second largest population?

07 What is South West Africa now called?

08 What is the predominant religion in Mexico?

09 What is the most northerly town in Europe?

10 In which country would you pay in Schilling?

11 Which is the most southerly point of the UK?

12 Which is New York's largest borough?

13 In which country does the Danube rise?

14 In which city is the Hagia Sofia situated?

15 Which is the only predominantly Moslem state in India?

16 Which country do the Faeroe Islands belong to?

17 In which sea is the Crimea situated?

18 What is the name of the mountain overlooking Capetown?

19 In which Australian state is Sydney?

20 Which three countries form the Baltic states?

118

21 In which mountain range is Andorra situated?

22 What is the capital of Indonesia?

23 What is the name of the group of islands off the southern tip of South America?

24 Which is the highest mountain in Japan?

25 On which river is Rome situated?

26 In which city can you find St Basil's cathedral?

27 Which town is further north – Oslo or St. Petersburg?

28 Which is China's largest city?

29 Can you name the three Balearic Islands?

30 In which city can you find the statue of the Little Mermaid?

31 On which border lies the Principality of Liechtenstein?

32 Which Scottish island group do Skye and Iona belong to?

33 What is the name of the strait between the European and Asian part of Turkey, connecting the Sea of Marmara with the Black Sea?

34 What is the capital of Morocco?

35 In which country is the ancient city of Carthage?

36 Which is the most northerly of the Great Lakes in North America?

37 In which city would you find the Taj Mahal?

38 Which is the largest province in Canada?

39 Which is the most sparsely populated state in the USA?

40 Which is the most northerly county in England?

41 In which mountain range would you find the Matterhorn?

42 On which island is Tokyo situated?

43 Which two former African countries formed Tanzania?

44 Where would you find the Prado?

45 What is the capital of Colorado?

46 What island group do Cuba and Jamaica belong to?

47 In which Italian region is Florence situated?

48 Which of the following countries is not in the northern hemisphere: Thailand, Ethiopia, Venezuela, Philippines, Zambia?

49 On which river is Cologne situated?

50 Which country do the Azores belong to?

119

Medicine

Answers to this quiz are on page 241

MEDIUM 😕 MEDIUM 😕 MEDIUM

Player 1	Player 2
12	20
33	24
07	03
46	45
01	28
21	02
23	25
04	32
35	39
14	50
31	08
48	17
11	40
27	43
15	29
06	41
10	30
47	34
26	16
38	05
36	49
13	09
19	18
42	37
44	22

01 Which eye disorder is caused by inadequate drainage of excess fluid?

02 Why do human beings not develop an immunity against the common cold?

03 What disease does a person suffer from who has the protein factor VIII missing from the plasma?

04 What are people with agoraphobia frightened of?

05 In a person with periodontal disease, what is inflamed?

06 In a person suffering from Down's syndrome, how do the body cells differ from those of normal people?

07 What type of cancer is malignant melanoma?

08 What are people with anaemia lacking?

09 What is thrombosis?

10 In which allergic disease do the muscles of the bronchi and bronchioles contract, resulting in the narrowing of the air passages?

11 The disease rickets implies that there is a bone defiency in what?

12 Mammography is used for screening for which disease?

13 What is the cause of angina pectoris?

14 What is a person with osteoporosis suffering from?

15 What does AIDS stand for?

16 What type of disease is psoriasis?

17 What does 'grand mal' mean?

18 Which widespread viral infection has been eradicated since 1979 due to a worldwide vaccination programme?

19 In a person suffering from emphysema, which organ is affected?

20 What does ECG stand for?

21 Which disease does the ades mosquito transmit?

22 In leukaemia, which cells are affected?

23 If a person is short-sighted, what type of lens would he need to correct this?

24 Which virus causes chicken pox?

25 In a person suffering from hepatitis, which organ is affected?

26 What permanent condition can an infection of poliomyelitis lead to?

27 What are the main symptons of a tetanus infection?

28 In encephalitis, which part of the body is inflamed?

29 Which serious condition can be caused by a burst appendix?

30 Which are the main glands affected by an attack of mumps?

31 Which part of the body does the bacterium vibrio cholerae affect?

32 In tuberculosis, which are the main organs affected?

33 What is German measles also called?

34 Which virus causes a cold sore?

35 Which infectious disease is caused by the spirochete Treponema pallidum?

36 Which condition describes the lesion of the mucous membrane of the stomach accompanied by inflammation?

37 What is infectious mononucleosis also called?

38 Which degenerative nervous disease is associated with the destruction of brain cells that produce dopamine?

39 Which serious contagious disease is caused by the bacterium Bordetella pertussis?

40 What type of infection is ringworm?

41 In which part of the body does gout usually start?

42 What is the purpose of a vagotomy?

43 How is a stroke caused?

44 What condition describes the inflammation of the membranes of the cavities in the skull?

45 What are haemorrhoids also known as?

46 What is a sty caused by?

47 Spondylitis is an inflammation of which part of the body?

48 What is icterus also called?

49 What do doctors examine by use of an angiography?

50 What is the effect of a cataract?

Sport

Answers to this quiz are on page 241

MEDIUM 😊 **MEDIUM**

Player 1	Player 2
12	20
33	24
07	03
46	45
01	28
21	02
23	25
04	32
35	39
14	50
31	08
48	17
11	40
27	43
15	29
06	41
10	30
47	34
26	16
38	05
36	49
13	09
19	18
42	37
44	22

122

01 What was the location of the 1994 Winter Olympics?

02 Which male tennis player won the Australian Open Singles Championship in 1989 and 1990?

03 With which sport is Max Schmeling associated?

04 Who was the first woman to swim the English Channel?

05 Which American football team did 'Red' Grange play for professionally?

06 What is the main difference between the decathlon and the modern pentathlon?

07 What type of sport is aikido?

08 Who became the first British golfer in 50 years to win the US Open in 1970?

09 Where is the Longchamp racecourse situated?

10 What sport do you associate with Damon Hill?

11 With which sport is Peggy Fleming associated?

12 In which sport would you find the James Norris Trophy?

13 Which golfer won the British Open in 1979, 1984, and 1988?

14 With which sport is Anita Lonsbrough associated?

15 Who founded the modern Olympic Games?

16 Which British runner became the first person to run a mile in under four minutes in 1954?

17 How long is a marathon race?

18 Which country won the football World Cup in 1966?

19 How many singles titles did Martina Navratilova win at Wimbledon?

20 Which US team did the Brazilian football player Pelè play for from 1975 to 1977?

21 Who was the first black American major-league baseball player?

22 Which American swimmer won five gold medals in the 1924 and 1928 Olympics and went on to become a film actor?

23 With which sport is Bobby Jones associated?

24 Which British athlete won gold medals in the decathlon in 1980 and 1984?

25 Which US speed skater won all five men's gold medals at the 1980 Winter Olympics?

26 What does the biathlon winter event consist of?

27 What is the name of the Argentinian football star who admitted to taking drugs?

28 At which modern Olympic Games was the torch first introduced?

29 In which American city would you find the football team The Steelers?

30 With which major sporting event is the Jules Rimet Trophy associated?

31 Which female tennis player became the French Open Singles Champion in 1993?

32 Name the stadium that was built in honor of baseball player Babe Ruth?

33 With which sport is Gene Tunney associated?

34 Why did 32 black countries boycott the 1976 Olympic Games at Montreal?

35 In which country was the first Football World Cup held?

36 Which are the two events in international gymnastics in which both men and women take part?

37 In which Olympic event did Abebe Bikila gain a medal?

38 In which sport would you be awarded the Dunhill Cup?

39 Which tennis player won the men's singles at Wimbledon in 1993 and 1994?

40 Who won the 1988 World Snooker Championship?

41 Which sport is associated with the Uber Cup?

42 Which athlete was referred to as 'The Flying Finn'?

43 What type of sport is Bill Shoemaker associated with?

44 For which event did David Hemery win a gold medal at the 1968 Olympics, setting a new world record?

45 How many players are there in a Rugby League team?

46 Which sport is Franz Klammer associated with?

47 What was the location of the 1968 Summer Olympics?

48 Which female tennis player became the US Open Champion in 1990?

49 What is Britain's Rugby Union team popularly known as?

50 Which event is Le Mans famous for?

123

Places

Answers to this quiz are on page 241

MEDIUM MEDIUM MEDIUM

Player 1	Player 2
12	20
33	24
07	03
46	45
01	28
21	02
23	25
04	32
35	39
14	50
31	08
48	17
11	40
27	43
15	29
06	41
10	30
47	34
26	16
38	05
36	49
13	09
19	18
42	37
44	22

01 Where is the coldest town in the world?

02 Which country is the odd one out: (a) Mexico, (b) Brazil, (c) Argentina, (d) Venezuela, (e) Chile?

03 Which of the following cities is furthest south: (a) Madrid, (b) New York,(c) San Francisco, (d) Cairo, (e) Tokyo?

04 In which country would you pay in escudos?

05 Which is the main religion in Brazil?

06 With which of the following countries does Germany not form a border: (a) Belgium, (b) Switzerland, (c) Hungary, (d) The Czech Republic, (e) Denmark?

07 What is the capital city of New Zealand?

08 In which country would you find Cork, Waterford, and Galway?

09 In which US state is New Orleans situated?

10 Which Chinese city has the highest population?

11 Which of the following states is the odd one out: (a) Manchuria, (b) Estonia, (c) Ukraine, (d) Byelorussia, (e) Kazakhstan?

12 What is the capital of Massachusetts?

13 Name the independent principality in south-eastern France near the Italian border?

14 Which Pacific islands are famous for their unusual wildlife, such as flightless birds and giant tortoises?

15 Where is the largest cave system in the world and what is it called?

16 Which is the largest coral reef in the world?

17 What is the capital of Zimbabwe?

18 Which street in London was famous for its association with newspaper publishing?

19 Which of the following countries is the odd one out: (a) Pakistan, (b) India, (c) Iraq, (d) Egypt, (e) Morocco?

20 Which is the largest active volcano in the world?

21 In which city would you find Madison Square Garden?

22 The Strait of Messina separates Italy from which island?

23 In which country would you find Stavanger, Bergen, and Trondheim?

24 In which city would you find The Spanish Steps?

25 In which country would you hear Catalan spoken?

26 Which country is referred to as the Emerald Isle?

27 With which of the following states does Florida not have a border: (a) Georgia, (b) Alabama, (c) Tennessee?

28 What is the capital of Peru?

29 Where can you find The Giant's Causeway?

30 With which cloth do you associate the French town of Chantilly?

31 Which city is further south – Buenos Aires or Brisbane?

32 On which river would you find the Victoria Falls?

33 In which country is the shekel the official currency?

34 Which Australian state lies to the north-east of the country?

35 What is the name of the large area of wetlands in Florida?

36 Which of these countries does not have a coastline on the Mediterranean: (a) Israel, (b) Greece, (c) Saudia Arabia?

37 Which city is commonly known as the The Big Apple?

38 With which other West Indian island did Trinidad join to form a state?

39 Havana is the capital of which country?

40 Which US state lies to the west of Colorado: (a) Utah, (b) Wyoming, (c) Arizona?

41 Which Canadian province borders Hudson Bay, Ontario, and the Gulf of St. Lawrence?

42 In which city would you find the Capitol?

43 What is the capital of the Philippines?

44 Which of the following countries does not have a coastline on the North Sea: (a) Great Britain, (b) The Netherlands, (c) Poland?

45 Which European country is divided into 23 cantons?

46 In which European city would you find St. Peter's Square?

47 In which Italian city would you find the Uffizi Gallery?

48 In which city would you find Carnaby Street?

49 Which US state is commonly known as the Sunshine State?

50 Orange Free State is a province of which country?

The Weather

Answers to this quiz are on pages 241-242

MEDIUM QUIZ

Player 1	Player 2
12	20
33	24
07	03
46	45
01	28
21	02
23	25
04	32
35	39
14	50
31	08
48	17
11	40
27	43
15	29
06	41
10	30
47	34
26	16
38	05
36	49
13	09
19	18
42	37
44	22

01 In the atmosphere, is the stratosphere, mesosphere, or troposphere nearest to the Earth's surface?

02 What are zones of transition from one air mass to another called?

03 What is another name for the 'absolute temperature scale'?

04 What instrument is used to measure wind speed?

05 What is an anemograph?

06 What name is given to a wind speed of above 119km (74 miles) per hour according to the Beaufort scale?

07 What name is commonly given to the equatorial belt of calms?

08 What name is given to a dark, funnel-shaped cloud containing violently rotating air that develops within a cumulonimbus cloud mass and extends to the earth?

09 What is a dust devil?

10 What is a hygrometer used for?

11 What sort of barometer is a statoscope?

12 Which metal has been widely used in the manufacture of thermometers and barometers?

13 In which part of the atmosphere would you find the ozone layer?

14 What is the meteorological use of silver iodide?

15 What is 'corn snow'?

16 What is a neve?

17 What is a whiteout?

18 What is rain-wash?

19 What is a pluviometer?

20 How much rain must a rainforest have in order to qualify for that description?

21 What is acid rain?

22 What is an isohyet?

23 What primitive aeronautical devices are often used to carry meteorological equipment?

24 What is a freshet?

25 In Southern Asia, what is the Monsoon?

26 What is the meaning of 'diluvial'?

27 What, in meteorological terms, is a bore?

28 What is a cloud forest?

29 What is the scientific name for a thundercloud?

30 What are noctilucent clouds?

31 What is a ceilometer?

32 What is a downburst?

33 What is cirrostratus?

34 What are virga?

35 What is an atmospherium?

36 What is a mackerel sky?

37 What is mare's-tail?

38 What, in relation to clouds, is flocculation?

39 What was Tiros 1?

40 What is relative humidity?

41 What is a thermocline?

42 What is a wind-chill factor?

43 What, in atmospheric terms, is the lapse rate?

44 What is the dew point?

45 What is a heat island?

46 What is a meteorograph?

47 What is the difference between weather and climate?

48 Approximately how much snow is equal to 2.5cm (1 in) of rainfall?

49 At what level does an increase in wind speed have very little additional effect on the wind chill factor?

50 What is the outermost layer of the atmosphere called?

Popular Music & Musicals

Answers to this quiz are on page 242

Player 1	Player 2
12	20
33	24
07	03
46	45
01	28
21	02
23	25
04	32
35	39
14	50
31	08
48	17
11	40
27	43
15	29
06	41
10	30
47	34
26	16
38	05
36	49
13	09
19	18
42	37
44	22

01 Who wrote the music to the film *The Mission*?

02 Whose real name is Richard Starkey?

03 Who wrote the score to the musical *Annie Get Your Gun*?

04 What are the names of the two albums that Bruce Springsteen released simultaneously in 1992?

05 What was the name of the French-American dancer and singer who appeared in the revue *Shuffle Along*?

06 From which musical does the song 'Hey, Big Spender' come?

07 Which song contains the words 'Cold cold heart, hard done by you, some things look better baby, just passing through'?

08 On which Boomtown Rats album is the song 'I Don't Like Mondays'?

09 Who wrote the theme to the film *Chariots of Fire*?

10 Robert Plant was the lead singer of which group?

11 On which original Beatles album is the song 'When I'm 64'?

12 The lyrics to the musical *Cats* were adapted from the poems of which writer?

13 Which song contains the words 'Dirty old river, must you keep rolling'?

14 Which musical does the song 'Another Op'nin', Another Show' come from?

15 On which Phil Collins album is the song 'One More Night'?

16 Which female singer recorded the song 'Don't Go Breaking My Heart' with Elton John?

17 Who wrote the score to the musical *Showboat*?

18 What is the name of the song Cliff Richard came second with in the 1973 Eurovision Song Contest?

19 Which instrument does Chris Barber play?

20 On which original Queen album is the song 'I Want to Break Free'?

21 Where did Simon and Garfunkel's reunion concert in 1981 take place?

22 Which Spanish singer revived the Cole Porter song 'Begin the Beguine' in 1981?

23 Which singer brought out his autobiography entitled *Moonwalk*?

24 Which musical does the song 'I Feel Pretty' come from?

25 Which song contains the words 'And when the night is cloudy there is still a light that shines on me'?

26 Which singer was born Reginald Dwight?

27 Who wrote the score to the musical *Carousel*?

28 Which instrument does Lester Young play?

29 Which band did Ritchie Blackmore form after leaving Deep Purple?

30 What style of music was Mahalia Jackson known for?

31 Which John Lennon song went to No. 1 in the UK and USA following his death?

32 Where did Hillbilly music originate?

33 Which team wrote most of the songs for the Sweet, Suzi Quatro, and Mud?

34 Complete the line 'This ain't no technological breakdown...'.

35 Who wrote the score to the musical *Joseph and the Amazing Technicolour Dreamcoat*?

36 Which style of instrumental jazz was associated with New Orleans?

37 What was Elvis Presley's first No. 1 hit?

38 Who was the female lead singer of Vinegar Joe?

39 Which Tina Turner song was on the soundtrack of *Mad Max Beyond Thunderdome*?

40 Who wrote 'Alexander's Ragtime Band'?

41 On which REM album is the song 'Losing My Religion'?

42 Which band was Brian Wilson involved with?

43 Who created the 'Duck Walk' dance step?

44 Who recorded the album *The Rise and Fall of Ziggy Stardust*?

45 Which jazz musician brought out the album *Bahia*?

46 With which female singer did George Michael sing 'I Knew You Were Waiting'?

47 In which group did Rod Stewart play in in the early 70s?

48 Which musical style were the Supremes known for?

49 Which song contains the words 'No help below us, above us only sky'?

50 From which musical comes the song 'Sitting Pretty'?

129

Costume

Answers to this quiz are on pages 242-243

MEDIUM

Player 1	Player 2
12	20
33	24
07	03
46	45
01	28
21	02
23	25
04	32
35	39
14	50
31	08
48	17
11	40
27	43
15	29
06	41
10	30
47	34
26	16
38	05
36	49
13	09
19	18
42	37
44	22

01 The tie originated from neckties worn by 17th-century Croatian soldiers. What was this type of wide tie first called?

02 **Name the set of petticoats worn in the 19th century under a woman's full skirt.**

03 In which region would you see people wearing a kaftan?

04 **What were men's hose replaced with in the 17th century?**

05 In which decade did women wear shorter skirts for the first time?

06 **What is the name of the scarf worn by American cowboys over their nose and mouth?**

07 Name the sleeveless garment, similar to an apron, which is usually worn as an overdress, in particular by little girls?

08 **What traditional headcovering did Muslim men wear?**

09 Which garment of the 1920s became known as 'Oxford Bags'?

10 **What was the shape of a 1920s woman's dress in the West?**

11 What is the name given to long drawers for men, originating in the 1920s, which are still worn today in cold weather?

12 **Name the undergarment worn by women in the late 19th and early 20th centuries to support their waistline, hips, and bust?**

13 What type of hat is a sou'wester?

14 **What is the name of the traditional skirt made from woven flax which is worn by the Maoris of New Zealand?**

15 What type of skirt do the hula dancers of Hawaii wear?

16 **What does an aloha shirt, a less traditional garment worn by Hawaiians, look like?**

17 What type of garment are lederhosen?

18 **What type of garment were pantaloons?**

130

19 What material is a kilt usually made from?

20 What is the name given to women's trousers cut to resemble a skirt?

21 What do you call the traditional full-skirted dress from Bavaria and Austria with a tight bodice, low neck and apron, often made from a flower-patterned material?

22 What did the farthingale, worn by women in the 16th and 17th centuries, try to achieve?

23 What is a jumpsuit?

24 What was the purpose of wearing pattens as footwear?

25 What special feature distinguished lorgnettes from other eyeglasses?

26 What do you call the elasticated band worn around the leg to hold up a stocking?

27 How long are Bermuda shorts?

28 The arrival of which material in the 1940s made stockings much cheaper and more hard-wearing than silk?

29 Which type of shoe featuring high heels and thick soles became fashionable in the 1970s?

30 What type of footwear was a solleret?

31 What would you call a stiff, starched, circular collar, either frilled or pleated, worn by people in the 16th and 17th centuries?

32 What sort of people wear a cassock?

33 What is the name of the rectangular linen or woollen cloak worn by men and women in Ancient Greece?

34 What colour biretta would a bishop wear?

35 Which round, rimless cap is often worn angled to one side?

36 What sort of hat is a trilby?

37 Which decade saw the introduction of the mini–skirt?

38 What is a tuxedo also called?

39 What colour tie would you normally wear with a tuxedo?

40 What type of person wears a dog collar?

41 What colour is a Panama hat?

42 What is the name for a waterproof overshoe?

43 What is the upper part of an espadrille usually made from?

44 In which country would a sarafan be worn?

45 What sort of dress is a chemise?

46 What type of clothing is a dashiki?

47 What is the name for a tight-fitting permeable suit worn by surfers and divers in order to retain body heat?

48 What is a boater made from?

49 What do you call the protective glove worn with medieval armour?

50 What do you call a roll made of cloth with an opening at each end for warming your hands?

Mountains

Answers to this quiz are on page 243

MEDIUM 😊 **MEDIUM**

Player 1	Player 2
12	20
33	24
07	03
46	45
01	28
21	02
23	25
04	32
35	39
14	50
31	08
48	17
11	40
27	43
15	29
06	41
10	30
47	34
26	16
38	05
36	49
13	09
19	18
42	37
44	22

01 In which country are the Southern Alps?

02 Which is the highest mountain in the USA?

03 In which mountain range is the Yosemite National Park situated?

04 Which is the highest peak of the Caucasus?

05 Mount Everest is situated on the border of which two countries?

06 Rock Creek Butte is the highest peak of which mountain range?

07 Which of the following US States do the Rocky Mountains not cross: (a) Wyoming, (b) Montana, (c) Nebraska?

08 In which country is Kilimanjaro situated?

09 Which mountain range lies to the south of Brisbane?

10 In which country would you find the Grampian Mountains?

11 Which mountain range is situated to the south of Stuttgart in Germany?

12 Which plateau extends through South East Belgium, Luxembourg, and northern France?

13 Which is the highest peak of the Austrian Alps?

14 In which country are the Transylvanian Alps?

15 Which mountain ranges do the Carpathian Mountains link?

16 In which country is Table Mountain situated?

17 Where in Africa would you find the Ahagger mountain massif?

18 Through which countries do the Alps not extend: (a) The Czech Republic, (b) Germany, (c) Italy?

132

19 Jebel Toubkal is the highest peak of which mountain range?

20 The Jura Mountains extend along which border?

21 Which mountain range lies to the south of Strasbourg?

22 Which mountain range lies along the northern border of Czechoslovakia and Germany?

23 In which mountain range is the Annapurna massif situated?

24 What is Mount Godwin Austen also called?

25 In which country is Nanga Parbat situated?

26 Which is the highest mountain in Canada?

27 The Kanchenjunga is situated on the border between which two countries?

28 The Dolomites are part of which mountain range?

29 The Brenner Pass links which two countries?

30 In which part of Great Britain are the Cambrian Mountains situated?

31 Which is the second highest mountain in Africa, after Kilimanjaro?

32 Between which seas are the Caucasus mountains situated?

33 Through which of the following countries do the Himalayas not extend: (a) Pakistan, (b) Afghanistan, (c) Nepal?

34 Which is the highest mountain in Great Britain?

35 The Tatra Mountains are part of which larger mountain range?

36 Lake Geneva lies on the border of which two mountain ranges?

37 Which mountain is said to be the landing place of Noah's ark?

38 Which is the highest peak in the Americas?

39 On which continent would you find the Vinson Massif?

40 Which is the highest peak in Australia?

41 The Blue Ridge is part of which mountain range?

42 In which country does the Sierra Madre Oriental rise?

43 In which US National Park is Mount Whitney situated?

44 The Matterhorn is situated on the border of which two countries?

45 In which part of the Alps is Monte Rosa situated?

46 Which is the highest peak in Hawaii?

47 Krakatoa is situated between which two islands?

48 Which is the highest peak in Japan?

49 Lourdes, known as a place of pilgrimage, is situated on the slopes of which mountain range?

50 Mount Corno is situated in which mountain range?

133

Pop Music

Answers to this quiz are on page 243

MEDIUM 😵 MEDIUM MEDIUM

Player 1	Player 2
12	20
33	24
07	03
46	45
01	28
21	02
23	25
04	32
35	39
14	50
31	08
48	17
11	40
27	43
15	29
06	41
10	30
47	34
26	16
38	05
36	49
13	09
19	18
42	37
44	22

01 What was the first album Michael Jackson released after his million-seller *Thriller*?

02 Who wrote the musical *South Pacific*?

03 Which singer released the album *No Jacket Required*?

04 Which English group derived their name from a Muddy Waters song?

05 What is the title of Roxette's Greatest Hits album?

06 What was the debut album of Sade?

07 Who sang the title song to the film *Waiting to Exhale*?

08 From which musical does the song 'Sixteen Going On Seventeen' come?

09 With which group is Marti Pellow associated?

10 Which group released the album *Achtung Baby*?

11 Which female singer sang the theme tune to the Bond film *GoldenEye*?

12 On which UB40 album would you find the song 'Kingston Town'?

13 Together with which female singer did James Taylor record the song 'Mockingbird'?

14 Which group released the album *Breakfast in America*?

15 In 1983 Irene Cara had a hit with 'What a Feeling'. From which film does the song come?

16 Who wrote the song 'Raindrops Keep Falling On My Head'?

17 With which instrument do you associate Kenny Ball?

18 Which film features the songs 'Stayin' Alive' and 'How Deep Is Your Love'?

19 Who wrote the theme music to *The Good, the Bad and the Ugly*?

20 What is the title of the Greatest Hits album of Tears For Fears?

21 Which singer released the album *Born in the USA*?

22 On which original Simon & Garfunkel album would you find 'The Boxer'?

23 From which musical is the song 'Pick a Pocket or Two'?

24 Who wrote the songs to the film *Toy Story*?

25 Which singer released the album *Mercury Falling*?

26 Which Simply Red album contains the song 'Something Got Me Started'?

27 In which year did the Rolling Stones have a hit with 'Satisfaction'?

28 With which instrument do you associate Gheorge Zamfir?

29 Together with which male singer did Barbra Streisand record the song 'You Don't Bring Me Flowers'?

30 Which group recorded the songs 'Georgy Girl' and 'The Carnival Is Over'?

31 Who wrote the song 'Ev'ry Time We Say Goodbye'?

32 Which French female singer became known as the 'Little Sparrow'?

33 What is the title of The Best of Bob Marley album?

34 Which female soul singer brought out the album *I Feel For You*?

35 With which group is Heather Small associated?

36 Which musical featured the songs 'Summer Nights' and 'You're the One That I want'?

37 From which Walt Disney film does the song 'The Bare Necessities' come?

38 Which Celtic group brought out the album *The Cutter and the Clan*?

39 Who released the album *The Return of the Space Cowboy*?

40 Who was the lead singer of the Commodores?

41 Who was the female singer of Yazoo?

42 Who was Richard Wayne Penniman?

43 In which year did Dire Straits record their album *Brothers In Arms*?

44 Which female singer brought out the album *It's A Man's World*?

45 Which original Bon Jovi album contains the song 'Livin' on a Prayer'?

46 What was the title of Kate Bush's debut album?

47 On which original Queen album would you find the song 'Who Wants to Live Forever'?

48 Which group did Marc Almond sing with before going solo?

49 Which original Beatles Album contains the song 'Strawberry Fields Forever'?

50 Which female singer released the album *Boys For Pele*?

135

Science

Answers to this quiz are on page 243

MEDIUM ☹ **MEDIUM**

Player 1	Player 2
12	20
33	24
07	03
46	45
01	28
21	02
23	25
04	32
35	39
14	50
31	08
48	17
11	40
27	43
15	29
06	41
10	30
47	34
26	16
38	05
36	49
13	09
19	18
42	37
44	22

136

01 Which gas is the major constituent of ordinary air?

02 At what speed do freely falling bodies descend under the influence of gravity?

03 It's said that Archimedes shouted 'Eureka!' upon discovering a scientific principle (while in the bath). What was the principle?

04 What is the popular name for an acid mixture capable of dissolving gold?

05 What does TNT stand for?

06 From what expression was the word radar derived?

07 Which Frenchman is regarded as the founder of modern chemistry?

08 What is litmus?

09 What approximate percentage of the atmosphere is composed of oxygen?

10 What metal is found in both brass and bronze?

11 What is used to galvanize iron?

12 Which gas is well known for its smell of rotten eggs?

13 In computer parlance, what does RAM stand for?

14 What property does cobalt have in common with iron?

15 What is thunder?

16 Of which creature are there most species on Earth?

17 What is the substance that makes plants green?

18 What is a metal composed of two or more others called?

19 The gene for having six fingers is dominant over the gene for having five fingers. True or false?

20 Are there land tides as well as sea tides?

21 What is meant by 'Panspermia'?

22 What is the name for a protein that functions as a biological catalyst?

23 What is another name for the star Polaris?

24 What is the closest spiral galaxy to the Milky Way?

25 Which is the farthest planet visible to the unaided eye?

26 Which is the largest planet?

27 Which planet is nearest the Sun?

28 Which is the most widely used of all solvents?

29 Amalthea, Io, Europa, Ganymede, and Callisto are all satellites of which planet?

30 Which metal, much used in jewellery, is more valuable than gold?

31 What is the speed of light?

32 How far is the Sun from Earth?

33 Is the Moon's diameter (a) 3,327.50 km (5,324 miles), (b) 552 km (345 miles), or (c) 3,456 km (2,160 miles)?

34 What, in modern physics, is the name applied to an abrupt change from one energy level to another?

35 What name is given to the treatment of food with heat to destroy disease-causing organisms?

36 What is the name given to the partial or complete obscuring, relative to a designated observer, of one celestial body by another?

37 What is the scientific term for a state of complete emptiness?

38 In 1938 a revolutionary writing device was invented. What was it?

39 Which machine, invented by J. Murray Spangler in the early 1900s, has become a household word under another name?

40 What name is given to an artificial device used to replace a missing body part?

41 What is prophylaxis?

42 What name is given to the field of study devoted to processes that behave in a complex, apparently random way?

43 What is the process by which plants create food using sunlight as an energy source?

44 What is the process by which plants develop without chlorophyll through lack of exposure to sunlight?

45 What is the material used as a base for bacterial culture media?

46 What basic laboratory tool was invented at Heidelberg University in 1850?

47 By what common name do we call a unit of power equal to 108,900 m-pounds/minute (33,000 foot-pounds/minute)?

48 What is the freezing point of water on the Celsius scale?

49 What is the freezing point of water on the Fahrenheit scale?

50 With what science do you associate the Austrian monk Gregor Mendel?

137

Food & Drink

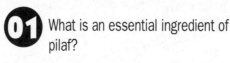

MEDIUM ☺ MEDIUM

Player 1	Player 2
12	20
33	24
07	03
46	45
01	28
21	02
23	25
04	32
35	39
14	50
31	08
48	17
11	40
27	43
15	29
06	41
10	30
47	34
26	16
38	05
36	49
13	09
19	18
42	37
44	22

01 What is an essential ingredient of pilaf?

02 What is a croquette?

03 Which family does the herb angelica come from?

04 With which herb is saltimbocca flavoured with?

05 What is polenta made with?

06 Which vegetables would you find in gazpacho?

07 What do you call the Spanish drink made from wine mixed with brandy, fruit juice, and sugar?

08 Which country does the wine retsina come from?

09 What type of meat would you use for Irish stew?

10 Which spice is used to flavour cevapcici?

11 What is a roulade?

12 What do you call the fatty tissues which are located around the kidneys of cattle or sheep and often used as cooking fat?

13 What part of the animal does hock come from?

14 Which fish does caviar usually come from?

15 Which vegetable is used in humus?

16 What is a profiterole filled with?

17 Where does shortbread originate?

18 What drink is a carbonade flavoured with?

19 What is a tandoor used for?

20 What sort of sauce is a remoulade?

21 In which area of France are truffles grown?

22 What type of drink is stout?

23 What is a Screwdriver made with?

24 What do you call large tubes of pasta, filled with meat or cheese, and cooked in a tomato sauce?

25 What sort of tortilla is a taco?

26 What is the name of the Creole rice dish containing chicken, ham or shrimps with added herbs and spices?

27 What do you call an espresso coffee mixed or topped with frothy cream or milk?

28 What sort of fruit is an ugli?

29 Which region of France does chardonnay come from?

30 What is a gimlet made with?

31 What type of meat is prosciutto?

32 What vegetable family does calabrese (broccoli) come from?

33 Which herb is used for making pesto sauce?

34 Which country does the dish biryani come from?

35 What type of fish is a rollmop?

36 What would you make with an endive?

37 What is tofu made from?

38 Which fruit is slivovitz made from?

39 What is zwieback?

40 What is made from pinot noir and pinot blanc?

41 What is naan?

42 Which country does the chorizo sausage come from?

43 What grain is pumpernickel made from?

44 Which is the main vegetable in a spanakopita?

45 What is a brioche?

46 What sort of cake is a devil's food cake?

47 What is amaretto flavoured with?

48 What type of dish is a chowder?

49 What part of the animal is a tournedos cut from?

50 What type of dish is shashlik?

The Bible

Answers to this quiz are on page 244

MEDIUM ☺ **MEDIUM**

Player 1	Player 2
12	20
33	24
07	03
46	45
01	28
21	02
23	25
04	32
35	39
14	50
31	08
48	17
11	40
27	43
15	29
06	41
10	30
47	34
26	16
38	05
36	49
13	09
19	18
42	37
44	22

01 What does the word 'Bible' actually mean?

02 What is the Pentateuch?

03 How many books are there in the Old Testament?

04 How many books are there in the Old and New Testaments together?

05 What is the name given to the 15 books which were not accepted into the Hebrew Bible?

06 What name was given to the Greek translation of the Five Books of Moses?

07 Why was the Septuagint so called?

08 Which are the oldest manuscripts of the Bible now in existence?

09 What name is given to a manuscript in the form of a modern book with writing on both sides of the page?

10 What is the Hebrew name for the Pentateuch?

11 Which two books tell the story of King David?

12 What did the writing on the wall at Belshazzar's feast say?

13 Why did Abraham lead the Hebrews into Egypt?

14 Who were the first two sons of Abraham?

15 Which is the world's oldest city?

16 Name the sons of Noah.

17 Who were the sons of Isaac and Rebekah?

18 Which prophet was cast into a den of lions?

19 Which son of David and Bathsheba was renowned for his wisdom?

20 Who had Samson's hair cut while he slept?

21 Who was the Philistine giant from Gath?

22 When the Jewish kingdom was split in two, what was the southern part called?

23 Which two seas are connected by the River Jordan?

24 Which Babylonian king captured Jerusalem in 597 BC?

25 What was the name of the priestly sect who lived at Qumran and wrote the Dead Sea Scrolls?

26 Who led the children of Israel out of Egypt?

27 Who occupied the promised land when the Israelites arrived?

28 Deliverance from which of the Plagues of Egypt is commemorated by the Passover?

29 Which queen came to test the wisdom of Solomon?

30 Of which nation was Sargon king?

31 Which Persian conqueror of Babylon allowed the Israelites to return home?

32 What name is given to the land between the rivers Tigris and Euphrates?

33 Who was king when Jesus was born?

34 Where is Nazareth?

35 What was the other name for the Sea of Galilee?

36 Who is regarded as the founder of Christianity?

37 Who was the first Christian martyr?

38 Name the four gospels of the New Testament.

39 What is the full name of the book often wrongly called The Book of Revelations?

40 What is the biblical significance of the number 666?

41 On which hill did the crucifixion take place?

42 Who were the magi?

43 Who lived on locusts and honey?

44 Who danced for John the Baptist's head?

45 Who were the Four Horsemen of the Apocalypse?

46 What are the gospels of Matthew, Mark, and Luke called?

47 Name three of Paul's letters.

48 What is strange about the census mentioned in the story of the nativity?

49 Which book comes after the three books of John?

50 Who was chosen to take Judas Iscariot's place amongst the Apostles?

The USA

Answers to this quiz are on page 244

MEDIUM

	Player 1	Player 2
	12	20
	33	24
	07	03
	46	45
	01	28
	21	02
	23	25
	04	32
	35	39
	14	50
	31	08
	48	17
	11	40
	27	43
	15	29
	06	41
	10	30
	47	34
	26	16
	38	05
	36	49
	13	09
	19	18
	42	37
	44	22

01 Which US state is known as the bluegrass state?

02 Which is the smallest US state?

03 Which river does the Ohio flow into?

04 In which year was the Constitution of the United States drawn up?

05 Which is the legislative branch of the federal government?

06 How many colonies declared their independence from Britain in 1776?

07 Which US state has the highest population?

08 Which was the first permanent European settlement in the present USA?

09 Who was the seventh president of the USA?

10 Which two houses does the US Congress comprise?

11 Which are the three largest cities in the USA?

12 What is the capital of Florida?

13 Which war took place between 1835 and 1842?

14 In which part of the USA do Apaches live nowadays?

15 Which event precipitated the Mexican War?

16 What is the name given to the 11 southern states that seceded from the USA in 1860?

17 Which political party did Theodore Roosevelt stand for?

18 What is the maximum term for a US president?

19 What is the minimum age for someone to become US president?

20 What is the capital of Maine?

21 Who succeeded John F. Kennedy as president?

22 Which west-coast state forms its northern border with Canada?

23 What was the name of the independent candidate in the 1992 presidential election?

24 What is the name given to the domestic reform program of President Roosevelt during the Great Depression?

25 On which river is Washington D.C. situated?

26 Which festival is celebrated in New Orleans on Shrove Tuesday?

27 What is the name of the US national anthem?

28 What is the capital of Alaska?

29 Geronimo was the leader of which tribe?

30 On which river is Memphis situated?

31 Where in the USA can you find Creoles?

32 In which city is the John Hancock Tower?

33 What did the Volsted Act, passed in 1919, prohibit?

34 Beverly Hills and Santa Monica are part of which city?

35 Which is the principal river flowing through New Mexico?

36 Which island is situated to the south-east of New York and contains two boroughs of New York City?

37 Which island served as the main entry station for US immigrants from 1892 to 1943?

38 Which two native American tribes were involved in The Battle of Little Bighorn?

39 What is the capital of Arkansas?

40 Which canal links New York with the Great Lakes?

41 Which holiday is celebrated on 12 October?

42 Who was US president at the outbreak of World War II?

43 Where is the most southerly point of the USA?

44 Which is the oldest American college?

45 Which city was originally called Yerba Buena?

46 What is the name of the historical overland route from the Missouri river to the north-west ?

47 Which state does Louisiana border on to the west?

48 What is the capital of New Mexico?

49 New York City is situated on the mouth of which river?

50 Which division of the US Department of Justice is responsible for dealing with all violations of federal law?

143

Recreation

Answers to this quiz are on pages 244-245

MEDIUM

Player 1	Player 2
12	20
33	24
07	03
46	45
01	28
21	02
23	25
04	32
35	39
14	50
31	08
48	17
11	40
27	43
15	29
06	41
10	30
47	34
26	16
38	05
36	49
13	09
19	18
42	37
44	22

01 Which side moves first in a game of chess?

02 By what name is Hsiang Ch'i known in the west?

03 What is the casino game of Black Jack called when played for fun?

04 What feature do American football, rugby, and Australian Rules football have in common?

05 Which boxer boasted he could 'float like a butterfly and sting like a bee'?

06 In which game can you 'huff'?

07 In which game might you capture a piece 'en passant'?

08 Which cousin of snooker and pool uses only three balls?

09 In which game might you play a 'full house'?

10 In which sport might you occupy the position of 'silly mid on'?

11 In which sport would you hope to score a strike?

12 In which sport would you try to avoid three strikes?

13 What name is given to the pitch on which American football is played?

14 In which game is the ball thrown with the aid of a large wicker scoop worn on the hand?

15 In which sport might you use ashi-waza?

16 In American football, what is the maximum number of men who can play for each team during a single match?

17 What is the name of the 'human spider' that forms such an important part of a rugby match?

18 Rugby balls used to be made of camelskin. True or false?

19 Which very dangerous Native American game, once known as 'the little brother of war', is now played mainly by women?

20 Which is the fastest team sport in the world?

21 What is the popular name for the place where ice hockey players are sent for breaking the rules?

22 Which popular game was invented by a Canadian clergyman using two peach baskets?

23 How many players are there in a netball team?

24 In which sport is a ball knocked back and forth across a net by hand?

25 Joe DiMaggio was a legendary player of which sport?

26 Are aluminium bats allowed in Major League baseball?

27 In baseball, spiked boots are not allowed. What are used instead?

28 In cricket, what is a sequence of six or eight balls called?

29 From what wood are cricket bats traditionally made?

30 What form of tennis was once the sport of kings?

31 The French game of Jeu de Paume was the precursor of what modern sport?

32 In which century was lawn tennis first played?

33 Which top-class tennis players now use wooden rackets?

34 Which game began with Cambridge students using cigar boxes and champagne corks?

35 Is it true that the Chinese name for table tennis is 'ping pong'?

36 What do the tinted dots on squash balls denote?

37 In which sport do you 'tee off'?

38 By what other name is Association Football commonly known?

39 By what geometrical-sounding name is fishing sometimes known?

40 Which ancient games were revived in Athens in 1896?

41 The Persian game 'As Nas' was combined with the French game 'Poque'. What was the resulting game called?

42 'A gambling game in which players bet on which slot of a rotating disk a small ball will come to rest in.' Of which game is this a definition?

43 By what other name is 'petanque' known?

44 What is the Irish game that resembles lacrosse?

45 In which Scottish game would you slide large 'stones' across ice?

46 Which Chinese game swept America as a craze in 1922?

47 Name a card game that sounds like two alcoholic drinks.

48 Which word game was originally called Criss-Cross?

49 Which popular type of puzzle first appeared in the USA in the December 1913 issue of New York World?

50 Which village lying north-east of Athens gave its name to a battle and a famous race?

Food & Drink

MEDIUM 😋 MEDIUM

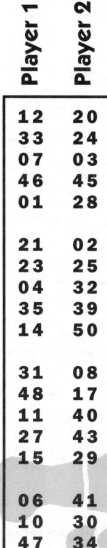

Player 1	Player 2
12	20
33	24
07	03
46	45
01	28
21	02
23	25
04	32
35	39
14	50
31	08
48	17
11	40
27	43
15	29
06	41
10	30
47	34
26	16
38	05
36	49
13	09
19	18
42	37
44	22

01 What is an aubergine (eggplant) parmigiana be topped with?

02 What type of vegetable is a capsicum?

03 What is rutabaga also known as?

04 What is sushi traditionally wrapped in?

05 What type of fish is scampi?

06 Where does marsala originate from?

07 What type of food is Monterey Jack?

08 Name the cold dessert of stewed or puréed fruit mixed with cream or custard.

09 What is sake made from?

10 Which type of pepper is used as a stuffing for green olives?

11 What do you call a dish of ice-cream with a topping of nuts, sauce, or whipped cream?

12 What is a vol-au-vent usually filled with?

13 What is mayonnaise made of?

14 What is a blancmange?

15 What type of sauce would a chicken à la king be cooked in?

16 What is an alligator pear also known as?

17 What is whisky made from?

18 Which spice is sambal seasoned with?

19 What type of alcohol does a pink lady contain?

20 What type of dairy product does beef stroganoff contain?

21 What type of food is a shiitake?

22 What type of fruit is mace made from?

23 To make a Scotch egg, what is the egg wrapped in?

24 What is a meringue made of?

25 What is aquavit flavoured with?

26 What type of food is a madeleine?

27 To make beef Wellington, what is the beef covered with?

28 What type of cake is a strudel?

29 If you sauté potatoes, how do you cook them?

30 What is the main ingredient of a guacamole?

31 What is a curaçao flavoured with?

32 What type of food is a pirog?

33 What is the name for a white sauce made with butter, flour, and milk or cream?

34 What is piccalilli?

35 What is a pina colada made of?

36 Which country does Limburger cheese come from?

37 What do you call the fragrance of a wine or liqueur?

38 What does the word 'florentine' after a dish imply?

39 Which herbs is Béarnaise sauce flavoured with?

40 What type of dish is chicken jalfrezi?

41 What is carob used as a substitute for?

42 What is crème de cassis made from?

43 Where does the dish teriyaki come from?

44 Which sauce are eggs Benedict topped with?

45 What do you call a mixture of flour and fat cooked together, usually as a base for sauces?

46 What sort of drink is manzanilla?

47 What part of the animal does sweetbread come from?

48 In what type of cooking would you use hoisin sauce?

49 What type of sauce is a satay usually dipped in?

50 Which part of the pig are chitterlings?

The Human Body

Answers to this quiz are on page 245

Player 1	Player 2
12	20
33	24
07	03
46	45
01	28
21	02
23	25
04	32
35	39
14	50
31	08
48	17
11	40
27	43
15	29
06	41
10	30
47	34
26	16
38	05
36	49
13	09
19	18
42	37
44	22

01 Which part of the eye controls the amount of light entering it?

02 In which organ would you find the following three bones: hammer, anvil and, stirrup?

03 Which blood vessels carry the blood away from the heart?

04 What are neurons?

05 What is the name of the membranes surrounding the brain?

06 What is the name of the nervous tissue linking the two halves of the brain?

07 Which muscle controls the bending of the arm?

08 What is the purpose of cartilage?

09 What is the name of the fluid in which the red and white blood cells are suspended?

10 What exactly do the two figures in measuring blood pressure refer to?

11 By what are muscles attached to the skeleton?

12 Which blood vessels allow blood to flow between the arteries and veins?

13 What is the main purpose of the lymphocytes?

14 What does the atrial septum divide?

15 Which hormone maintains the blood sugar level?

16 How much blood does the average person have?

17 Where is the pituitary gland situated?

18 In which part of the body would you find the phalanges?

19 In which tissue are the red blood cells produced?

20 Which is the longest bone in the body and where is it situated?

21 Which two sets of muscles are used for breathing in air?

22 What is the name of the membranes surrounding the lungs?

23 What is the windpipe also called?

24 Which muscle flexes the knee joint?

25 Which enzyme in the stomach is responsible for breaking down proteins?

26 Which organ has the function to store the bile produced by the liver?

27 Why is bile essential for the functioning of the digestive system?

28 Which organ controls the amount of sugar in the body?

29 The small intestine is made up of which three parts?

30 Which is the largest organ of the body?

31 What function does the appendix have?

32 What are the fluid contents of the small intestine called?

33 Of what smaller chemical units are proteins made up?

34 In which organ are the hepatocytes situated?

35 What is the name of the organelles responsible for cell metabolism, for example converting food into energy?

36 Which organ produces urine?

37 What do the letters DNA stand for?

38 What substance do the sebaceous glands produce?

39 How many teeth are in an adult full set?

40 Which parts of the body contain keratin?

41 What is the name of the tubes leading from the kidneys to the bladder?

42 Against what does the pigment melanin protect the skin?

43 What is the cranium?

44 What is the white part of the eye called?

45 What is the cochlea responsible for?

46 What is joined together by the corpus callosum?

47 What happens if melanocytes in the skin are clumped together?

48 In which part of the body would you find the calcaneus?

49 Which mechanism are the platelets responsible for?

50 What is the voice-box also called?

149

Pot Luck

Answers to this quiz are on page 245

MEDIUM MEDIUM **MEDIUM**

Player 1	Player 2
12	20
33	24
07	03
46	45
01	28
21	02
23	25
04	32
35	39
14	50
31	08
48	17
11	40
27	43
15	29
06	41
10	30
47	34
26	16
38	05
36	49
13	09
19	18
42	37
44	22

150

01 Who wrote the novel *From Russia With Love*?

02 **What is the name of Rome's airport?**

03 Which US political party has the donkey as its symbol?

04 **In Rome, which flight of 137 stairs leads from Piazza di Spagne to the Church of the Trinita dei Monti?**

05 With which sport do you associate Imran Khan?

06 **Name the woman who has been prime minister of Pakistan twice.**

07 Of which political party was Zhou Enlai a leader?

08 **How, in olden days, did the Chinese most commonly refer to their country?**

09 The name of the Australian airline QANTAS is an acronym. What does it stand for?

10 **Which is the largest lake in Africa?**

11 To which country does the word Singhalese refer?

12 **In Asian countries, the word 'singh' is commonly used. What does it mean?**

13 In which subcontinent would you hear Urdu, Hindi, and Bengali spoken as native languages?

14 **Which English university city stands on the river Cam?**

15 Cellist Jacqueline du Pré died of which illness?

16 **Who wrote *Far From the Madding Crowd*?**

17 Which organs of the body produce urine?

18 **What substance is produced by the gall bladder?**

19 What boon to gardeners was invented by Mr Budding and Mr Ferrabee?

20 Why is a mausoleum so-called?

21 What were the pre-communist rulers of Russia called?

22 What, in military terms, is a SAM?

23 Which country is the home of the Sony electronics company?

24 Which US poet broadcast Fascist propaganda during World War II?

25 What is the more formal name of London's Old Bailey?

26 Who shot John Lennon?

27 Who tried to assassinate President Ford in Sacramento?

28 Which US president withdrew US forces from Vietnam?

29 What is a locum?

30 What is the charleston?

31 Edward VIII of England abdicated to marry an American divorcee. What was her name?

32 Of which country is Vientiane the capital?

33 In which country would you find political parties called Fianna Fail and Fine Gael?

34 Which literary character made famous the phrase, 'Tomorrow is another day'?

35 What other name is used for the Erse language?

36 Who wrote Catch-22?

37 In which year did the Six Day War take place?

38 Was Munich in East or West Germany?

39 Which fictional character would have made you an offer you could not refuse?

40 Whose house was moved by Pooh and Piglet?

41 What is an obsequy?

42 Who was the last woman to be hanged in Britain?

43 In which year was the Panama Canal completed?

44 What sort of music do you associate with Nashville, Tennessee?

45 Who wrote For Whom the Bell Tolls?

46 What is the connection between Truman Capote, Audrey Hepburn, and a morning meal?

47 How often are the Olympic Games held?

48 A funeral director is called different things in British and American English. Can you give both versions?

49 In English, we use the French phrase cul de sac to mean a street closed at one end. Why is the phrase not used in France?

50 What was tennis star Evonne Cawley's maiden name?

History

Answers to this quiz are on page 246

TOUGH · TOUGH · TOUGH

Player 1	Player 2
12	20
33	24
07	03
46	45
01	28
21	02
23	25
04	32
35	39
14	50
31	08
48	17
11	40
27	43
15	29
06	41
10	30
47	34
26	16
38	05
36	49
13	09
19	18
42	37
44	22

152

01 In which year were England and Scotland united?

02 Who was president of the USA between 1877 and 1881?

03 Which prison was stormed at the start of the French Revolution?

04 The people of Rome drove out a king in 510 BC and formed a republic. Name the king.

05 To what does the adjective Carolingian refer?

06 Who beat the Roman army at the Battle of Cannae in 216 BC?

07 What was remarkable about the way Rome was ruled in AD 68–9?

08 When the Chinese invented gunpowder they used it only for fireworks. Is this true?

09 Where were the Normans from originally?

10 What famous Australian landmark was opened in 1932?

11 In which year was the survey for establishing the Mason-Dixon line concluded?

12 Which city, the original home of Abraham, was the hub of Sumerian civilization?

13 Which family ruled Milan from 1277 to 1447?

14 Who were the Valois family?

15 Which notable building was started by the Emperor Vespasian and finished by his son Domitian?

16 To which Native American tribe did Geronimo belong?

17 Which civilization did Pizzaro destroy when he invaded Peru?

18 By what name did the 'louisette' become infamous?

19 The first talking movie was *The Jazz Singer*, but what was the first British talkie?

20 How was the French legal system reformed in 1804?

21 What horror stalked the streets of the East End of London in 1888?

22 Name the French Jewish soldier falsely accused of selling secrets to the Germans in 1894.

23 Which revolutionary was killed with an ice-pick in Mexico in 1940?

24 What happened at Kill Devil Hill in 1903?

25 Which Spanish knight seized Valencia from the Moors in 1094?

26 What name connects a blouse, a Californian fish, a biscuit, and an Italian general?

27 Which British general and his French opponent were both killed at the Battle of the Plains of Abraham (Quebec) 1759?

28 To whom does the following mnemonic refer: Divorced, Beheaded, Died, Divorced, Beheaded, Survived?

29 Which royal dynasty was named after its gentian flower emblem?

30 What was Alexander the Great's horse called and what did the name mean?

31 Name Mary Queen of Scots' preferred Italian musician, who was murdered in Holyrood Palace.

32 Which event first took place in New Orleans in 1827?

33 Which French premier was known as 'The Tiger'?

34 What was remarkable about the Rochdale Society of Equitable Pioneers founded in 1844?

35 The island of Tortuga played host to people of a notorious profession. What were they?

36 Which Christian priest and king, according to medieval reports, was supposed to rule an empire in Africa or Asia?

37 Which British general was killed by the Mahdi's soldiers at the siege of Khartoum (1885)?

38 A stream near Washington DC gave its name to two American Civil War battles. Name it.

39 Of which town was Samuel Langhorne Clemens a boyhood resident?

40 Who said: 'The only thing we have to fear is fear itself'?

41 Who said: 'A man who is good enough to shed his blood for his country is good enough to be given a square deal afterwards'?

42 Name the stone upon which all British monarchs are crowned.

43 Who said: 'I beseech you, in the bowels of Christ, think it possible you may be mistaken'?

44 What did US Generals George Crook, Henry Ware Lawton, and Nelson Miles have in common?

45 Who served with distinction in the Mexican War, was superintendent at West Point, and led (1859) the US marines who captured John Brown at Harpers Ferry?

46 Name the German theologian and leader of the Reformation who died in 1546.

47 The phrase 'hocus pocus' is a corruption of what Latin phrase from the Eucharist?

48 Which South American hero was made president of Greater Colombia (now Colombia, Venezuela, and Ecuador), and helped liberate (1823–34) Peru and Bolivia?

49 What was Tokyo formerly called?

50 Which African lake was first sighted by John Speke and Sir Richard Burton in 1858?

153

Money

Answers to this quiz are on page 246

TOUGH **TOUGH**

Player 1	Player 2
12	20
33	24
07	03
46	45
01	28
21	02
23	25
04	32
35	39
14	50
31	08
48	17
11	40
27	43
15	29
06	41
10	30
47	34
26	16
38	05
36	49
13	09
19	18
42	37
44	22

01 What is the site of the US Gold Bullion Depository?

02 What do you call the process of imprinting a blank coin with a design?

03 Where were the earliest known coins made?

04 What is the basic unit of currency in Poland?

05 In 1979, a dollar coin was withdrawn due to lack of popularity. Who did the coin portray?

06 In US currency, how many cents is a dime worth?

07 Before Wilhem I became Emperor of Germany in 1871, which was the main unit of currency?

08 In which year did the full decimalization of the British currency take place?

09 Which is the basic unit of currency in Morocco?

10 Which three places in the UK use different coins from the rest of the country?

11 What is the name of the famous gambling center situated on the Mediterranean coast?

12 Where was an obol used and what was it made from?

13 In German currency, how much is one mark worth?

14 What is the name given to the study or collection of money?

15 What material was a sovereign made from?

16 In which country did the ecu coin originate?

17 Which was the first coin to be issued in the USA?

18 Prior to decimalization, how many old pennies was the English shilling worth?

19 What types of leaf were used as money in Virginia and Maryland in the 17th and 18th centuries?

20 Which country issued the first printed paper money in Europe?

21 Which is the basic unit of currency in Hungary?

22 In French currency, into which smaller currency unit is the franc divided?

23 What type of printing plate is used for printing banknotes?

24 Which nation first started to handle money in the form of printed paper documents?

25 After the Gold Rush, in which form was gold first used as a method of payment?

26 What is the basic unit of currency in India?

27 What was the name of the paper money issued during the French Revolution?

28 Which English gold coin issued between 1663 and 1813 was worth one pound and one shilling?

29 In US currency, what was the face value of an eagle?

30 What is the basic unit of currency in South Africa?

31 Which people issued pieces of eight?

32 What has been the main feature on French coins since the revolution?

33 Which is the main currency unit in Sweden?

34 Name the coin used in Great Britain that was worth a fourth of an old penny?

35 In which country is the yen the basic unit of currency?

36 Which Scandinavian country has a different coinage system from the others?

37 Which people first developed a round coin with a design on both sides?

38 In which countries was the doubloon formerly used?

39 Which were the biggest coins ever made?

40 Which European city issued ducats and sequins in the 13th century?

41 During the Roman Empire, what was the main design on most coins?

42 What was the first Roman money made from?

43 Where did the practice of banking first begin?

44 Nowadays, which language appears on Belgian coins?

45 In which three countries is the ore in use?

46 What is the basic unit of currency in Turkey?

47 During the 1970s there was a shortage of small-denomination coins in Italy. What types of coin did shopkeepers give out instead?

48 Which smaller unit is the Dutch gulden divided into?

49 What do you call the type of trade where one type of goods is swapped for another type without money transactions?

50 What is the name for the South African bullion coins made of solid gold?

Transport

Answers to this quiz are on pages 246-247

TOUGH 😐 **TOUGH** 🙁 **TOUGH**

Player 1	Player 2
12	20
33	24
07	03
46	45
01	28
21	02
23	25
04	32
35	39
14	50
31	08
48	17
11	40
27	43
15	29
06	41
10	30
47	34
26	16
38	05
36	49
13	09
19	18
42	37
44	22

01 What record did the American Voyager aircraft achieve in 1986 in its nine-day flight around the world?

02 **What is the name of the French high-speed train going into service in 1981?**

03 Where was the world's first underground railway line built?

04 **In which year did Concorde go into service?**

05 Which popular car was stopped being made in Germany in 1977?

06 **Which new era in transport was started by the French Montgolfier brothers in 1783?**

07 What was the name of Charles Lindbergh's plane in which he made the first solo non-stop transatlantic flight?

08 **Which incident put an end to the use of passenger airships in 1937?**

09 What were the Big Boys?

10 **Who designed the first successful American helicopter?**

11 What was the name of the world's first jet airliner, and when did it enter service?

12 **What new type of water transport did Christopher Cockerell design?**

13 Which new device did Gottfried Daimler produce in 1885 that started the development of the automobile industry?

14 **Which was the first-mass produced car in the USA?**

15 What is the major advantage of the stealth bomber?

16 **What is the name of a bicycle which two people can ride together, sitting one behind the other?**

17 On an aircraft, what is the purpose of a spoiler?

18 **Which was the first steam-powered sailing ship to cross the Atlantic?**

19 Both the hovercraft and the hydrofoil lift themselves above the surface of the water. What is the main difference between them?

20 Which part of a ship is the hull?

21 What type of aircraft did Otto Lilienthal design?

22 What are most large ships powered by?

23 Which is the main difference between a rocket and a jet engine?

24 What type of vessel is a galleon?

25 What is the difference between the ignition of a petrol engine and that of a diesel engine?

26 Who put New York's first public transit facility into service, and what was it?

27 Which famous navigator and explorer sailed on the Endeavour?

28 Who built the first pedal-ridden bicycle?

29 What was the name of the ship Christopher Columbus sailed on to America?

30 What do you call a glider with a small engine driving a propeller?

31 What are the majority of heavy-goods vehicles powered by?

32 Which was the first ship to complete a voyage around the world?

33 What type of vessel is a cog?

34 What is the name of the horse-drawn carriage which appeared for hire in London in the early 17th century?

35 Why do aeroplanes land into the wind?

36 Which was the main feature of a 'penny farthing' bicycle?

37 Which is the longest rail tunnel in the world?

38 Who built the first motorcycle?

39 What was the main disadvantage of steam-powered vehicles?

40 Which country operated the first public railway?

41 Which major new feature did the Draisienne bicycle, invented by Baron von Drais de Sauerbrun, have?

42 In motorcycles, how is the gearbox linked to the wheels?

43 Which major advance did Richard Trevithick introduce to rail travel?

44 Between which two cities did the Orient Express run?

45 Who was the first aviator to cross the English Channel by plane?

46 What type of vehicle did Francis and Freelan Stanley develop?

47 In a car, what is the function of the carburettor?

48 Which was the first railroad tunnel going through the Alps?

49 Which was the predecessor of the American Greyhound bus?

50 Which was the first underwater ship used in war and in which conflict did it take part?

The Arts

Answers to this quiz are on page 247

TOUGH 😞 TOUGH

	Player 1	Player 2
	12	20
	33	24
	07	03
	46	45
	01	28
	21	02
	23	25
	04	32
	35	39
	14	50
	31	08
	48	17
	11	40
	27	43
	15	29
	06	41
	10	30
	47	34
	26	16
	38	05
	36	49
	13	09
	19	18
	42	37
	44	22

01 Who wrote, directed, and starred in *The Navigator and The General*?

02 **Who starred in *The Kid, The Goldrush,* and *The Great Dictator*?**

03 Who directed the 1957 film *A Farewell to Arms*?

04 **Which opera did Borodin leave unfinished at his death?**

05 What sort of creature was Gizmo?

06 **In Britain it was known as music hall, but what was the American name?**

07 Who played the beleaguered sheriff in *High Noon*?

08 **In which 1975 film did a group of Australian schoolgirls mysteriously vanish?**

09 Who wrote *The Cask of Amontillado*?

10 **Who wrote *Beyond the Wall of Sleep*?**

11 Who starred in *The Blue Angel*?

12 **Who starred as Sir Thomas More in both the stage and film versions of *A Man For All Seasons*?**

13 For what did Eugene O'Neill get his 1957 Pulitzer Prize?

14 **Who wrote *A Streetcar Named Desire*?**

15 Which famous American playwright was married to Marilyn Monroe?

16 **Who wrote *On the Road*?**

17 Who was the author of *Leaves of Grass*?

18 **For what work is Geoffrey Chaucer chiefly remembered?**

19 Which jazz musician was known to his fans as 'Satchmo'?

20 Which girl singer gained fame with 'Ruby Tuesday'?

21 Who won three Oscars for his animated films featuring Wallace and Gromit?

22 Who won an Oscar for her adaptation of Jane Austen's *Sense and Sensibility*?

23 Who played Ophelia to Mel Gibson's Hamlet?

24 Which film star was suffocated by his best friend in *One Flew Over the Cuckoo's Nest*?

25 Two people combined to make one formidable villain in *Mad Max – Beyond Thunder Dome*. What name did they go by?

26 Which actor was *Down and Out* in Beverly Hills?

27 Which country is invaded in Spielberg's *Empire of the Sun*?

28 Which glittering role did Gert Frobe land in a Bond movie?

29 From which film did the song 'Everybody's Talkin' At Me' come?

30 Which actors traded places in a film version of a Mark Twain story?

31 In which TV series did we meet the Log Lady?

32 In which TV series do we meet Eugene Tooms?

33 In which round did Mike Tyson defeat Frank Bruno in the 1996 World Heavyweight Championship?

34 James Mason played Brutus, John Gielgud played Cassius, but who played Mark Antony in this film of *Julius Caesar*?

35 In which film did Tom Cruise and Demi Moore play naval lawyers?

36 Who played Rooster Cogburn in *True Grit*?

37 What was the subtitle of *Superman IV*?

38 Which actor was swindled by Paul Newman and Robert Redford in *The Sting*?

39 Under what other name does the crime novelist Ruth Rendell write?

40 Who mounted the stage to criticize Michael Jackson's performance of 'Earth Song' at the 1996 Brit Awards?

41 Which American author of *The Bell Jar* committed suicide in England?

42 Which American pop artist was noted for his large-scale depictions of comic book panels?

43 What is the link between the Guggenheim Museum and Simon & Garfunkel?

44 Who wrote the song 'American Pie'?

45 In which Neil Simon play did a couple of men, separated from their wives, share an apartment to their mutual discomfort?

46 Which tale, set in Paris and featuring a monstrous musician, became a hit musical?

47 In which Australian film were two children, lost in the outback, rescued by a young aborigine?

48 What profession does Bill Cosby's character follow in The Cosby Show?

49 In which TV family would you find Morticia?

50 Which collie dog starred in numerous films and TV programmes?

Foreign Phrases

Answers to this quiz are on page 247

TOUGH TOUGH TOUGH

Player 1	Player 2
12	20
33	24
07	03
46	45
01	28
21	02
23	25
04	32
35	39
14	50
31	08
48	17
11	40
27	43
15	29
06	41
10	30
47	34
26	16
38	05
36	49
13	09
19	18
42	37
44	22

01 Which country do you associate with the motto 'E pluribus unum'?

02 What item was sometimes kept as a 'memento mori'?

03 Which order of chivalry was founded with the words 'Honi soit qui mal y pense'?

04 Who said 'Veni, vidi, vici' and of what occasion?

05 What is meant by 'Mens sana in corpore sano'?

06 What would you be doing if you acted ultra vires?

07 What does the phrase 'Borgen macht sorgen' mean?

08 What is schadenfreude?

09 Which military body has the motto 'Per Ardua ad Astra'?

10 What does the expression 'O tempora! O mores!' mean?

11 What is the Latin expression which means 'So passes away earthly glory'?

12 Where would you hear the expression 'Faites vos jeux!'?

13 What is meant by the saying 'Plus ça change, plus c'est la meme chose'?

14 What is the meaning of the expression 'Delenda est Carthago'?

15 What is the meaning of the philosophical proposition 'Cogito, ergo sum'?

16 What does the instruction 'Divide et impera' mean?

17 How would you translate 'Dulce et decorum est pro patria mori'?

18 The Chinese greeting 'Hen jiu, bu jian' is sometimes used in the English language. What is the translation?

19 What did Archimedes mean when he shouted 'Eureka!'?

20 What does 'Gott mit uns' mean?

21 Whose motto is 'Ich dien' and what does it mean?

22 What is meant by the expression 'Fiat lux'?

23 What does the instruction 'Carpe diem' mean?

24 What did Heraclitus mean by the saying 'Panta rhe'i?

25 What does 'Que sera, sera mean'?

26 How would you translate the greeting 'Salaam aleikum'?

27 What do you understand by the saying 'Keine antwort is auch eine antwort'?

28 What do you understand by 'La donna e mobile'?

29 What do you understand by the expression 'Enfants s'amusent'?

30 What is meant by the Irish expression 'Erin go bragh'?

31 'Fortuna favet fatuis' and 'Fortuna favet fortibus' give very different impressions of how Fortune distributes her favors. What are they?

32 Why would you not fear a 'fulmen brutum'?

33 What is a 'coup de foudre'?

34 What is a 'coup de théâtre'?

35 What is a 'coup de poing'?

36 What is meant by 'In vino veritas'?

37 What hopeful sentiments are contained in the phrase 'Dum spiro, spero'?

38 What did Galileo mean when he is alleged to have said 'Eppur si muove'?

39 What is the meaning of the phrase 'J'y suis, j'y reste'?

40 What is meant by a vote of non placet?

41 What does a Muslim mean by the expression 'Inshallah'?

42 What would you expect to find under a sign containing the words 'Hic iacet...'?

43 Would the expression 'Festina lente' encourage you to hurry?

44 What do you understand by the expression 'Tempus fugit'?

45 Would you be encouraged by a colleague who said 'Volo, non valeo'?

46 How would you render the German abbreviation u.s.w. in English?

47 Is the expression 'Vedi Napoli, e poi muori' an encouragement to visit Naples?

48 What is meant by 'O sancta simplicitas'?

49 What is 'a deus ex machina'?

50 What was meant by the expression 'C'est magnifique mais ce n'est pas la guerre'?

Current Affairs

Answers to this quiz are on page 248

TOUGH 😦 TOUGH

Player 1	Player 2
12	20
33	24
07	03
46	45
01	28
21	02
23	25
04	32
35	39
14	50
31	08
48	17
11	40
27	43
15	29
06	41
10	30
47	34
26	16
38	05
36	49
13	09
19	18
42	37
44	22

164

01 By which political group was Rajiv Ghandi assassinated?

02 Who was the world's first ever woman prime minister?

03 Which Greek head of state abolished his country's monarchy in 1973?

04 Who was the Argentinian president during the Falklands War?

05 Why did the Arab League move their headquarters from Cairo to Tunis in 1989?

06 Who was the first freely elected Marxist leader of the Americas?

07 What was the name of the guerrilla army in Namibia before the country became independent in 1990?

08 Which two members of the American National Security Council were predominantly involved in the Iran-Contra Affair?

09 Which country did the Gaza Strip belong to before it was occupied by Israel?

10 The Schuman Plan lead to the formation of which organization?

11 When was the Iran-Iraq War?

12 What was the name of the Swedish prime minister assassinated in 1986?

13 Which Polish head of state banned Solidarity in 1982?

14 Where was Rudolf Hess held until his death in 1987?

15 Who signed the INF Treaty?

16 What was the aim of the hunger strikers in the Maze Prison in Belfast?

17 Who succeeded Harold Wilson as British prime minister in 1976?

18 Who was the last viceroy of India before it became an independent nation?

19 In which country did Hafez al-Assad seize power in 1970?

20 Who is the leader of the first Spanish Socialist government since the Civil War?

21 Why did Willy Brandt resign as German chancellor in 1974?

22 Who was US vice president under George Bush?

23 Name the Panamanian general who was captured in 1989 and convicted of drug-trafficking?

24 Who turned Albania into a republic in 1946?

25 Which three countries joined the European Economic Community in 1973?

26 Name the spacecraft that Neil Armstrong used for his flight to the moon in 1969?

27 When did the Cultural Revolution in China take place?

28 Who was UN general secretary during the Gulf War?

29 Who was Tunisia's first president after independence?

30 What was François Duvalier, dicator of Haiti, commonly known as?

31 Which German Nazi official was tried and subsequently hanged by Israel in 1960?

32 When was Amnesty International founded?

33 Who became Chinese premier after the formation of the People's Republic in 1949?

34 Who preceded Nasser as Egyptian head of state?

35 Name of the world's first man-made Earth satellite?

36 Which country became a US state in 1958?

37 Who did François Mitterrand appoint as French premier in 1986?

38 With which state was Armenia at war after the disintegration of the USSR?

39 Who became the first prime minister of Bangladesh?

40 Who succeeded Juan Perón as leader of Argentina?

41 What was Winnie Mandela convicted of in 1991?

42 In which year did the IRA bomb Harrod's in London?

43 Which three former Soviet states formed the Commonwealth of Independent States?

44 Which position did Jimmy Carter hold before becoming US president?

45 Who became prime minister of Fiji in 1992, having previously led two military coups?

46 Name the first black prime minister elected in Southern Rhodesia in 1979?

47 Which party did the Irish prime minister Charles Haughey lead?

48 When did the first direct election to the European Parliament take place?

49 Who was Norway's first woman prime minister?

50 The followers of which religious cult committed mass suicide in the Guyana jungle in 1978?

165

Odd One Out

Answers to this quiz are on page 248

TOUGH ☹ TOUGH

Player 1	Player 2
12	20
33	24
07	03
46	45
01	28
21	02
23	25
04	32
35	39
14	50
31	08
48	17
11	40
27	43
15	29
06	41
10	30
47	34
26	16
38	05
36	49
13	09
19	18
42	37
44	22

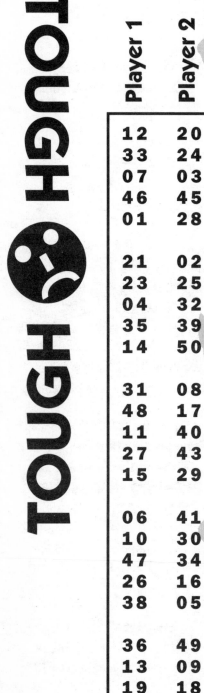

01 Which snake is the odd one out: (a) cobra, (b) viper, (c) python, (d) rattlesnake?

02 Which composer is the odd one out: (a) Schubert, (b) Vivaldi, (c) Handel, (d) Bach?

03 Which drink is the odd one out: (a) amaretto, (b) sherry, (c) marsala, (d) port?

04 Which does not form part of the brain: (a) cerebrum, (b) cortex, (c) thalamus, (d) ileum?

05 Which artist is the odd one out: (a) Vincent van Gogh, (b) Paul Cézanne, (c) Claude Monet, (d) Paul Rubens?

06 Which tree does not belong to the same family as the others: (a) copper beech, (b) weeping willow, (c) oak, (d) chestnut?

07 Which musical instrument is the odd one out: (a) saxophone, (b) trumpet, (c) tuba, (d) trombone?

08 In which country would you not pay in dollars: (a) Jamaica, (b) South Africa, (c) Singapore, (d) Australia?

09 Which US state is the odd one out: (a) Virginia, (b) Florida, (c) Pennsylvania, (d) Oklahoma?

10 Which drink is the odd one out: (a) calvados, (b) beaujolais, (c) chianti, (d) claret?

11 Which of the following is not a constellation: (a) Ceres, (b) Great Bear, (c) Orion, (d) Delphinus?

12 Which musician is the odd one out: (a) Anne-Sophie Mutter, (b) Yehudi Menuhin, (c) Claudio Arrau, (d) Pinchas Zukerman?

13 Which of the following dishes is the odd one out: (a) vindaloo, (b) rogan gosht, (c) pasanda, (d) gazpacho?

14 Which animal is the odd one out: (a) lion, (b) giraffe, (c) rhinoceros, (d) elephant?

15 Which country is the odd one out: (a) Ghana, (b) Ivory Coast, (c) Malawi, (d) Honduras?

16 Which of the following political figures is the odd one out: (a) Kerensky, (b) Trotzky, (c) Khrushchev, (d) Lenin?

17 Which US state was not part of the Confederacy in the Civil War: (a) Massachusetts, (b) Louisiana, (c) Florida, (d) Tennessee?

18 Which is the odd one out: (a) Obstetrician, (b) Pediatrician, (c) Podiatrist, (d) Pedagogue?

19 Which flower belongs to a different family from the others: (a) auricula, (b) cyclamen, (c) snapdragon, (d) cowslip?

20 **Which is the odd one out: (a) The Bartered Bride, (b) Kiss Me Kate, (c) Sunset Boulevard, (d) Miss Saigon?**

21 Which fish is the odd one out: (a) mackerel, (b) carp, (c) trout, (d) pike?

22 **Which is the odd one out: (a) crossword, (b) rebus, (c) jigsaw, (d) patience?**

23 Which sports personality is the odd one out: (a) Carl Lewis, (b) Mark Spitz, (c) Johnny Weissmuller, (d) Matt Biondi?

24 **Which city is the odd one out: (a) La Paz, (b) Islamabad, (c) Casablanca, (d) Manila?**

25 Who was not awarded the Nobel Peace Prize: (a) Nelson Mandela, (b) Mikhail Gorbachev, (c) Martin Luther King, (d) John F. Kennedy?

26 **Which fungus is not edible: (a) fly agaric, (b) chanterelle, (c) champignon, (d) morel?**

27 Which singer is the odd one out: (a) Eddie Cochran, (b) Chuck Berry, (c) Frank Sinatra, (d) Little Richard?

28 **Which country is the odd one out: (a) Jamaica, (b) Barbados, (c) Puerto Rico, (d) Madeira?**

29 Which film is the odd one out: (a) Roman Holiday, (b) Charade, (c) To Kill a Mockingbird, (d) Breakfast at Tiffany's?

30 **Which musical form is the odd one out: (a) oratorio, (b) chorale, (c) cantata, (d) opera?**

31 Who is the odd one out: (a) Jacques Cousteau, (b) Graham Greene, (c) James A. Michener, (d) Ernest Hemingway?

32 **Which is the odd one out: (a) ruby, (b) topaz, (c) amber, (d) sapphire?**

33 Which animal is the odd one out: (a) chameleon, (b) gecko, (c) alligator, (d) salamander?

34 **Which island is the odd one out: (a) Sardinia, (b) Corsica, (c) Sicily, (d) Elba?**

35 In which country would you not pay in francs: (a) Tunisia, (b) Cameroon, (c) Belgium, (d) Switzerland?

36 **Which is the odd one out: (a) pizza margherita, (b) ratatouille, (c) coq au vin, (d) eggs florentine?**

37 Which part of the body is the odd one out: (a) triceps, (b) hamstring, (c) clavicle, (d) flexor?

38 **Who is the odd one out: (a) Leonard Bernstein, (b) Placido Domingo, (c) Herbert von Karajan, (d) Sir Georg Solti?**

39 Which region is the odd one out: (a) Umbria, (b) Normandy, (c) Tuscany, (d) Lombardy?

40 **Which of the following is not a Greek god: (a) Apollo, (b) Tartarus, (c) Ares, (d) Dionysus?**

41 Which civilization is the odd one out: (a) Inca, (b) Aztec, (c) Egyptian, (d) Maya?

42 **Which city is the odd one out: (a) Miami, (b) Boston, (c) Salt Lake City, (d) Nashville?**

43 Who is the odd one out: (a) Sir Isaac Newton, (b) Emile Berliner, (c) Thomas Alva Edison, (d) Alexander Graham Bell?

44 **Which drink is the odd one out: (a) cognac, (b) slivovitz, (c) cassis, (d) kirsch?**

45 Who is the odd one out: (a) Richard Burton, (b) Michael Wilding, (c) Stewart Granger, (d) Eddie Fisher?

46 **Which bird is the odd one out: (a) chaffinch, (b) robin, (c) plover, (d) thrush?**

47 Who of the following US presidents is the odd one out: (a) Jimmy Carter, (b) Dwight Eisenhower, (c) Ronald Reagan, (d) Richard Nixon?

48 **Which of the following countries does not belong to the Commonwealth: (a) Canada, (b) Bahamas, (c) Thailand, (d) Kenya?**

49 Which of the following battles did not take place during World War II: (a) Battle of Verdun, (b) Battle of Stalingrad, (c) Battle of El Alamein, (d) Battle of Tobruk?

50 **Which is the odd one out: (a) iodene, (b) magnesium, (c) calcium, (d) retinol?**

167

Rivers

Answers to this quiz are on page 248

TOUGH TOUGH TOUGH

Player 1	Player 2
12	20
33	24
07	03
46	45
01	28
21	02
23	25
04	32
35	39
14	50
31	08
48	17
11	40
27	43
15	29
06	41
10	30
47	34
26	16
38	05
36	49
13	09
19	18
42	37
44	22

01 By what other name is the Delaware River known?

02 Of what major river is the Jefferson River a headwater?

03 Which disconcertingly named waterway joins the Wabash River?

04 On which river is London situated?

05 St. Louis, Missouri, is situated near the confluence of two great rivers. Which are they?

06 Which is the longest river in the world?

07 Which is the longest river in China?

08 The delta of which river was the scene of bitter battles during the Vietnam War?

09 Jericho was originally a stronghold commanding the valley of which river?

10 The Mississippi is navigable by ocean-going vessels as far as which town?

11 Which is the chief river of central and south-east Europe?

12 Through which countries does the Elbe flow?

13 Near which town does the Seine reach the English Channel?

14 The Danube flows into which sea?

15 On which river is Düsseldorf situated?

16 Which Bavarian city is situated on the Isar River?

17 Which American river connects Tanana with Holy Cross and passes by the Kaiyuh Mountains?

18 Buenos Aires and Montevideo are to be found on which river?

19 Which river flows through the city of Moscow?

20 Which famous Russian river flows into the Caspian Sea?

21 What is the sacred river of India?

22 Which river flows through America's Grand Canyon?

23 On which river does New York stand?

24 Beside which river would you find the Bois de Boulogne?

25 The Tiergarten in Berlin is next to which river?

26 Which river in Thailand starred in a famous film?

27 Which city does the Chao Phraya flow through?

28 Which river connects the Sea of Galilee and the Dead Sea?

29 Which river flows through Kinshasa on its way to the Atlantic?

30 The river that separates Texas from Chihuaha has two names (depending on which bank you are standing on). What are they?

31 Which river connects Lake Ontario with the sea?

32 Which is the most important river in Brazil?

33 Which river flows through Colombia and Venezuela?

34 Liverpool is famous for its river. What is its name?

35 Name the two great rivers that flow through Portugal.

36 By what name do the citizens of Vienna know the Danube?

37 Which Indian city is situated on the Hugli River?

38 Which river of Pakistan flows through Hyderabad and into the Arabian Sea?

39 Near which river would you find Sheffield, Florence, and Athens?

40 Cincinnatti stands on the banks of which river?

41 Name the river that connects the Great Slave Lake with the Beaufort Sea?

42 On which river does Mobile, Alabama, stand?

43 On which river would you find Athens, Nanticoke, Berwick, and Columbia?

44 Which river, with the name of a fruit, forms the border between South Africa and Namibia?

45 Which river valley forms a north-south split in California?

46 Which river flows through North and South Dakota?

47 The upper course of which river is called the Isis?

48 What is the name of the main river that flows through New South Wales?

49 Which river forms the border between Thailand and Laos?

50 Cambridge, England, lies on the River Cam. On which river does Cambridge, Massachusetts, lie?

Current Affairs

Answers to this quiz are on pages 248-249

TOUGH

TOUGH

Player 1	Player 2
12	20
33	24
07	03
46	45
01	28
21	02
23	25
04	32
35	39
14	50
31	08
48	17
11	40
27	43
15	29
06	41
10	30
47	34
26	16
38	05
36	49
13	09
19	18
42	37
44	22

01 What was the Palestinian uprising which started in 1988 called?

02 Nelson Mandela is the leader of which party?

03 Who succeeded Jimmy Carter as US president?

04 What was the name of the Egyptian president who was assassinated by Islamic fundamentalists in 1981?

05 Which German chancellor was awarded the Nobel Peace Price for his efforts to reduce tensions between the East and West?

06 From which country did Biafra try to secede?

07 Who came to power in Chile following a military coup in 1973?

08 Which African country became independent from France in 1962, after more than seven years of war?

09 Which incident resulted in the Suez crisis?

10 Who was president of Zambia from 1964 to 1991?

11 What happened on June 17 1953 in East Berlin?

12 What were the Communist-backed South Vietnamese guerillas called?

13 Who was India's first prime minister after independence?

14 What was the name of the peace treaty signed in 1979 by Menachem Begin, Anwar Sadat, and Jimmy Carter?

15 Where was Martin Luther King assassinated?

16 Of which country was Idi Amin dictator?

17 What was the name of the US space shuttle which exploded soon after take-off in 1986?

18 Which incident provoked the USA to bomb Libya in 1986?

19 Where was the Treaty on European Union signed?

20 When was the Berlin Wall dismantled?

21 For which city was the Pan Am Boeing bound that exploded over Lockerbie in 1989?

22 Which were the founder states of the European Economic Community?

23 Which Communist leader was overthrown in 1989 and executed, together with his wife?

24 Who lost the 1960 US presidential election to John F. Kennedy?

25 Where was the toxic gas leak at an insecticide plant that killed over 6,000 people in 1984?

26 Who was the longest-serving British prime minister of the 20th century?

27 What does OPEC stand for?

28 Who was the Soviet secretary of state during the Cuban missile crisis?

29 During which war did Israel capture the Golan Heights?

30 Which were the first two states of the former Yugoslavia to declare independence?

31 When was NATO established?

32 Which Soviet head of state was awarded the Nobel Peace Prize in 1990?

33 To which movement did the former Cambodian leader Pol Pot belong?

34 In which year did Margaret Thatcher become Britain's first woman prime minister?

35 What was the location of the unsuccessful CIA-sponsored invasion of Cuba?

36 Which surgeon completed the first human heart transplant?

37 Which Mediterranean island was invaded by Turkish troops in 1974?

38 What was the aim of the SALT treaties?

39 Who declared Iran an Islamic Republic in 1979?

40 What was Perestroika?

41 Which international organization was founded in 1945 to promote peace, security, and economic development?

42 During the Korean War which outside forces joined the North Korean army?

43 Who headed the Polish trade union Solidarity?

44 Who became Zimbabwe's first prime minister after it gained independence?

45 Which African emperor was deposed in 1974?

46 Who was the longest-serving French president in history?

47 In which year was the oil crisis that resulted from an embargo by Arab Nations?

48 What was the Communist equivalent to NATO during the Cold War?

49 What was the period of reform and liberalization in Czechoslovakia in 1968 called?

50 Who became first president of Cyprus after it gained independence in 1960?

171

"Quotations

Answers to this quiz are on page 249

TOUGH TOUGH TOUGH

Player 1	Player 2
12	20
33	24
07	03
46	45
01	28
21	02
23	25
04	32
35	39
14	50
31	08
48	17
11	40
27	43
15	29
06	41
10	30
47	34
26	16
38	05
36	49
13	09
19	18
42	37
44	22

172

01 Who said: 'That woman speaks eighteen languages and can't say "No" in any of them'?

02 Who described military glory as 'the attractive rainbow that rises in showers of blood'?

03 Which historian said: 'This filthy twentieth century. I hate its guts'?

04 'It is not from the benevolence of the butcher, the brewer, or the baker, that we expect our dinner, but from their regard to their own interest.' Which 18th-century economist wrote that?

05 Which American industrialist said: 'We don't want tradition. We want to live in the present'?

06 Which dictator remarked: 'To choose one's victims, to prepare one's plan minutely, to slake an implacable vengeance, and then to go to bed... there is nothing sweeter in the world'?

07 Who said: 'In peace the sons bury their fathers, but in war the fathers bury their sons'?

08 Which American actor said: 'A lot of people have asked me how short I am. Since my last divorce, I think I'm about $100,000 short'?

09 Which Scottish religious leader referred to 'the monstrous regiment of women'?

10 Who wrote: 'If your morals make you dreary, depend upon it they are wrong'?

11 Which fictional character said: 'My spelling is Wobbly. It's good spelling but it Wobbles, and the letters get in the wrong places'?

12 Which American author wrote: 'The hangover became a part of the day as well allowed-for as the Spanish siesta'?

13 Who said of Scott Fitzgerald: 'Scott took literature so solemnly. He never understood that it was just writing as well as you can and finishing what you start'?

14 Who said: 'We must use time as a tool, not as a couch'?

15 Which author, English of course, said: 'I do not know the American gentleman, God forgive me for putting two such words together'?

16 Who said: 'God never did make a more calm, quiet, innocent recreation than angling'?

17 Which American actress said: 'I was born at the age of twelve on a Metro-Goldwyn-Mayer lot'?

18 At whom did Dorothy Parker direct this barb: 'She runs the gamut of emotions from A to B'?

19 Which fat man said: 'Guns will make us powerful; butter will only make us fat'?

20 Which French missionary said: 'The African is my brother – but he is my younger brother by several centuries'?

21 Which Albanian woman said: 'I try to give to the poor people for love what the rich could get for money'?

22 Which novelist wrote of girls: 'They say "No" when they mean "Yes", and drive a man out of his wits for the fun of it'?

23 Which 'ism' is: 'Americanism with its sleeves rolled'?

24 Who said: 'Whoever lights the torch of war in Europe can wish for nothing but chaos'?

25 Which British actor said: 'I do not live in the world of sobriety'?

26 'Do you realize the responsibility I carry? I'm the only person between ... and the White House.' Who said this, and of whom did he speak?

27 Which US military leader said of Congress: 'They do not seem to be able to do anything except to eat peanuts and chew tobacco, while my army is starving'?

28 Who said: 'The remarkable thing about Shakespeare is that he is really very good – in spite of all the people who say he is very good'?

29 Which British actor, writer, and director said: 'Laughter would be bereaved if snobbery died'?

30 According to Humphrey Bogart, what is necessary to become a star?

31 Who called England: 'a nation of shopkeepers'?

32 'They are decidedly the most servile imitators of the English it is possible to conceive.' Who was Edgar Allan Poe describing?

33 When, according to the saying, will 'New York be a great place'?

34 Which Roman said: 'I come to bury Caesar, not to praise him. The evil that men do lives after them; the good is oft interr'd with their bones'?

35 Who wrote: 'The past is a foreign country; they do things differently there'?

36 Who said: 'I'm trying to die correctly, but it's very difficult, you know'?

37 Which Canadian novelist wrote: 'Lord Ronald said nothing; he flung himself from the room, flung himself upon his horse and rode madly off in all directions'?

38 Who wrote: 'I went out to Charing Cross to see Major-General Harrison hanged, drawn and quartered – which was done there – he looking as cheerful as any man could do in that condition'?

39 How did the poet Shelley describe Italy?

40 Which American author wrote: 'A Jewish man with parents alive is a fifteen-year-old boy, and will remain a fifteen-year-old boy until they die!'?

41 Which showman remarked: 'There's a sucker born every minute'?

42 What, according to Proudhon, is property?

43 Who wrote: 'Sex is the last refuge of the miserable'?

44 Who wrote: 'Down these mean streets a man must go who is not himself mean, who is neither tarnished nor afraid'?

45 Which city did Ezra Pound describe as 'a fit abode for a poet'?

46 Which American writer said: 'Sex is. There is nothing more to be done about it'?

47 Which British soldier said of homosexuality: 'This sort of thing may be tolerated by the French – but we are British, thank God'?

48 Which Roman wrote: 'Trust not the horse, O Trojans. Be it what it may, I fear the Greeks, even when they offer gifts'?

49 'He's like an express train running through a tunnel.' Who was Virginia Woolf describing?

50 Who wrote: 'God is not on the side of the big battalions, but on the side of those who shoot best'?

173

Space

Answers to this quiz are on page 249

TOUGH TOUGH TOUGH

Player 1	Player 2
12	20
33	24
07	03
46	45
01	28
21	02
23	25
04	32
35	39
14	50
31	08
48	17
11	40
27	43
15	29
06	41
10	30
47	34
26	16
38	05
36	49
13	09
19	18
42	37
44	22

01 Name the planets of the solar system in order, starting nearest the Sun.

02 Name the moons of Mars.

03 Of which planet is Charon a satellite?

04 What are Perseids?

05 Where would you find Humboldt's Sea?

06 Which of the following is not a lunar sea: (a) Sea of Showers, (b) Sea of Mysteries, or (c) Sea of Geniuses?

07 What is the English name for the constellation Monoceros?

08 In which year was Sputnik 1 launched?

09 Who flew in Vostok 1?

10 Who was the first woman in space?

11 What was special about the Voshkod 2 mission?

12 What was remarkable about the Soyuz 19 mission?

13 What happened to Soyuz T10-1?

14 Who was the first British cosmonaut?

15 What was unusual about the American astronaut Enos?

16 Who flew in the first US manned suborbital flight?

17 Who was in command of the first US manned orbital flight?

18 What is the name of the planetary nebula in the constellation Lyra?

19 What is a space shuttle?

20 When did operational flights of the space shuttle Columbia begin?

174

21 What is the name of the gaseous nebula in the constellation Taurus?

22 What was the purpose of the 1985 European Space Agency Giotto mission?

23 Which mission carried out the first successful flyby of Venus?

24 Which were the missions which first successfully landed on Mars and sent back TV pictures of the Martian surface?

25 What problem, later corrected, was experienced with the Hubble Space Telescope?

26 What shape is the Milky Way galaxy?

27 What is our Moon's diameter?

28 What is zodiacal light?

29 What is the chief gas of the Venusian atmosphere?

30 Which are the most distant and most luminous objects in the universe?

31 What is the solar wind?

32 What is an aurora?

33 Name the two auroras.

34 What is a solar eclipse?

35 What is the ecliptic?

36 What is a white dwarf?

37 What is a red giant?

38 What sort of star is Antares?

39 Which is the closest spiral galaxy to our Milky Way?

40 Where would you find the constellation Perseus?

41 In which constellation is the star Betelgeuse?

42 What is a supergiant?

43 What is a nebula?

44 What is a black hole?

45 What is a white hole?

46 What is dark matter?

47 What is an antigalaxy?

48 What is the metagalaxy?

49 Where would you find the constellation Andromeda?

50 What are the Megallanic Clouds?

Words

Answers to this quiz are on pages 249-250

TOUGH 😦 **TOUGH**

Player 1	Player 2
12	20
33	24
07	03
46	45
01	28
21	02
23	25
04	32
35	39
14	50
31	08
48	17
11	40
27	43
15	29
06	41
10	30
47	34
26	16
38	05
36	49
13	09
19	18
42	37
44	22

176

01 Satrap means: (a) Eastern prince, (b) stirrup, (c) cloth.

02 Fuliginous means: (a) defamatory, (b) poetic, (c) sooty.

03 Calumny means: (a) war club, (b) defamation, (c) bridle.

04 Calabash means: (a) musical instrument, (b) flower, (c) gourd.

05 Gravid means: (a) pregnant, (b) heavy, (c) serious.

06 Apse means: (a) snake, (b) part of a church, (c) drop.

07 Malady means: (a) lies, (b) villain, (c) sickness.

08 Libretto means: (a) opera text, (b) debaucher, (c) singer.

09 Ululation means: (a) apotheosis, (b) howling, (c) rectification.

10 Pistil means: (a) firearm, (b) bat, (c) flower ovary.

11 Fedora means: (a) workman, (b) hat, (c) gypsy.

12 Recondite means: (a) explosive, (b) hidden, (c) pregnant.

13 Gibbous means: (a) half-witted, (b) quaint, (c) humped.

14 Fulgurate means: (a) explode, (b) flash, (c) detonate.

15 Moratorium means: (a) undertaker, (b) temporary ban, (c) piece of music.

16 Nictate means: (a) blink, (b) argue, (c) smoke.

17 Prosthesis means: (a) gratitude, (b) artificial body part, (c) poem.

18 Locum means: (a) place, (b) deputy, (c) doctor.

19 Morass means: (a) treacle, (b) marsh, (c) stew.

20 Meiosis means: (a) a disease of rabbits, (b) a literary device, (c) cell division.

21 Grandiloquent means (a) effulgent, (b) bombastic, (c) abusive.

22 Lepidote means: (a) rabbit-like, (b) stony, (c) scaly.

23 Gimcrack means: (a) gewgaw, (b) unsafe, (c) glittering.

24 Lachrymose means: (a) unhappy, (b) tearful, (c) dismal.

25 Depict means: (a) gloat, (b) glean, (c) describe.

26 Impuissant means: (a) smelly, (b) powerless, (c) powdery.

27 Cricoid means: (a) ring-shaped, (b) flower, (c) mineral.

28 Frenetic means: (a) speedy, (b) frenzied, (c) acute.

29 Grosgrain means: (a) illegal alcohol, (b) computer language, (c) fabric.

30 Kapok means: (a) fibre, (b) china clay, (c) guard.

31 Transmogrify means: (a) change shape, (b) send, (c) translate.

32 Crepuscular means: (a) crinkled, (b) diseased skin, (c) dim.

33 Jejune means: (a) uninteresting, (b) worthless, (c) yellowed.

34 Inchoate means: (a) outraged, (b) imperfectly formed, (c) speechless.

35 Frambesia means: (a) shrub, (b) yaws, (c) card game.

36 Treponema means: (a) spirochetes, (b) worms, (c) beetles.

37 Tantalum means: (a) Greek king, (b) metallic element, (c) spinning wheel.

38 Deflagarate means: (a) lose air, (b) burn suddenly, (c) criticize.

39 Evagation means: (a) wandering, (b) losing fluid, (c) reducing fat.

40 Gabelle means: (a) musical instrument, (b) tax, (c) form of torture.

41 Galant means: (a) style of music, (b) polite, (c) chivalrous.

42 Monotroch means: (a) solitude, (b) wheelbarrow, (c) one-handed.

43 Pholas means: (a) piddock, (b) philabeg, (c) phillipsite.

44 Rogation means: (a) ploughing, (b) asking, (c) forgiving.

45 Procerity means: (a) tallness, (b) propinquity, (c) celerity.

46 Quey means: (a) heifer, (b) hairstyle, (c) strange.

47 Perstringe means: (a) to reduce, (b) to constrain, (c) to subtract.

48 Peduncle means: (a) relative, (b) flower part, (c) architectural term.

49 Passim means: (a) everywhere, (b) peaceful, (c) rarely.

50 Passus means: (a) canto, (b) footstep, (c) shoe.

Current Affairs

Answers to this quiz are on page 250

TOUGH TOUGH TOUGH

Player 1

Player 2

Player 1	Player 2
12	20
33	24
07	03
46	45
01	28
21	02
23	25
04	32
35	39
14	50
31	08
48	17
11	40
27	43
15	29
06	41
10	30
47	34
26	16
38	05
36	49
13	09
19	18
42	37
44	22

178

01 Which terrorist organization kidnapped and murdered the Italian prime minister Aldo Moro?

02 Which prime minister resigned after the Yom Kippur War?

03 Which nun founded the Missionaries of Charity in 1950?

04 Name the US senator who investigated communist activity amongst army officials and public figures?

05 What was the name of the US-supported rebels during the Afghan War?

06 What was the location of a protest in 1960 of 20,000 blacks against passlaws which led to a massacre by South African police?

07 Which South African president removed the ban on the African National Congress?

08 Who ran against Ronald Reagan in the American presidential election in 1981?

09 What was the name of the US-backed movement during the civil war in Angola?

10 Which area did Israel agree to return to Egypt after the Camp David Accords?

11 How did the Pakistani president Zia Ul-Haq die?

12 Which dissident writer was the first Soviet citizen to be expelled by the government?

13 Name of the Eastern European organization founded to coordinate economic policies?

14 Which African head of state became an emperor in 1976?

15 Name of the West German terrorist organization who were active in the early 1970s?

16 Who sentenced Salman Rushdie to death for the publication of his *Satanic Verses*?

17 Who was the first president of Israel?

18 Which political party did Indira Gandhi lead?

19 Who was Soviet foreign minister under Gorbachev?

20 What accusation forced Ferdinand Marcos to leave the Philippines in 1986?

21 Which British king died in 1952?

22 Who is the head of the Zulu-based Inkatha Freedom Party?

23 Who commanded the Allied Forces during the Gulf War?

24 Which Chinese Nationalist Party leader was driven out of China by the Communists?

25 In which country were the Sandinistas based?

26 What was the *Exxon Valdez* involved in?

27 When was the Anglo–Irish agreement drawn up?

28 Which disease of cattle caused friction between Britain and her European partners?

29 Who was the first president of Kenya after it gained independence?

30 Who succeeded de Gaulle as French president?

31 What measures, introduced in Northern Ireland in August 1971, led to riots in Republican areas?

32 Where is ETA based?

33 Which political party did Menachem Begin lead?

34 In which year was the Hungarian uprising?

35 Who founded Pakistan?

36 Which American president broke off diplomatic relations with Cuba?

37 Who was the leader of the Al Fatah guerrilla movement?

38 Which is the main launching site for US space missions?

39 Who was the Iraqi foreign minister during the Gulf War?

40 Which political party does Helmut Kohl lead?

41 Which town was the birthplace of the Solidarity movement?

42 In which year was the Berlin Wall erected?

43 What was the name of the Greenpeace ship blown up in Auckland Harbour?

44 Which former UN general secretary was accused of German intelligence activities during World War II?

45 Which Canadian prime minister proposed the Constitution Act, which gave Canada complete independence?

46 Who was president of the European Commission from 1985 to 1995?

47 Who succeeded Menachem Begin as prime minister of Israel?

48 Name the ferry that capsized outside the port of Zeebrugge in 1987, killing 186 people?

49 When did the USA withdraw its troops from Vietnam?

50 Where are the headquarters of the Council of Europe?

179

Islands

Answers to this quiz are on page 250

TOUGH 😕 **TOUGH**

Player 1	Player 2
12	20
33	24
07	03
46	45
01	28
21	02
23	25
04	32
35	39
14	50
31	08
48	17
11	40
27	43
15	29
06	41
10	30
47	34
26	16
38	05
36	49
13	09
19	18
42	37
44	22

01 Which is the world's largest island?

02 Which island, to the south of Corsica, once belonged to the House of Savoy?

03 An island called the Malagassy Republic was renamed in 1975. What is it now called?

04 On which island does the famous yachting venue of Cowes lie?

05 From which island did the tailless Manx cat originate?

06 By what name was Taiwan formerly known?

07 By which name is the island and holiday resort of Kerkira better known?

08 Which island is infamously linked with the Mafia?

09 What is the large island found in the Gulf of Tongkin?

10 By what name does Argentina, which claims ownership of the territory, refer to the Falkland Islands?

11 Which group of islands would you find north of Crete?

12 Which island lies off the southern tip of India?

13 The ownership of which island is contested by Turkey and Greece?

14 Which islands lie north-east of Cuba?

15 What is the capital of the Philippines?

16 On which 'island' would you relax in Brooklyn, New York?

17 Which island, south of Java, has a festive name?

18 Who was the most famous, though unwilling, resident of the Isle of Elba?

19 The island of Patmos is traditionally considered to be the place where one of the books of the Bible was written. Which one?

20 Which island has been referred to as 'The Pearl of the Antilles'?

21 What is the English name for what the French call the Isles Normandes?

22 The island of Sjelland contains the capital of a European country. Name both the country and the capital.

23 Children are often taught to recognize the map of Italy by looking for a boot kicking a ball. Which island forms the ball?

24 Which island was ceded to France by Genoa in 1768?

25 Which famous peninsula juts into the Black Sea?

26 On which island does the Chinese Nationalist Government hold power?

27 On which island do Malaysia and Indonesia meet?

28 Which group of islands would you find due south of the Bay of Bengal?

29 Of which island group is Mindanao a part?

30 Of which island is Colombo the capital?

31 On which island would you find Larnaka?

32 Which group of islands would you find north-east of Madagascar?

33 Off which continent would you find the Galapagos Islands?

34 On which island would you find Suffolk?

35 With which island state do you associate Maui and Oahu?

36 Is Nova Scotia an island?

37 The island of New Guinea is split into two halves. One half is Irian Jaya. Name the other half?

38 By what name were the Hawaiian Islands formerly known?

39 What name is given to a large group of islands?

40 Of what island group is Okinawa a part?

41 Where would you find Kodiak Island?

42 Which country in the Persian Gulf between Qatar and Saudi Arabia is actually an archipelago?

43 Which country lies next to Haiti?

44 What is the capital of Haiti?

45 On which island do Haiti and the Dominican Republic exist side by side?

46 Between which pair of islands does the Windward Passage run?

47 What interest did the USA have in Guantanamo, Cuba?

48 Where does the mainland of Great Britain rank in the world's ten largest islands?

49 Which island has a name implying that it suffers from strong winds?

50 The Virgin Islands belong to two countries. Which are they?

181

People

Answers to this quiz are on page 250

TOUGH TOUGH TOUGH TOUGH

Player 1	Player 2
12	20
33	24
07	03
46	45
01	28
21	02
23	25
04	32
35	39
14	50
31	08
48	17
11	40
27	43
15	29
06	41
10	30
47	34
26	16
38	05
36	49
13	09
19	18
42	37
44	22

01 Who was seduced by the god Zeus in the shape of a swan?

02 Which Greek hero was vulnerable only at his heel?

03 Of which country was Chang Kai-Shek head of state?

04 Which romantic legendary figure later became plain Aircraftsman Ross?

05 Who said: 'Die, my dear doctor, that is the last thing I shall do'?

06 Holmes had his Watson, but who was aided and abetted by Dr Petrie?

07 Pheidippides was famous as the originator of which race?

08 Which blind poet wrote *Paradise Lost*?

09 Who was the hero of *The Catcher in the Rye*?

10 Who united Germany by a policy of 'blood and iron'?

11 Which Georgian ran Stalin's secret police?

12 Which queen of the Iceni fought against the Roman invaders of Britain?

13 Name the Roman god of the sea?

14 Which Roman presided over the trial of Jesus.

15 Name the 19th-century French artist who was famous for his small stature?

16 Who is famous for a painting protraying the destruction of Guernica?

17 In which story by J.D. Salinger did Seymour Glass kill himself?

18 Who was the youngest member of J.D. Salinger's fictional Glass family?

19 Who is the odd one out of the Gandhi family: Mohondas, Indira, Sanjay, and Rajiv.

20 Name the cyclops of Greek legend.

21 Who was the evil god of Norse legend?

22 Who was the wife of the Indian hero Rama?

23 Which famous doctor was created by Boris Pasternak?

24 Who was the brother of the Anglo-Saxon chieftain Hengist?

25 Who was the Scottish mathematician who invented logorithms?

26 Who was the first Chancellor of post-war West Germany?

27 In the Bible two people are given credit for killing the Philistine Goliath. The most famous was David, who was the other?

28 The skeleton of a man called Yehohanan was discovered in Israel in 1968. What was his unfortunate distinction?

29 For what was Joseph Grimaldi famous?

30 By what name did Archibald Leach find fame?

31 Mr Austerlitz and Miss McMath became partners under other names. What were they?

32 Who was the director of the 1968 film *Romeo and Juliet*?

33 Who was responsible for inventing dynamite and gelignite?

34 Who pioneered the pneumatic tyres fitted to the Model T Ford?

35 Which Spaniard had delusions of knightly glory?

36 Which explorer was known as 'Il Millioni'?

37 Who was famous for going over Niagara Falls in a barrel?

38 What was unusual about the hanging of John 'Babacombe' Lee?

39 Aleksandr Solzhenitsyn wrote a novel about a day in the life of one man. Who was he?

40 Which Chinese philosopher wrote *The Analects*?

41 Which Indian political and religious leader defied the British by making salt?

42 Which king of Egypt rejected the old gods and initiated a new form of sun worship?

43 Who was 'mad, bad and dangerous to know'?

44 He was severely disabled and had a speech impediment but became emperor of Rome. Who was he?

45 Who was popularly known as 'The Virgin Queen'?

46 Who brought the Christmas tree to the British?

47 How was Admiral Nelson's body preserved following his death at the Battle of Trafalgar?

48 Who reputedly fell in love with his own reflection?

49 Which legendary ladies were named Medusa, Stheno, and Euryale?

50 Who assassinated Jean Paul Marat?

Pot Luck

Answers to this quiz are on pages 250-251

TOUGH 😦 **TOUGH**

Player 1	Player 2
12	20
33	24
07	03
46	45
01	28
21	02
23	25
04	32
35	39
14	50
31	08
48	17
11	40
27	43
15	29
06	41
10	30
47	34
26	16
38	05
36	49
13	09
19	18
42	37
44	22

01 How many googols make a googolplex?

02 What have an outcast group in Japan and a Basque separatist organization got in common?

03 The statue of Eros in Piccadilly Circus, London, commemorates a Victorian reformer. Who was he?

04 The Ngorogoro national park has an explosive connection. What is it?

05 Everyone has heard of the 'waters of Babylon' but which river ran through the city?

06 Soweto, in South Africa, is not an African word. What does it mean?

07 In which film did Gene Kelly dance with an umbrella?

08 What explanation did W.C. Fields give when found reading the Bible on his deathbed?

09 By what name was wartime English broadcaster William Joyce better known?

10 By what name was the European Union originally known?

11 Which Egyptian leader precipitated the Suez Crisis?

12 What is the name of the Israeli parliament?

13 In which country did the Boxer Rebellion take place?

14 What is collagen?

15 What, according to Dante, was the inscription at the entrance to Hell?

16 Who is traditionally considered to have founded Taoism?

17 Apart from its religious merit, what special distinction does The Diamond Sutra possess?

18 What distinction do Edward V and Edward VIII share?

19 Who was the famous queen of the Iceni?

20 Which emperor made his horse a Roman consul?

21 What impossible building task were the Hebrews set by their Egyptian captors?

22 For what purpose was natron used?

23 What is the more polite name for the act of ritual suicide known as *hara kiri*?

24 What instrument was the precursor of the trombone?

25 Where was the composer Frederick Delius born?

26 Which appropriately named English painter killed his father?

27 Which French mathematician died in a duel at the age of 21?

28 Which religious group worship the Ethiopian emperor Haile Selassie?

29 Would you drink a Molotov cocktail?

30 What did Howard Carter discover in 1922?

31 What inflammatory act did Marinus van der Lubbe commit in 1933?

32 Which Georgian became known as Uncle Joe?

33 What were kulaks?

34 What notable event took place at Appomattox Court House in 1865?

35 What are the people who follow the teachings of a Zoroaster called.

36 Which Spanish naval disaster was commanded by the Duke of Medina Sidonia?

37 For what military blunder was General Galtieri of Argentina responsible?

38 By what name did Siddartha Gautama become well known?

39 For which literary work did Sei Shonagon become famous?

40 Who said: 'Speak softly and carry a big stick'?

41 In which country would you find guerrillas of the Shining Path?

42 In which country did the Red Army Faction operate?

43 What happened at the Battle of Actium in 31 BC?

44 Which English MP was a member of the Hellfire Club?

45 Whose execution prompted Voltaire's remark that the English occasionally shoot an admiral to encourage the others?

46 Why would a Basenji make a poor watchdog?

47 Which pigment does the cuttlefish secrete?

48 What is a haiku?

49 What is a malapropism?

50 Who wrote *Six Characters in Search of an Author*?

Classical Music

Answers to this quiz are on page 251

TOUGH TOUGH TOUGH

Player 1	Player 2
12	20
33	24
07	03
46	45
01	28
21	02
23	25
04	32
35	39
14	50
31	08
48	17
11	40
27	43
15	29
06	41
10	30
47	34
26	16
38	05
36	49
13	09
19	18
42	37
44	22

01 What is the type of German opera of the 18th century called where songs are interspersed with dialogue?

02 **How many strings does a cello have?**

03 Who orchestrated *Pictures at an Exhibition*?

04 **'The Polovtsian Dances' are part of which opera?**

05 Who wrote the 'Egmont Overture'?

06 **Which nationality was Béla Bartók?**

07 Which instrument does Anne-Sophie Mutter perform on?

08 **Which musical work is the Young Person's Guide to the Orchestra based on?**

09 Which orchestral work is based on *A Thousand and One Nights*, and who wrote it?

10 **The 'Ode to Joy' is part of which musical work?**

11 How many symphonies did Bruckner write?

12 **Who wrote the 'Reformation Symphony'?**

13 Which word describes a vocal and orchestral work telling a sacred story without dramatic effects?

14 **What is a bass viola also called?**

15 Who wrote the 'German Requiem'?

16 **Which musical work is 'Anitra's Dance' part of?**

17 How many semitones are there in a scale?

18 **Who created a catalogue of Mozart's music?**

19 Which composer established the 12-tone technique of Serial Music?

20 Who composed 'My Fatherland'?

21 Which family does the English horn belong to?

22 How many symphonies did Brahms write?

23 Riccardo Muti is the director of which opera house?

24 Who composed 'The Creation'?

25 What is the difference between an interval and a chord?

26 On a piano, what are the strings struck by?

27 In which work would you find a secion entitled 'Fortuna Imperatrix Mundi'?

28 By what other name is Mendelssohn's 'Hebrides Ouverture' also known?

29 What do you call an interval of eight full tones?

30 Mendelssohn's 'Wedding March' is part of which musical work?

31 Who wrote the opera *Russlan and Ludmilla*?

32 Which composer was regarded as the architect of impressionism?

33 Which instrument was Fritz Kreisler famous for?

34 Which was Richard Wagner's only comic opera?

35 Which type of instrument did Henry Steinway build?

36 Who wrote *In the Steppes of Central Asia*?

37 What type of singing voice is Elisabeth Schwarzkopf known for?

38 In a tempo direction, what does the word 'assai' stand for?

39 What is unusual about Beethoven's Eighth Symphony?

40 Which country does the polonaise come from?

41 Which instrument does Narciso Yepes perform on?

42 Who wrote *Till Eulenspiegel's Merry Pranks*?

43 What type of singing voice is Dame Janet Baker known for?

44 What is the name given to Beethoven's Fifth Piano Concerto?

45 What is a sarabande?

46 Who wrote *The Swan of Tuonela*?

47 Which three of Verdi's operas are based on plays by Shakespeare?

48 What is the title of Schubert's Fourth Symphony?

49 Which instrument did Arthur Grumiaux perform on?

50 What type of instrument is a sousaphone?

Wars & Battles

Answers to this quiz are on page 251

Player 1	Player 2
12	20
33	24
07	03
46	45
01	28
21	02
23	25
04	32
35	39
14	50
31	08
48	17
11	40
27	43
15	29
06	41
10	30
47	34
26	16
38	05
36	49
13	09
19	18
42	37
44	22

01 During the conflict in North America, whio was defeated in the Seven Years' War?

02 **During the French Revolution, which country did France declare war on in 1792?**

03 Which army did Napoleon defeat at Austerlitz in 1805?

04 **Which two towns saw the first battles of the American Revolution?**

05 During the Korean War, which major powers supported the North Koreans?

06 **During which war did the Battle of Edgehill take place?**

07 The Thirty Years' War was fought on which main issue?

08 **Which army was defeated in the Second Battle of Bull Run during the American Civil War?**

09 Where was the Spanish Armada fought?

10 **Name the coalition, headed by Germany, Italy, and Japan, during World War II?**

11 Who were the Central Powers in World War I?

12 **Where was the first battle in the American Civil War?**

13 In which year did the USA enter World War I?

14 **Who was the German Field Marshall who commanded the Afrika Korps in North Africa during World War II?**

15 What did the Russian February Revolution achieve?

16 **In which year did the Vietnam War start?**

17 In which year did the USA start sending troops to Vietnam?

18 **Which was the opposing branch of Russian socialism that was in conflict with the Bolsheviks before and during the revolution?**

19 Which general led the Union army in the Battle of Fair Oaks in the American Civil War?

20 In which year did the Battle of Trafalgar take place?

21 The French Revolution started during the reign of which king?

22 Which treaty ended the Seven Years' War?

23 During the American War of Independence, where did the British troops finally surrender?

24 Where was Robert E. Lee's army defeated on July 3 1863 in the American Civil War?

25 In which war was poison gas first used successfully?

26 Which part of Egypt was captured in the Six Day War?

27 What was the codename of the US bombing campaign during the Vietnam War?

28 Name of the major offensive of the Vietcong and North Vietnamese troops on South Vietnamese cities in 1968?

29 Which war did the Treaty of Vereeniging end?

30 Which state was created as a result of the First Balkan War?

31 What was the name of the German statesman who provoked the Franco-Prussian War?

32 What was the aim of the Boxers during their uprising in 1900?

33 During which war did Hannibal invade Italy?

34 Which commander, during the American Civil War, led Union troops toward Richmond?

35 Who were the three colonial powers in North America at the start of the Seven Years' War?

36 During the Napoleonic Wars, which army was defeated at Friedland?

37 During which war did the Battle of Lutzen take place?

38 Where did the Confederate Army surrender at the end of the American Civil War?

39 Which French king was captured during the Battle of Poitiers during the Hundred Years' War?

40 What was the location of a major evacuation of British and French troops by British ships and boats in 1940?

41 Which war started on the Jewish Holy Day of Atonement in 1973?

42 During which battle were tanks first used?

43 Which were the disputed areas in the Russian–Japanese War?

44 In which year did the Russian Revolution begin when troops fired on workers marching towards the Winter Palace of the czar and what name was given to the day?

45 When was the Boer War?

46 What did the Balkan League try to achieve during the First Balkan War?

47 Which city was destroyed during the Third Punic War?

48 During which war did the Battle of Sluys take place?

49 What was the name of the peninsula at the entrance to the Dardanelles that British troops and their allies tried to capture in World War I?

50 What was the location of Henry V's victory over an army of French knights in 1415?

189

Books

Answers to this quiz are on pages 251-252

TOUGH TOUGH

Player 1	Player 2
12	20
33	24
07	03
46	45
01	28
21	02
23	25
04	32
35	39
14	50
31	08
48	17
11	40
27	43
15	29
06	41
10	30
47	34
26	16
38	05
36	49
13	09
19	18
42	37
44	22

190

01 Who wrote *Persuasion*?

02 Mary Renault's *Fire From Heaven*, *The Persian Boy* and *Funeral Games* describe the life and death of which historical figure?

03 For many years Samuel Richardson's novel *Clarissa* had a claim to fame not strictly based on its literary merit. What was it?

04 Who was the mortal foe, and eventual killer, of Mervyn Peake's character Swelter?

05 Which young man about town would you expect to find in the company of Bingo Little, Gussie Fink-Nottle and Stinker Pinker?

06 Who wrote *Gravity's Rainbow*?

07 A loud, overdecorated hat was often called a Dolly Varden. Why?

08 The Marquis de Sade wrote a novel entitled *Justine*. What was its subtitle?

09 In which novel were some animals more equal than others?

10 In which novel would you find Adela Quested?

11 Whose book, entitled *The Doors of Perception*, was criticized for encouraging young people to take drugs?

12 For what literary work is Anne Frank remembered?

13 Which is the world's best-selling book of all time?

14 Who invented the character Allan Quartermain?

15 Which work by Homer tells the story of the siege of Troy?

16 In which huge work does the Guermantes Way figure?

17 Which funereal-sounding man wrote the supposed autobiography of the Emperor Claudius?

18 Of which modern country is James Michener's *The Source* a fictionalized history?

19 Which novel begins with Joad hitching a ride after being released from prison?

20 Which fictional character arrived at Whitby having travelled from eastern Europe in a box?

21 What was the name of the Hunchback of Notre Dame?

22 What was the real name of the author of *Burmese Days*?

23 Which British author invented the term 'the two cultures'?

24 Which American poet wrote: 'A politician is an arse upon which everyone has sat except a man'?

25 What is the best-known novel of Raphael Sabatini?

26 In which novel does a word-processor called Abulafia appear?

27 What was the name of the computer in *2001: A Space Odyssey*?

28 Who wrote *Earthly Powers*?

29 What manner of person was Rabelais' character Gargantua?

30 Which Dane is famous for his collection of fairy tales?

31 Name the John Buchan hero who appears in *The Thirty-Nine Steps*.

32 Which character is responsible for the line: 'All is for the best in the best of all possible worlds'?

33 For what work is the mother of Mary Shelley known?

34 Who was the creator of the lawyer Perry Mason?

35 Which fictional butler was a member of the Junior Ganymede Club?

36 Complete the line, 'Full fathom five...'

37 Which boy, disguised as a girl, was detected by the way he threw a lump of iron at a rat?

38 Name the villainous plantation owner from Uncle Tom's Cabin.

39 Which Dickens character was always confident that something would turn up?

40 An expensive computer was described in the title of a Len Deighton novel. What was it called?

41 'Ill met by moonlight, proud Titania' comes from which play?

42 Who describes his wound as: 'tis not so deep as a well, nor so wide as a church door; but 'tis enough, 'twill serve'?

43 'A horse! A horse! My kingdom for a horse!' is uttered by which Shakespeare character?

44 Complete the line: 'St Agnes' Eve – Ah! bitter chill it was'

45 Name the horrid housekeeper in Daphne Du Maurier's *Rebecca*.

46 In which novel would you find Stephen Daedalus, Leonard Bloom and Molly Bloom?

47 In Len Deighton's *A Funeral in Berlin*, which character complains just before he dies that his suit has been ruined?

48 Who said: 'If I had a half share in that dog I'd kill my half'?

49 Who wrote *The Glass Bead Game*?

50 Which tragic heroine is arrested at Stonehenge?

191

Crime & Punishment

Answers to this quiz are on page 252

TOUGH

Player 1	Player 2
12	20
33	24
07	03
46	45
01	28
21	02
23	25
04	32
35	39
14	50
31	08
48	17
11	40
27	43
15	29
06	41
10	30
47	34
26	16
38	05
36	49
13	09
19	18
42	37
44	22

01 What were stocks used for?

02 What was a gallows?

03 What did it mean if criminals were 'transported'?

04 What was the rack?

05 What punishment was inflicted on Guy Fawkes?

06 Is it true that criminals used to have to pay for their keep in prison?

07 What was the iron maiden?

08 What does the expression 'to let the cat out of the bag' refer to?

09 What fate befell Anne Boleyn?

10 What was strange about the execution of John 'Babacombe' Lee?

11 What happened to people who refused to plead in a criminal case?

12 What was a ducking stool used for?

13 What title was given to Matthew Hopkins?

14 Who were the tricoteuses?

15 What happened to the prankster Til Eugenspiel?

16 What official body was appointed by the Roman Catholic Church to root out heresy?

17 What was Alcatraz?

18 Which gang were the chief opponents of the Kray twins?

19 What was Al Capone finally convicted of?

20 What were the full names of Bonnie and Clyde?

21 What were pilliwinks?

22 How did Sitting Bull die?

23 Who tried to steal the British Crown jewels?

24 For what crime is Charles Manson infamous?

25 What crime was Lizzie Borden suspected of?

26 Who was the first murderer to be caught by wireless telegraphy?

27 Who were the Moors murderers?

28 What was a tawse?

29 Of what crime was Dreyfus falsely accused?

30 Who was known as the Demon Barber of Fleet Street?

31 What mythical character was punished by having his liver repeatedly torn out by eagles yet magically renewed itself each day?

32 What was keel hauling?

33 What, at least in stories, was the traditional punishment meted out by pirates to their captives?

34 What is the name for the Muslim legal code which prescribes severe punishments for crime?

35 Which country used the 'death of a thousand cuts'?

36 In which country could a prominent man order a guilty subordinate to disembowel himself?

37 In which country was the knout used as an instrument of punishment?

38 What punishment, inflicted upon Captain Jenkins, sparked off a war?

39 What was so bad about being made Keeper of the White Elephants by the King of Siam?

40 How are criminals executed in modern Thailand?

41 In which country is the electric chair a method of execution?

42 What was the Gulag?

43 There are many accounts of crucifixion, but how many crucified bodies have ever been discovered?

44 Which Roman slave was crucified after leading a slave rebellion?

45 What was the strappado?

46 What is 'falaka'?

47 For what crime was Socrates punished?

48 Who had to push a stone uphill for ever?

49 What was the name given to the practice of making a criminal prove his innocence by carrying a red-hot bar of metal in his bare hands?

50 What was Bridewell famous for?

Classical Music

Answers to this quiz are on page 252

TOUGH TOUGH TOUGH

Player 1	Player 2
12	20
33	24
07	03
46	45
01	28
21	02
23	25
04	32
35	39
14	50
31	08
48	17
11	40
27	43
15	29
06	41
10	30
47	34
26	16
38	05
36	49
13	09
19	18
42	37
44	22

194

01 Which type of scale has been the most widely used since the Baroque period?

02 Which composer first performed the *St. Matthew's Passion* after Bach's death?

03 Which signs were used for the notation of Gregorian Chant?

04 Which instrumentation did Max Bruch write 'Kol Nidrei' for?

05 Which musical piece is Beethoven's 'Turkish March' part of?

06 Who wrote the opera *Hary Janos*?

07 What is Karl Czerny best known for?

08 Who wrote the 'Sabre Dance' and what is it part of?

09 Where would you find the 'Merry Gathering of Peasants'?

10 Which instrument does David Popper mainly write for?

11 Which name has been given to Haydn's Symphony No. 101?

12 Which of his other operas is Wagner's *Parsifal* related to?

13 Who wrote the *Warsaw Concerto*?

14 In which keys are orchestral clarinets made?

15 Which country does the *csárdás* come from?

16 Which Frenchman wrote the music for an opera called Ivan the Terrible?

17 Who wrote the opera *The Love of Three Oranges*?

18 Which musical term indicates the prolongation of a sound or pause beyond its indicated time value?

19 Which instrument did Dietrich Buxtehude mainly write for?

20 Which Italian composer is regarded as the founder of opera?

21 Which type of instrument is a *toccata* usually written for?

22 Which type of singing voice is Dietrich Fischer-Dieskau known for?

23 Which type of instrument did the Guarneri family make?

24 What does the instruction *ritardando* mean?

25 Who wrote *Fantasia Para un Gentilhombre*?

26 Which instrument is Heinz Holliger best known for?

27 What is the name of Alban Berg's unfinished opera?

28 Which musical work is 'Clair de Lune' part of?

29 Which composition is Paul Dukas best known for?

30 What is the name given to Tchaikovsky's Symphony No. 2?

31 Which type of singing voice is Kirsten Flagstad known for?

32 Which nationality was Heitor Villa-Lobos?

33 Who wrote *The Snow Maiden*?

34 Which of Puccini's operas was unfinished at the time of his death?

35 Who was the founder of the London Philharmonic Orchestra?

36 Apart from his compositions, what is Carl Orff known for?

37 Who wrote the opera *Cavalleria Rusticana*?

38 Which is the term for a change of key within a composition?

39 IWhich type of singing voice is Jon Vickers known for?

40 Which two composers completed Borodin's *Prince Igor*?

41 Who was director of the Philadelphia Orchestra from 1938 to 1980?

42 Arthur Rubinstein was particularly known for the interpretation of the works of which composer?

43 Who wrote the opera *Iphigénie en Tauride*?

44 What is the name of musical notation by way of letters or numbers, as originally used for the lute, but nowadays mainly for the guitar?

45 For which instrument did Ravel write his piece *Le Tombeau de Couperin*?

46 Who wrote *Wedding Day at Troldhaugen*?

47 What type of music is a *bourée*?

48 What works of music is Giovanni Palestrina especially known for?

49 Who wrote the *Hungarian Rhapsodies*?

50 Which composer had the nickname 'Il prete rosso'?

World War II

Answers to this quiz are on page 253

TOUGH TOUGH TOUGH

	Player 1	Player 2
	12	20
	33	24
	07	03
	46	45
	01	28
	21	02
	23	25
	04	32
	35	39
	14	50
	31	08
	48	17
	11	40
	27	43
	15	29
	06	41
	10	30
	47	34
	26	16
	38	05
	36	49
	13	09
	19	18
	42	37
	44	22

01 The invasion of which country precipitated World War II?

02 What name did the Germans give to the annexation of Austria?

03 With whom did Hitler negotiate a Non-Aggression Pact prior to his invasion of Poland?

04 What does the German expression Blitzkrieg mean?

05 Which German general was mainly responsible for applying the principles of Blitzkrieg?

06 Prior to the war, the British had tried to negotiate a settlement with Hitler. What was this policy called?

07 What were German submarines called?

08 Which British liner was sunk by the Germans early in the war in the mistaken belief that it was an armed merchant ship?

09 Apart from Germany, which other country attacked Poland?

10 On which date did Britain and France declare war on Germany?

11 On November 30 1939 the Soviets carried out an attack on which country?

12 When did Churchill become British prime minister?

13 From where was the British Expeditionary Force evacuated?

14 In which battle did the Luftwaffe pit its strength against that of the RAF?

15 Which of the major combatants in the war suffered no civilian casualties?

16 The USA and Great Britain suffered an almost identical number of military casualties in the conflict. How many men were lost by each country?

17 Which country bore the heaviest military and civilian losses of the war?

18 Who commanded the Soviet military forces?

19 Which Japanese admiral, although opposed to involving Japan in the war, planned the attack on Pearl Harbor?

20 What nickname was given to the German V-1 rocket bomb?

21 What was the name of the French government which collaborated with the Germans?

22 Who led the Free French?

23 Who was leader of the Italian fascists during the war?

24 In which theater of operations was Rommel the German commander?

25 Which scientist was chiefly responsible for the German rocket bomb programme?

26 Why was the letter V used when naming rocket bombs?

27 What was a PIAT used for?

28 The Russians had a rocket weapon, named after a girl, which is still in use in some parts of the world. What is it called?

29 What was a Nebelwerfer?

30 What was regarded as spooky about the explosion of a V-2?

31 Give the US and British names of the underwater detection systems similar in operation to RADAR?

32 What weapon was chiefly used against submerged submarines?

33 What was the purpose of 'degaussing'?

34 What was the code name given to the German invasion of the USSR?

35 Which Soviet city was subjected to a 900-day siege?

36 What was a T34?

37 What stopped the German advance into Russia?

38 Did the Germans occupy Moscow?

39 What event brought the USA into the war?

40 What name was given to groups of German U-boats operating together?

41 Who commanded the U-boats?

42 Who commanded the Luftwaffe?

43 What name was given to Rommel's force in North Africa?

44 What symbol were Jews forced to wear to distinguish them from 'Aryans'?

45 What was the name given to the illegal trade in rationed goods?

46 What was the purpose of the Einsatzgruppen?

47 Who carried out the task of unifying the French Resistance organizations?

48 Who was the German commander in charge of the attack on Stalingrad?

49 What did Paulus finally do that was against Hitler's orders?

50 What was the codename given to the Normandy landings?

199

Books

Answers to this quiz are on page 253

TOUGH TOUGH TOUGH

Player 1	Player 2
12	20
33	24
07	03
46	45
01	28
21	02
23	25
04	32
35	39
14	50
31	08
48	17
11	40
27	43
15	29
06	41
10	30
47	34
26	16
38	05
36	49
13	09
19	18
42	37
44	22

01 The character Natty Bumpo has two nicknames, one English and the other French. What are they?

02 What scandalous tale was written by Lucius Apuleius?

03 What novel by Richard Adams was devoted to the adventures of a group of rabbits?

04 What was the name of Ray Bradbury's tale of an evil travelling fair?

05 Which of Anthony Burgess's novels concerned early Christianity?

06 Most people know only the film of Breakfast at Tiffany's, but who wrote the novel?

07 What is the name of the series of novels for which Anthony Powell became famous?

08 Name David Lodge's novel concerning a catastrophe at a well-known British institution?

09 Sinclair Lewis wrote a novel about an evangelical preacher. What was the title?

10 What dangerous-sounding novel was written by Laclos?

11 Who wrote the novels in which the spy George Smiley appears?

12 Name the British professor who wrote a novel apparently opposing cannibalism.

13 In which Graham Greene novel did he describe small-time crooks at a seaside resort?

14 Which F. Scott Fitzgerald hero had a past cloaked in mystery?

15 Which of Christopher Isherwood's Berlin characters was noted for her emerald green nail polish?

16 Which novelist walked out on a midsummer's morning and had cider with a girl called Rosie?

17 What was the real name of Ettrick Shepherd?

18 Which of Stephen King's characters used psychokinetic powers to gain revenge?

19 Ruth Prawer Jhabvala had parents of two nationalities but was born in a third country. Can you name all three?

20 Who created the detective Lord Peter Wimsey?

21 Which Nigerian novelist wrote *The Famished Road*?

22 Which American scholar wrote a series of books on the mythologies of the world, entitled *The Masks of God*?

23 Which Robert Louis Stevenson novel used characters reminiscent of Robin Hood and his merry men?

24 What name was given to a series of four books by Lawrence Durrell set in Egypt?

25 What event was dramatized in John Masters' novel *The Night Runners of Bengal*?

26 What was Bram Stoker's occupation at the time he wrote *Dracula*?

27 What brief book did Stephen Hawking write?

28 In which science fiction novel, written by which scientist, do we read of an intelligent cloud?

29 Who wrote a book entitled *The Unbearable Lightness of Being*?

30 In which American novel, and by which author, did Mrs Robinson appear?

31 In which book, with a floral title, are monks murdered by means of a poisoned book?

32 In a J.D. Salinger book a story is dedicated 'For Esme'. What is the rest of the dedication?

33 Which novel, in the form of two diaries, tells the story of a girl held prisoner by an entomologist?

34 Which Frenchman wrote about a revolution in New York?

35 Who wrote *The Naked Ape*?

36 Which writer created the character Captain Nemo?

37 Who wrote a book entitled *Ethics*?

38 Who wrote *Utopia*?

39 For what literary work is Cellini chiefly remembered?

40 Name the US town made famous by Garrison Keillor.

41 Which science fiction story tells the story of a laboratory mouse and a mentally subnormal human?

42 Which psychiatrist wrote the book *Games People Play*?

43 Which Asimov novel starts by stating the *Three Laws of Robotics*?

44 What was the name of the walking, carnivorous plants created by John Wyndham?

45 In which Norman Mailer novel is the protagonist mummified?

46 A book called *The English Governess at the Siamese Court* was turned into a musical. What was it called?

47 Which novel, with a Chinese connection, was written by Simone de Beauvoir?

48 Which Graham Greene novel was set in French Vietnam?

49 Who wrote *The Descent of Man*?

50 Who wrote: 'The mind is its own place, and in itself can make a heav'n of hell, a hell of heav'n'?

201

Pot Luck

Answers to this quiz are on page 253

TOUGH ● TOUGH

Player 1	Player 2
12	20
33	24
07	03
46	45
01	28
21	02
23	25
04	32
35	39
14	50
31	08
48	17
11	40
27	43
15	29
06	41
10	30
47	34
26	16
38	05
36	49
13	09
19	18
42	37
44	22

01 In which constellation would you find the star Bellatrix?

02 In Ancient Greece, games were held in Delphi every four years in honour of Apollo. What were they called?

03 Which country's national flag has two horizontal stripes, one red and one white of the same width?

04 What type of animal is a pangolin?

05 During the Hundred Years War, in which battle did the English capture John the Good?

06 What is the basic unit of currency in Korea?

07 Which composer wrote the ballet *Appalachian Spring*?

08 What is the capital of Laos?

09 Who became Spanish prime minister in 1975, following General Franco's death?

10 Which Austrian engineer designed the VW Beetle?

11 What can you examine with an otoscope?

12 Which hormone, produced by the adrenal cortex, regulates the salt and water balance in the body?

13 Jakob Grimm (of the Brothers Grimm) had a profession aside from writing. What was it?

14 What is etymology.

15 What do Jews celebrate on Rosh Hashanah?

16 What type of animal is an ichneumon?

17 What do you call a left-hand page of a book?

18 The ranunculus is a type of wildflower. By what name is it more commonly known?

19 Who directed the film *Bugsy Malone*?

20 Which period in prehistory saw the disappearance of dinosaurs?

21 In which country does the Atacama desert lie?

22 Which US president succeeded Andrew Johnson?

23 Who wrote the opera *Tancredi*?

24 Of which Frankish dynasty was Pepin the Short king?

25 Which is Carlo Collodi's most famous piece of literature?

26 Who won the Nobel Peace Prize in 1983?

27 Which city in northern Italy is famous for its white marble?

28 Which invention is René Laënnec famous for?

29 What are cumulonimbus clouds composed of?

30 Jonas Salk developed the first vaccine against which disease?

31 Which singer had a hit in 1974 with his reggae version of 'Everything I own'?

32 On which river is Stuttgart situated?

33 Who wrote the novel *Zorba the Greek*?

34 Who did Paul von Hindenburg succeed as leader of the Weimar Republic?

35 What do you call the positively charged particles within the nucleus of an atom?

36 What is the unit for measuring sound intensity?

37 In which organ is the Bowman's capsule situated?

38 Where are the Comoro Islands situated?

39 Who plays the part of Charles Smithson in the film *The French Lieutenant's Woman*?

40 Which artist painted *The Funeral at Ornans*?

41 What is the name given to the warm surface current off the western coast of South America which occurs every 4 to 12 years blocking the upwelling of cold currents?

42 Who wrote the music to the TV series 'Twin Peaks'?

43 The Mosquito Coast is divided between which two countries?

44 What does the *stratum corneum* consist of?

45 What is the name of the dry, dusty wind that originates in the Sahara and blows north toward the Mediterranean?

46 Which South American volcano erupted in 1985 killing over 20,000 people?

47 How are you most likely to catch trichinosis?

48 What is the capital of Azerbaijan?

49 Who directed the film *Back to the Future*?

50 What did Urban II bring about by his sermon at Clermont?

203

Places

Answers to this quiz are on pages 253-254

TOUGH **TOUGH** **TOUGH**

Player 1	Player 2
12	20
33	24
07	03
46	45
01	28
21	02
23	25
04	32
35	39
14	50
31	08
48	17
11	40
27	43
15	29
06	41
10	30
47	34
26	16
38	05
36	49
13	09
19	18
42	37
44	22

204

01 Which town did Tel Aviv merge with in 1950?

02 Which waterway connects the Southern Atlantic and Pacific Oceans?

03 Where is the St. George's Channel?

04 Which sea is Bombay situated at?

05 Which river flows along the German-Polish border?

06 Of which country is Guayaquil the largest city?

07 Which stretch of water lies between Iceland and Greenland?

08 What is the capital of Uruguay?

09 What river is Montreal situated on?

10 What is the predominant religion in Nepal?

11 In which country would you pay in forint?

12 Where is Wilkes Land?

13 Which South American country achieved independence from Spain in 1824?

14 In which mountain range is Lake Titicaca situated?

15 On which river is Warsaw situated?

16 Which country does Gotland belong to?

17 Which country does Ethiopia form its eastern border with?

18 Which island group does Rhodes belong to?

19 At which sea is Palermo situated?

20 Which US state is St Paul the capital of?

21 On which Hawaiian island is Honolulu situated?

22 Which desert occupies parts of Botswana, Namibia, and northern South Africa?

23 What is the name of the islands situated at the western entrance of the English Channel, to the south-west of England?

24 On which sea is Baku situated?

25 Which two countries does the Brenner Pass connect?

26 What is the capital of Angola?

27 Where would you find the ancient city of Knossos?

28 Which is the lowest point on the Earth?

29 On which sea is Murmansk situated?

30 In which city is the cathedral of St. John the Divine?

31 Of which country was Zaire a colony before it became independent in 1960?

32 Which countries does the Gobi Desert occupy?

33 On which river is Toulouse situated?

34 Which country does the island of Bornholm belong to?

35 At which sea is Darwin situated?

36 Which capital city is laid out in the shape of an aeroplane?

37 What is the capital of Byelorussia?

38 What is the name of the waterway between Alaska and eastern Siberia?

39 Where does the river Ganges rise?

40 What is the East German town of Meissen famous for?

41 Which countries does Paraguay have borders with?

42 Between which two lakes are the Niagara Falls?

43 Which US state lies between Indiana and Pennsylvania?

44 Which is the highest peak of the Andes?

45 In which country can the former kingdom of Ashanti be found now?

46 What is Bechuanaland now called?

47 Which island lies at the entrance to the Gulf of Mexico?

48 Which is the world's smallest independent state?

49 Of which country is Maputo the capital?

50 Where would you find the Koutoubya Mosque?

"Quotations

Answers to this quiz are on page 254

TOUGH ☹

Player 1	Player 2
12	20
33	24
07	03
46	45
01	28
21	02
23	25
04	32
35	39
14	50
31	08
48	17
11	40
27	43
15	29
06	41
10	30
47	34
26	16
38	05
36	49
13	09
19	18
42	37
44	22

01 Which cartoon-strip character said: 'Big sisters are the crab grass in the lawn of life'?

02 Who said: 'How can anyone govern a nation that has two hundred and forty-six different kinds of cheese?'

03 Who said: 'Let reverence for the laws be breathed by every American mother to the lisping babe that prattles on her lap'?

04 What bargain involving the telling of lies did Adlai Stevenson offer to make with the Republicans?

05 Which American humourist wrote: 'Experiments with laboratory rats have shown that, if one psychologist in the room laughs at something a rat does, all of the other psychologists in the room will laugh equally.'

06 Who described the German annexation of the Sudetanland as 'a quarrel in a faraway country between people of whom we know nothing'?

07 Who said: 'So little done, so much to do'?

08 Which Marxist said: 'I think that a man should not live beyond the age when he begins to deteriorate'?

09 What did the American black leader Malcom X have to say about peace and freedom?

10 Which fictional American lawyer said: 'The one thing that doesn't abide by majority rule is a person's conscience'?

11 Lyndon B. Johnson mentioned two activities that Gerald Ford could not accomplish at the same time. What were they?

12 Which Italian said: 'Since it is difficult to join them together, it is safer to be feared than to be loved when one of the two must be lacking'?

13 What did Gertrude Stein say about being a genius?

14 Which American film actress said: 'If you have a vagina and an attitude in this town, then that's a lethal combination.'

15 What did Frank Sinatra call rock 'n' roll?

16 Who said: 'When it comes to the point, really bad men are just as rare as really good ones'?

17 What did Gore Vidal have to say on the subject of narcissism?

18 'It's like Britain, only with buttons.' Who described America in those words?

19 Who said: 'I believe that it's better to be looked over than it is to be overlooked'?

20 Which African leader said: 'Only free men can negotiate. Prisoners cannot enter into contracts'?

21 Who said: 'Whoever speaks of Europe is wrong: it is a geographical expression'?

22 Which, according to Jonathan Swift, are the best doctors in the world?

23 According to Robert Benchley, what does a dog teach a boy?

24 Which American film actor said: 'If you want to know about a man you can find out an awful lot by looking at who he married'?

25 Which Czech politician said: 'For us she is not the iron lady. She is the kind, dear Mrs Thatcher'?

26 Which English military hero and politician said: 'I hate the whole race. . . There is no believing a word they say – your professional poets, I mean there never existed a more worthless set than Byron and his friends for example'?

27 Which French dramatist defined business as 'other people's money'?

28 Who wrote: 'Proud people breed sad sorrows for themselves'?

29 Who said: 'No one can make you feel inferior without your consent'?

30 Which queen used the motto 'In my end is my beginning'?

31 Who described nationalism as 'the measles of the human race'?

32 Which Scottish poet wrote: 'A man's a man for a' that'?

33 Who coined the phrase 'How to win friends and influence people'?

34 Which comedian was famous for the line 'Another nice mess you've gotten me into'?

35 Which songwriter said that 'everything's coming up roses'?

36 What line, for which he was to become famous, did Johnny Weissmuller never utter whilst playing the part of Tarzan?

37 Where, according to the Duke of Wellington, was the battle of Waterloo won?

38 Who wrote: 'I sing the body electric'?

39 Which fictional character said: 'It's no good telling me there are bad aunts and good aunts. At core they are all alike. Sooner or later, out pops the cloven hoof'?

40 What is the shortest quotation for which Emile Zola was famous?

41 Who defined rock journalism as 'people who can't write, interviewing people who can't talk for people who can't read'?

42 Which character said: 'Everywhere I see bliss from which I alone am irrevocably excluded'?

43 Whose epitaph is this: 'Here lies one whose name was writ in water'?

44 Who wrote: 'I am the Love that dare not speak its name'?

45 Who wrote: 'Money doesn't talk, it swears'?

46 What were the last words of Isadora Duncan?

47 Who cried: *Sic semper tyrannis!* The South is avenged'?

48 Who asserted: 'Oh, East is East and West is West and never the twain shall meet'?

49 Who is reported as saying: 'The unexamined life is not worth living'?

50 What, according to Leon Trotsky, is the most unexpected of all things that happen to a man?

207

Popular Music and Musicals

Answers to this quiz are on page 254

Player 1	Player 2
12	20
33	24
07	03
46	45
01	28
21	02
23	25
04	32
35	39
14	50
31	08
48	17
11	40
27	43
15	29
06	41
10	30
47	34
26	16
38	05
36	49
13	09
19	18
42	37
44	22

01 With which song did Kate Bush become famous?

02 Who was the lead singer of The Doors?

03 What was the name of Paul McCartney's group after the break-up of the Beatles?

04 Who wrote the musical *Candide*?

05 Which song contains the words 'Behind the shelter in the middle of a roundabout the pretty nurse is selling poppies from a tray'?

06 What is the name of the song with which Abba won the Eurovision Song Contest?

07 Who wrote the piece 'In the Mood'?

08 Which original Queen album contains the song 'Bohemian Rhapsody'?

09 Who sang the title song to the film *Hello Dolly*?

10 Which ragtime song was used in the film *The Sting*?

11 Which song contains the words 'Take me on a trip upon your magic swirlin' ship, my senses have been stripped'?

12 On which original Dire Straits album is the song 'Walk of Life'?

13 From which musical comes the song 'Mr Mistoffelees'?

14 What was Madonna's first hit?

15 Who sang the title song to the film *What's New Pussycat*?

16 In which year did Elvis Presley die?

17 Who revived the Sonny & Cher song 'I Got You Babe' in 1986?

18 Who wrote the score to the musical *Evita*?

19 Who was the singer of the Eurythmics?

20 Which song contains the words 'Sitting on a sofa on a Sunday afternoon, going to the candidates' debate'?

21 Who wrote the song 'The Times They are a-Changin''?

22 What was the theme song to the film *Flashdance*?

23 In which musical can you find the song 'Food, Glorious Food'?

24 On which Fleetwood Mac album is the song 'Go Your Own Way'?

25 Who wrote the operetta *The Mikado*?

26 Who preceded Phil Collins as lead singer of Genesis?

27 What was the title of the first Beatles single?

28 Who wrote the score to the musical *Kiss Me Kate*?

29 Which song contains the words 'Beelzebub has a devil for a son'?

30 Who wrote the song 'This Land is Your Land'?

31 From which musical does the song 'There's no Business like Show Business' come from?

32 Who was the lead singer of The Police?

33 Who played the king in the film musical *The King and I*?

34 Who made the single 'Peggy Sue'?

35 Which was Bon Jovi's first top ten hit?

36 Who sang the theme song to the James Bond film *Goldfinger*?

37 For which type of music was Bob Marley famous?

38 Who made the album *Tubular Bells*?

39 Who made the recording 'Banana Boat Song'?

40 Who brought out the album *The Joshua Tree*?

41 Which song contains the words 'My father was a tailor, he sewed my new blue jeans'?

42 Who was the lead singer of T. Rex?

43 From which musical does the song 'All I Ask of You' come ?

44 Which Parisian singer was known for songs like 'Non, je ne regrette rien'?

45 Which was Elton John's first hit?

46 Who wrote the music to the film musical *Gigi*?

47 Which two singers had a massive hit in 1985 with the remake of 'Dancing in the Street'?

48 Through which film did Meat Loaf become a success?

49 Who is the singer of U2?

50 Who first performed the rock opera *Tommy*?

World Religions

TOUGH **TOUGH** **TOUGH**

Player 1	Player 2
12	20
33	24
07	03
46	45
01	28
21	02
23	25
04	32
35	39
14	50
31	08
48	17
11	40
27	43
15	29
06	41
10	30
47	34
26	16
38	05
36	49
13	09
19	18
42	37
44	22

210

01 What is the name of the classes and subclasses that constitute Hindu Society?

02 Who was the prophet of Islam?

03 Which book comprises all the teachings of Judaism?

04 What is the title given to Siddhartha Gautama?

05 Sikhism combines elements of which two major religions?

06 What are the three monotheistic world religions?

07 In the Roman Catholic Church, what do you call the partaking of wine and bread in remembrance of Jesus' last supper?

08 Which type of Christians accept the Bible as the sole source of information?

09 Which work is a compilation of Jewish oral law?

10 What is the name of the holy book of Islam?

11 In Judaism, which prayer would be recited by mourners after the death of a close relative?

12 What is the governing body of the Eastern Orthodox churches called?

13 Theravada is a school of which major religion?

14 Which religion was founded by the Bab?

15 In the Roman Catholic Church, by whom is High Mass celebrated?

16 What is the name given to the ninth month of the Muslim year?

17 Which former prince taught the doctrine that there is a path to the end of all suffering?

18 In the Eastern Orthodox and Roman Catholic Churches, who ranks just below the priest?

19 In Judaism, what is the Day of Atonement called?

20 How many times daily is a Muslim expected to pray?

21 What do you call a member of the Hindu priestly caste?

22 Which type of Buddhism teaches the state of sudden enlightenment, or satori?

23 Which event during the Middle Ages led to Christianity being split into numerous sects?

24 How many sacraments are there in the Orthodox church?

25 Who started the Methodist movement in the Christian Church?

26 What was the aim of the Ecumenical Movement?

27 Which place must each Muslim visit once in his life?

28 Which of the great gods of Hinduism has the function of a preserver?

29 Which Jewish festival marks the exodus of Jews from Egypt, led by Moses?

30 In Zen Buddhism, what is a koan?

31 What type of meat are Muslims not allowed to eat?

32 Which religion is based on the works of Lao-tzu?

33 What is the Roman Catholic Mass traditionally based on?

34 What are the names of the oldest sacred texts in Hinduism, which were written in Sanskrit and kept in four collections?

35 Which movement, established in the late 19th century, had the aim of establishing a Jewish State in Palestine?

36 In Islam, what does the Sunna consist of?

37 In the Christian Church, which period precedes Easter?

38 Does Easter fall on the same day in all the Christian Churches?

39 Which two branches of Protestantism developed from the Reformation?

40 What is the goal of Hinduism?

41 In Buddhism, what do you call the state of liberation from rebirth?

42 What do you call the branch of Islam that accepts the first four caliphs as rightful successors of Mohammed?

43 Where did Mohammed go after leaving Mecca?

44 What is the name given to Mohammed's departure from Mecca?

45 In the Christian Church, on which day is the departure of Jesus from Earth celebrated?

46 In Hinduism, which class is not recognized by the other four main castes because it is considered ritually unclean?

47 In the Christian Church, which festival commemorates the coming of the Holy Ghost to the disciples of Jesus?

48 What is the name of the Jewish festival that commemorates the revelation of the Law on Mount Sinai?

49 In the Christian Church, on which date is Epiphany observed?

50 Apart from Sunni, what are Muslims from the other main branch of Islam called?

Books

Answers to this quiz are on pages 254-255

TOUGH 🙁 **TOUGH**

Player 1	Player 2
12	20
33	24
07	03
46	45
01	28
21	02
23	25
04	32
35	39
14	50
31	08
48	17
11	40
27	43
15	29
06	41
10	30
47	34
26	16
38	05
36	49
13	09
19	18
42	37
44	22

212

01 Which 1939 novel is concerned with the economic and social plight of migrant farm workers in California?

02 Which writer invented Yoknapatawpha County?

03 Which English writer disguised his native Dorsetshire as 'Wessex'?

04 Beowulf slew Grendel but, or what, who slew Beowulf?

05 What was the name of the land of peace described in Pilgrim's Progress?

06 Robert MacGregor was the original name of which fictional hero?

07 Which Italian collection of 100 stories was set against the somber backdrop of the Black Death?

08 'I started out very quiet and I beat Mr Turgenev. Then I trained hard and I beat Mr de Maupassant. I've fought two draws with Mr Stendhal, and I think I had an edge in the last one. But nobody's going to get me in any ring with Mr Tolstoy unless I'm crazy or I keep getting better.' Who said that?

09 Which comic figure was created by Jaroslav Hašek?

10 Who wrote the novels *The Maltese Falcon* and *The Thin Man*?

11 Who created detective Philip Marlowe?

12 For what dramatic work is Jerome K. Jerome known?

13 In which story, by which author, does a man become a beetle?

14 Who wrote: 'The first breath of adultery is the freest; after it, constraints aping marriage develop'?

15 Who was the victim of Dr Svengali?

16 Who wrote *One Thousand and One Nights*?

17 Who wrote: 'I have hardly ever known a mathematician who was capable of reasoning'?

18 Which German writer spent 10 years as chief minister of state at Weimar?

19 Which 17th-century French playwright was famous for basing his work on classical themes?

20 Which great work of Japanese fiction was written by Murasaki Shikibu?

21 Which famous 'pillow book' was written by a lady-in-waiting to the late Japanese empress Sadako?

22 By what pen-name was Josef Korzeniowski better known?

23 Which story of Nero's Rome was written by a Polish author?

24 Who wrote *Dead Souls*?

25 Which was Dostoyevsky's last novel?

26 Who wrote *Les Fleurs du Mal*?

27 Which New Zealand writer is known for her detective stories?

28 Which Philip Roth novel takes a comic look at Jewish middle-class life?

29 Which fictional book had the words 'Don't Panic' on the cover?

30 In which period is Mary Renault's The Charioteers set?

31 Who wrote a collection of short stories entitled *The Dove's Nest*?

32 Which blind and deaf author was taught by Anne Sullivan?

33 Who wrote: 'Whipping and abuse are like laudanum: you have to double the dose as the sensibilities decline'?

34 What is the title of the Indian epic which tells the story of Rama?

35 Which Chinese story is often compared to the legend of Robin Hood?

36 What nationality was the detective Hercule Poirot?

37 *A Tale of the Riots of 'Eighty* is the subtitle of what famous book?

38 Which author travelled across the Atlantic Ocean in steerage and across the USA in an emigrant train to pursue Fanny Van de Graft Osbourne, a married woman 11 years his senior and mother of three?

39 'Kind man, brave man, wise soul, indomitable spirit of the indomitable Irishry.' Who was Sean O'Casey describing?

40 'The great majority of people in England and America are modest, decent and pure-minded and the amount of virgins in the world today is stupendous.' Which British author said that?

41 'Where there is no imagination there is no horror.' Who wrote this and in which novel?

42 Under which pen name did Arthur Sarsfield Ward write *Dr Fu Manchu*?

43 'When I think of this life I have led; the desolation of solitude it has been; the masoned, walled-town of a Captain's

exclusiveness, which admits but small entrance to any sympathy from the green country without. Oh, weariness! heaviness! Guinea-coast slavery of solitary command!' Which character said this, and in which novel?

44 'Going home must be like going to render an account.' Who wrote this, and in which novel?

45 Which of Jane Austen's novels were published posthumously?

46 Which name connects a Welsh pop singer with an 18th-century English novelist?

47 'You can always count on a murderer for a fancy prose style.' Who wrote this and in which novel?

48 Which film director wrote a book entitled *Getting Even*?

49 'Must we really see Chicago in order to be educated?' Who wrote this and in which book?

50 Which 19th-century American writer, famous for his works about Japanese life and culture, was allowed to become a Japanese citizen?

213

Botany

Answers to this quiz are on page 255

TOUGH TOUGH

	Player 1	Player 2
	12	20
	33	24
	07	03
	46	45
	01	28
	21	02
	23	25
	04	32
	35	39
	14	50
	31	08
	48	17
	11	40
	27	43
	15	29
	06	41
	10	30
	47	34
	26	16
	38	05
	36	49
	13	09
	19	18
	42	37
	44	22

01 Which common plant provided the poison that killed Socrates?

02 Which plant family do cow parsley, wild carrot and fennel belong?

03 What sort of plants are papavers?

04 Which plant is the source of the drug digitalis?

05 What do the following fungi have in common: (a) Amanita virosa, (b) Amanita phalloides, and (c) Cortinarius orellanus?

06 What is the common name for the fungus *Amanita muscaria*, and what was it used for in former times?

07 Which parasitic plant, once sacred to the Druids, is often found on apple trees?

08 From which part of the horseradish plant is a spicy sauce made?

09 Which poisonous substances would you find in Deadly Nightshade, Jimson Weed, and Greater Celandine?

10 What is the other common name for the herb rue?

11 From which plant is the liqueur Kummel derived?

12 By what common name is the condition urticaria known?

13 Which popular fruit is a member of the *Fragaria* family?

14 *Quercus robur* and *Quercus coccinea* are typical trees of their native lands. What are their common names and where do they grow?

15 What is the most unusual feature of the yew tree?

16 The tree *Araucaria araucana* has sharp, spiny leaves that would make it hard to climb. The common name of this tree suggests this feature. What is it?

17 What family of tress are known as Salix?

18 *Betula pendula* is well known for its light grey bark. What is it more commonly known as?

19 Which small evergreen tree, originating in the Far East, has become well known in the southern states of the US?

20 This tree comes from the south-eastern USA, grows up to 20m (60 ft), and has astringent fruit which are edible after exposure to autumn frost. What is it?

21 The bark of this tree, which bears a raspberry-like fruit, can be used to make cloth or paper. What is it?

22 Which tree provides an essential oil used in flavouring gin?

23 What is another name for the rowan tree?

24 On what part of a plant would you find stomata?

25 What is the name of the long, pollen-bearing stalk in the middle of a flower?

26 What is an inflorescence?

27 What is the name of the sticky part of the female stalk that receives pollen?

28 What is the name of the sweet, sugary liquid made inside a flower?

29 Why is it important for flowers to attract passing insects?

30 What happens if you kick a puffball fungus?

31 Litmus, the substance used to test for acidity or alkalinity, is produced from what sort of plant?

32 What man-made hazard is especially dangerous to lichen?

33 What is the most obvious feature of succulent plants?

34 What do so-called pitcher plants live on?

35 Which gas is produced during photosynthesis?

36 Are fungi capable of photosynthesis?

37 What is the venomous name sometimes given to Forget-me-not?

38 How are the seeds of the sycamore tree distributed?

39 What highly prized edible substance is produced from crocuses?

40 What is the function of chloroplast cells?

41 Salep, used as food and medicine, is made from the dried roots of which plant?

42 When plants are wounded they respond by producing a hormone called traumatin. What is its function?

43 What is the technical name for movement of part of a plant in response to an outside cause?

44 What is the word to describe how plants turn white through lack of light?

45 What is meant by a phototropic reaction in a plant?

46 What is strange about the Sensitive Plant (*Mimosa pudica*)?

47 What agricultural use has been found for kelp seaweeds?

48 What do saprophytic fungi live on?

49 Which insectivorous plant has a name suggesting unearthly origins?

50 Which are the commonest plants in the world?

215

Sport & Games

Answers to this quiz are on page 255

TOUGH

TOUGH

TOUGH

Player 1	Player 2
12	20
33	24
07	03
46	45
01	28
21	02
23	25
04	32
35	39
14	50
31	08
48	17
11	40
27	43
15	29
06	41
10	30
47	34
26	16
38	05
36	49
13	09
19	18
42	37
44	22

01 Name the Japanese board game played with black and white 'stones'?

02 In card games, what is the meaning of 'finesse'?

03 What is shogi?

04 Which Greek games were held in honor of the god Apollo?

05 What, in the context of games, is the meaning of the word 'rubber'?

06 What is Hoyle?

07 What is bezique?

08 What is hare and hounds?

09 What is fan tan?

10 What is shuffleboard?

11 In which game would you 'castle'?

12 What is the object of the game called knights?

13 What popular children's prank was called Knock Down Ginger?

14 With which festival do you associate the custom of Trick or Treat?

15 Who won the 1996 Wimbledon's men's singles tennis championship?

16 In which sporting event would a competitor wear the maillot jaune?

17 With which sport do you associate the expression 'slam dunk'?

18 How many men form a team in Australian football?

19 What is the difference between fives and squash?

20 What is the Irish game that vaguely resembles hockey?

21 In which country is golf thought to have originated?

22 For what sporting achievement is James Naismith remembered?

23 Where did chess originate?

24 How do you keep the score in a game of cribbage?

25 In which game might you attempt a carom?

26 The game of quoits is traditionally, though not necessarily, associated with a method of travel. What is it?

27 The Chinese name for table tennis is 'ping pong'. True or false?

28 In poker which of these hands is worth the most: (a) royal flush, (b) full house, or (c) four of a kind?

29 In which country did canasta originate?

30 In which country did badminton originate?

31 Which children's game uses a whip?

32 Which toy has Satanic connections?

33 Which sport uses a jack?

34 By what other name is the game of petanque known?

35 What form of roulette can have fatal consequences?

36 Which game, played on a chess board, goes by different names in the UK and the USA?

37 What is jokari?

38 What is a slalom?

39 With which sport do you associate the Cresta Run?

40 Which of these is not a martial art: (a) Tae Kwon Do, (b) Wing Chun, or (c) Basho?

41 Which country won the Euro 96 soccer competition?

42 The Japanese play a gambling game on a vertical pinball machine. What is its name?

43 In which sport would you find gutta percha used?

44 How do you croquet an opponent's ball?

45 What is a roquet shot?

46 What did the word croquet originally mean?

47 Which game is divided into 'chukkers'?

48 What is buzkashi?

49 The polka used to be a very popular dance. What does the name mean?

50 Edson Arantes do Nascimento was a famous Brazilian football player. By what name was he better known?

Popular Music & Musicals

Answers to this quiz are on pages 255-256

TOUGH TOUGH

	Player 1	Player 2
	12	20
	33	24
	07	03
	46	45
	01	28
	21	02
	23	25
	04	32
	35	39
	14	50
	31	08
	48	17
	11	40
	27	43
	15	29
	06	41
	10	30
	47	34
	26	16
	38	05
	36	49
	13	09
	19	18
	42	37
	44	22

01 Who joined Pink Floyd in 1968 after Roger Barrett left the group?

02 Who wrote the score to the musical *Guys and Dolls*?

03 Which jazz musician brought out the album *Touchstone*?

04 Who composed the soundtrack for the film *One Trick Pony*?

05 Which group did Pete Seeger and Lee Hays form in 1948?

06 Who originally recorded the Simply Red hit 'If You Don't Know Me by Now' in 1972?

07 On which Simple Minds album is the song 'The Belfast Child'?

08 Which musical contains the song 'You'll Never Walk Alone'?

09 Which group recorded the album *Commoner's Crown*?

10 Which singer was born Gordon Matthew Sumner?

11 Who wrote the theme to the film *Dangerous Liaisons*?

12 Which Spanish opera star did Freddie Mercury sing duets with?

13 Who wrote the USA for Africa song 'We Are the World'?

14 Who wrote the song 'I Get a Kick out of You'?

15 Which group released the album *Communiqué*?

16 Which instrument does Joe Henderson play?

17 Which singer released a cover version of the old Platters song 'Smoke Gets in Your Eyes' in 1974?

18 Which musical does the song 'Life Upon the Wicked Stage' come from?

19 Paul McCartney released an arrangement of which nursery rhyme in 1972?

20 With which song did Steve Miller have a hit in 1982?

21 Who wrote the piece 'A Harlem Symphony'?

22 On which John Lennon album is the song 'Number Nine Dream'?

23 Who sang the theme tune to the film *Endless Love*?

24 Who wrote the Janis Joplin hit 'Me and Bobby McGee'?

25 Which musical does the song 'I Don't Know How to Love Him' come from?

26 Which singer released the album *Spanish Train and Other Stories*?

27 What was the name of the musician, known for his electronic experiments, who played with Roxy Music from 1971 to 1973?

28 On which Foreigner album is the song 'Hot Blooded'?

29 Which teen band did Derek Longmuir belong to?

30 Which jazz musician brought out the album *Perfect Machine*?

31 Which was the name of Elvis Costello's backing group, formed in the late '70s?

32 In 1988 Phil Collins had a hit with 'Groovy Kind of Love'. Who recorded this song originally?

33 Which Belgian jazz guitarist, born in 1910, originated from a gypsy family?

34 Which Chubby Checker hit was re-released in 1975?

35 Which instrument does Miles Davis play?

36 Who recorded the theme song of the James Bond film *The Living Daylights*?

37 Which group backed Tony Sheridan in his 1961 recording of 'My Bonnie Lies over the Ocean'?

38 Who composed the song 'Strangers in the Night'?

39 From which musical does the song 'We Said We Wouldn't Look Back' come?

40 Which was Hawkwind's only hit?

41 Chet Atkins was responsible for creating which style of music?

42 Which singer recorded the double-album *Songs in the Key of Life*?

43 Which jazz musician wrote the song 'Crawlin' Kingsnake'?

44 The Paul McCartney song 'We All Stand Together' appeared on the soundtrack of which cartoon film?

45 Which guitarist replaced Eric Clapton in the Yardbirds in 1965?

46 Who wrote the theme tune for the film *Grease*?

47 'I'll Never Fall in Love Again' is a song from which musical?

48 In which film did Bing Crosby introduce his song 'White Christmas'?

49 Which group recorded the album *Colour by Numbers*?

50 Who sang the theme tune to the film *Arthur*?

219

? Pot Luck

Answers to this quiz are on page 256

TOUGH :(**TOUGH**

Player 1	Player 2
12	20
33	24
07	03
46	45
01	28
21	02
23	25
04	32
35	39
14	50
31	08
48	17
11	40
27	43
15	29
06	41
10	30
47	34
26	16
38	05
36	49
13	09
19	18
42	37
44	22

01 What does the Latin tag *Nil desperandum* mean?

02 In the city name Washington DC, what do the letters DC stand for?

03 Which of the tropics is north of the equator?

04 In which direction do tornadoes usually spin in the northern hemisphere?

05 Only two flowering plants grow in Antarctica. One is a relative of the carnation, what is the other?

06 How much of the Earth's ice is found in Antarctica?

07 Where is the deepest point in the oceans?

08 In AD 582 Paris experienced a shower of what was thought to be blood. What was it?

09 There is a fungus that can use jet fuel as a source of food. True or false?

10 What is the definition of the 'minimum lethal dose' of a toxin?

11 What is hypermertropia?

12 Why is a wound in your tongue far more painful than a wound of the same size on your back?

13 What percentage of the body's energy is consumed by the brain?

14 A British scientist once successfully used Coca Cola as a replacement for oil in a car. True or false?

15 When did Native Americans first get the vote?

16 Which was the first country to give the vote to women?

17 By what title was Augustina Domonech better known?

18 Which Irish adventurer tried to steal the British crown jewels?

19 What is alliteration?

20 What is the bony substance in a tooth just beneath the enamel?

21 What is a lectern?

22 What is the oldest alloy?

23 Why does a helium balloon rise in air?

24 What is a molecule?

25 Why can there never be a perfect vacuum?

26 Why is carbon monoxide so dangerous?

27 What is a 'mother lode'?

28 What is a saskatoon?

29 What is pemmican?

30 By what other name is the kinkajou known?

31 By what nickname is the American Stars and Stripes flag often known?

32 Which English leader's body was exhumed and hanged after his death?

33 What is the name of the race of dwarfs whose magic ring was stolen from them by Siegfried?

34 In the Nibelungen, which queen of Iceland was defeated by Siegfried?

35 What is the name for a Russian carriage drawn by three horses abreast?

36 What was a charabanc?

37 What was a travois?

38 'He was a Jeanne d'Arc, a saint. He was a martyr. Like many martyrs, he held extreme views.' Who was Ezra Pound describing?

39 St. George survived the dragon but, according to tradition, what fate eventually befell him?

40 Where did Albert Schweitzer establish his hospital?

41 Who won the Nobel Prize for Peace in 1989?

42 What is an andiron?

43 What is a trephine?

44 Where would you find the stratosphere?

45 What is a galley proof?

46 What, in railway terms, is a caboose?

47 Who was the founder of Presbyterianism?

48 For what is Matthew Vassar famous?

49 Giuseppi Garibaldi lived in the USA before becoming an Italian hero. What trade did he follow?

50 Who wrote the book *Death in Venice*?

Gotcha!

Answers to this quiz are on page 256

TOUGH TOUGH TOUGH

	Player 1	Player 2
	12	20
	33	24
	07	03
	46	45
	01	28
	21	02
	23	25
	04	32
	35	39
	14	50
	31	08
	48	17
	11	40
	27	43
	15	29
	06	41
	10	30
	47	34
	26	16
	38	05
	36	49
	13	09
	19	18
	42	37
	44	22

222

01 In the Bible, who danced for the head of John the Baptist?

02 What do Olga Korbut, John Keats, and Queen Victoria have in common?

03 What is odd about the love life of the earthworm?

04 Iron particles found on the Moon and brought back to Earth exhibited a strange characteristic. What was it?

05 How many people died during the construction of the Panama Canal?

06 What interesting feature was to be found in the trial of Thomas à Becket?

07 What were the Rosenbergs, the infamous Soviet spies, doing when arrested by the FBI?

08 The French king Charles VII reopened the case of a woman 24 years after her execution and found that there had been an atrocious miscarriage of justice. Who was the victim?

09 By what nickname was Albert de Salvo better known?

10 Where would you find Fairyland, complete with Cinderella Drive, Glass Slipper Trail, and Wendy Lane?

11 In the event of nuclear attack, which would be the safest state in the USA?

12 Had she lived, what age would Marylin Monroe have been in 1996?

13 According to the Bible, David killed Goliath. However, another lesser known reference gives victory to someone else. Who was it?

14 Under what strange circumstances was Charlie Chaplin kidnapped?

15 The Chinese poet Li Po died while attempting to bestow a kiss. Who was the recipient?

16 What did Daniel Boone, Mark Twain, and Alfred Nobel have in common?

17 Wallace Hume Carothers killed himself in 1937 because he thought he was a failure. Yet his major invention is still with us. What is it?

18 What do Christopher Marlowe, Charles Darwin, and Joseph Stalin have in common?

19 What connects Adam, Isaac Newton, and William Tell?

20 What did Charles de Gaulle, Sir Francis Bacon, and Teddy Roosevelt have in common?

21 In 1911 three men were hanged in London for the murder of Sir Edmund Berry at Greenberry Hill. What was odd about their names?

22 What sporting achievement have Paul Robeson, Erskine Caldwell, and Kris Kristofferson in common?

23 On average, how often during his life did Mozart write a new piece of music?

24 When General Napier captured Sind in 1843 he sent the Foreign Office a one-word telegram. What was the word and what did it mean?

25 Which actor has been portrayed on screen most times by other actors?

26 In which movie part did Tamara de Treaux achieve fleeting fame?

27 what do the writers Gertrude Stein, e e cummings, and Jerzy Adrezejewski have in common?

28 What did P.T. Barnum, Mark Twain, and Walt Disney have in common?

29 What do Maria Callas, Jacqueline Kennedy, and Eva Peron have in common?

30 According to the Bible, what do Lot and his daughters, Abraham and Sarah, and Amon and Tamar have in common?

31 What novel event took place between Indian film actors Shooshi Kapoor and Zeenat Aman?

32 W.H. Auden, Tchaikovsky, and Oscar Wilde were all gay. What else did they have in common?

33 What have the books *Dune*, *Lorna Doone*, and *Dubliners* in common?

34 What do Sarah Bernhardt, Winston Churchill, and Jean Harlow have in common?

35 What was a parasang?

36 What would you do with a roquelaure?

37 What would you do with a reguerdon?

38 What do you call a liquor vessel equivalent to two jeroboams?

39 Daffy Duck was famous for the expression, 'Sufferin' succotash!' What is succotash?

40 What would you do with a squail?

41 What is the difference between 'continual' and 'continuous'?

42 What did Juliet (of Romeo and Juliet) have in common with Pocahontas?

43 What does Tarzan have in common with the FBI?

44 What do Leonardo da Vinci, Charlie Chaplin, and Benjamin Franklin have in common?

45 Which daring feat was performed by Bobby Leach, Jean Lussier, and William Fitzgerald?

46 What was a bellibone?

47 What do the words aspirirn, corn flakes, and trampoline have in common?

48 What have Samuel Johnson, Colette, and Edgar Allan Poe in common?

49 What is hyperalgesia?

50 What is oroide?

Answers

EASY

EASY

History (8-9)

1 Six.
2 George Washington.
3 (b) Poland.
4 Joan of Arc.
5 (a) Egypt.
6 The ship struck an iceberg.
7 Napoleon.
8 Horatio Nelson.
9 General Francisco Franco.
10 Admiral Turpitz
11 Martin Luther King, Jr.
12 The Israeli army
13 Czars.
14 (b) Franklin D Roosevelt.
15 (a) Elizabeth I.
16 India.
17 (a) World War I.
18 Abraham Lincoln.
19 Adolf Hitler.
20 Judge Jeffries.
21 (c) Peru.
22 (a) Battle of the Little Bighorn.
23 (c) Charles Lindbergh.
24 The Great Fire of London.
25 Berlin.
26 (b) Brutus.
27 (c) Sarajevo.
28 (b) Wars of the Roses.
29 The Red Baron.
30 His invention of the rigid airship.
31 (a) Vikings.
32 Gold.
33 (a) 1776.
34 (c) the Byzantine Empire.
35 England and France.
36 (b) Virginia, in Jamestown.
37 (c) Dunkirk.
38 England.
39 (b) World War I.
40 Spanish military leaders conquering the New World.
41 Rasputin.
42 The Wall Street Crash.
43 The Italian Fascists in the 1920s and 1930s.
44 Al Capone.
45 (a) Treaty of Versailles.

46 Samurai.
47 It was the site of the largest concentration camp.
48 (b) Tutankhamen.
49 World War I.
50 Normandy.

Pot Luck (10-11)

1 The Plough.
2 Maid Marian.
3 King Arthur.
4 1,000.
5 Red and blue.
6 It comes from the north.
7 Coffee.
8 Sweden
9 (b) Apache.
10 Islam.
11 Paris.
12 c) mineral
13 Flock together.
14 Fish and sometimes frogs.
15 A revolver.
16 Badger hunting.
17 The Sundance Kid.
18 Armed robbery.
19 Jupiter.
20 A million.
21 The equator.
22 Peter Pan.
23 The Bible.
24 William Shakespeare.
25 Wind speed.
26 Captain Bligh.
27 They were detectives.
28 Russia.
29 Burma
30 Snoopy.
31 The British Prime Minister.
32 The President of the USA.
33 A World War II fighter plane.
34 Easter.
35 The cat.
36 Pulling sleds.
37 Deer.
38 Shark.
39 *A Christmas Carol*.
40 Egg plant.
41 Yes – when cooked they are considered

a delicacy.
42 They wet their beds.
43 Davy Crockett.
44 Dick Turpin.
45 The pyramids.
46 An Inuit.
47 Wood.
48 Melted sand.
49 It is the bell found in the clock tower of the Palace of Westminster in London, although the name is often used to refer to the whole tower.
50 Hands.

The Spectrum (12-13)

1 Truce or surrender.
2 Red.
3 Black and white in patches.
4 Blue.
5 Yellow.
6 Red, orange, yellow, green, blue, indigo, violet.
7 Infra–red and ultra–violet.
8 Bluish–violet.
9 Green.
10 They are all red, white, and blue.
11 Black.
12 Blue.
13 A red sky.
14 A blue dye.
15 Yellow.
16 Copper.
17 Green.
18 A yellow one.
19 Cowardice.
20 Bad weather.
21 White water.
22 The silver birch.
23 Pink.
24 The USA.
25 A white one.
26 Yellow.
27 A polar bear.
28 Scarlett O'Hara.
29 (a) white.
30 Gold.
31 Purple.
32 Silver.
33 A red cross on a white ground.

34 Black.
35 Silver.
36 A black one.
37 Green, white, and orange.
38 Red.
39 Blue and grey.
40 Blue.
41 China.
42 Red coats.
43 Khaki.
44 Greenwich.
45 The Red Army.
46 A red giant.
47 The silver screen.
48 Tartan.
49 Yellow.
50 Orange.

Transport (14-15)

1 A unicycle.
2 A tandem.
3 An omnibus.
4 A hovercraft.
5 A boat with two hulls.
6 By sail.
7 Trains.
8 As the last car.
9 Steam, diesel, and electricity.
10 A single-passenger electric car.
11 The camel.
12 Gears.
13 Roller blades.
14 A caravan.
15 One powered by three banks of oars.
16 Covered wagons.
17 Full speed ahead.
18 Stop doing it.
19 The paddle steamer.
20 On ships, using a plumb line to check the depth of water under the ship was regarded as an easy job.
21 Because it had to make its journey in stages, stopping frequently for fresh horses.
22 A type of horse-drawn carriage.
23 Long ships.
24 (a) Mercedes.
25 A surrey was a horse-drawn pleasure carriage with two or four seats.
26 The passenger seat.
27 Motorcycles.
28 (c) BMW.
29 Motor racing.
30 A mountain bike.
31 A covered wagon.
32 A rigid airship.
33 A steam train.
34 It was a ghost ship.
35 The crew disappeared without trace.
36 Amtrak.
37 A portable enclosed chair for one person, having poles in the front and rear, and carried by two other people.
38 To provide a swift transcontinental express coach service.
39 An open, flat-bottomed boat with squared

ends, propelled by a long pole and used in shallow waters.
40 An early bicycle with one large and one small wheel.
41 Bicycle moto-cross.
42 A moped.
43 A trick performed while riding a bicycle or motorcycle which involves balancing the vehicle on its rear wheel.
44 A submarine.
45 It can take off vertically.
46 A ferry.
47 A shuttle.
48 The Model T Ford.
49 Black.
50 It burst into flames at its moorings.

Pot Luck (16-17)

1 Diamond.
2 b) vegetable
3 A small, round boat for one occupant.
4 93,000,000.
5 Deciduous.
6 Atlantis.
7 The Khmer Republic.
8 He flew too near the sun and the wax of his artificial wings melted, causing him to fall to his death.
9 Brazil.
10 (c) tigers.
11 Matthew, Mark, Luke, John.
12 A Buddhist temple
13 Stratford on Avon.
14 William Tell.
15 Coniferous.
16 Pinnochio's.
17 The yellow brick road.
18 Jonah.
19 Oliver Twist.
20 Rome.
21 It can turn it completely round and look backwards.
22 Marsupials.
23 Openwork fabric made by plaiting, knotting, looping or twisting threads.
24 James Bond.
25 Hibernation.
26 Dr Watson.
27 The Red Baron.
28 Passion fruit, orange, and guava.
29 The little mermaid.
30 Oxygen and hydrogen.
31 Oxygen.
32 At night.
33 The centaur.
34 The Minotaur.
35 The Greeks.
36 Africa.
37 Walkabout.
38 Paris.
39 The Netherlands.
40 True.
41 Beer.
42 Wine.
43 December 21.
44 Cancer and Capricorn.

45 Basketball.
46 He is the emperor.
47 (a) Ikebana: it is a Japanese style of flower-arranging.
48 (b) Paparazzi: they are newspaper photographers.
49 Yes.
50 144.

Films (18-19)

1 101.
2 Jafar.
3 *Tramp.*
4 Julia Roberts.
5 Dustin Hoffman.
6 A car.
7 *Mary Poppins.*
8 *The Lion King.*
9 Scar.
10 Pumbaa and Timon.
11 Jasmine.
12 Cruella de Ville.
13 Triton.
14 Sebastian.
15 Ursula.
16 Fred.
17 Dede.
18 Dumbo.
19 He can use them as wings.
20 Toto.
21 Judy Garland.
22 'Over the Rainbow'.
23 Fat Sam and Dandy Dan.
24 Blousey Brown.
25 Kevin.
26 Paris.
27 The phones have been knocked out by a storm.
28 Harry and Marv.
29 *Lost in New York.*
30 Florida.
31 He uses his dad's credit card.
32 A dog.
33 A St Bernard.
34 He is a vet.
35 Vada.
36 He is a funeral director.
37 Pennsylvania.
38 Denmark.
39 Magic.
40 By delivering groceries.
41 Huey, Dewey, and Louis.
42 Tchaikovsky, Chubby, Dolly, and Mo.
43 Missy.
44 Regina.
45 A novice nun.
46 Von Trapp.
47 The Flintstones.
48 He asks them nicely to do what he wants.
49 Kids.
50 *The Never-ending Story.*

Odd One (20-21)

1 (c) crow: all the others are birds of prey.

2 (d) *Back to the Future*: all the others are James Bond films.

3 (a) Chinese, which is not based on an alphabet.

4 (d) Princess Diana: all the others have been political leaders of their countries.

5 (c) fig: all the others are dried grapes.

6 (a) salamander: all the others are crustaceans.

7 (c) Russia: the population of the other countries is predominantly Chinese.

8 (a) cypress: it is coniferous, whereas all the other trees are deciduous.

9 (c) Leonard Bernstein: all the others are authors.

10 (b) moped: none of the others is motorized.

11 (a) trumpet: all the others are woodwind instruments.

12 (d) film cartridge: all the others can reproduce sound.

13 (a) cuckoo: all the others are flightless birds.

14 (b) sarong: all the others are types of footwear.

15 (d) Alexander the Great: all the others were Roman emperors.

16 (a) water lily: it is a plant, whereas all the others are animals.

17 (d) Italy: all the others are groups of countries.

18 (c) harp: all the other instruments have keyboards.

19 (b) symphony: all the others are types of dance.

20 (a) marmoset: it is a monkey, whereas the others are apes.

21 (c) Westminster Abbey: all the others are situated in the USA.

22 (d) pear: all the others are types of plum.

23 (d) Jean Baptiste Molière: he was a playwright, whereas all the others were composers.

24 (b) geologist: all the others study living things.

25 (a) 11: it is the only prime number.

26 (a) milk: it is derived from animals, whereas the others are derived from plants.

27 (c) dolphin: it is a mammal.

28 (d) *The Magic Flute*: it is an opera, whereas all the others are musicals.

29 (c) bronchitis: all the others are skin diseases.

30 (d) cannelloni: it is a pasta dish – the others are made with rice.

31 (c) John F. Kennedy: all the others were Russians.

32 (b) mole: all the others are nocturnal.

33 (c) cotton: all the others are derived from animals.

34 (b) concerto: all the others contain singing.

35 (a) rain gauge: all the others are devices for measuring time.

36 (c) auricle: it is a part of the ear – all the others are part of the eye.

37 (d) cantata: all the others are singing voices.

38 (d) omelette: all the others contain bread or pastry.

39 (a) Isaac Newton: all the others were writers.

40 (a) J. R. R. Tolkien: all the others were writers of crime stories.

41 (d) banana: all the other fruit have stones.

42 (b) A Midsummer Night's Dream: it is a play, whereas all the others are operas.

43 (b) pelvis: all the others are part of the leg.

44 (a) gaiter: all the others are types of headgear.

45 (c) risotto: all the others are made with egg.

46 (b) Cuba: all the others are part of the USA.

47 (d) cavalry: all the others are connected with the navy.

48 (c) autogyro: all the others are types of boat.

49 (b) trachea: all the others are types of tooth.

50 (a) gruyère: it is a type of cheese, whereas all the others are sausages.

Pot Luck (22-23)

1 Ladislao Biro.
2 No, it's an ape.
3 (a) marble.
4 The ancient Egyptians.
5 (c) Thailand.
6 France.
7 Electricity.
8 Fossilized wood.
9 Apple.
10 The cuckoo.
11 Penicillin.
12 Hungary
13 (b) boa constrictor.
14 Mistletoe.
15 A person.
16 It was a sacred site and also acted as a calendar.
17 Thailand
18 Eight minutes.
19 (c) Spanish.
20 A meteor remains in space, whereas a meteorite survives contact with our atmosphere and strikes the ground.
21 A shuttlecock.
22 A googol.
23 Lightning.
24 Jealousy.
25 Its sweet smell.
26 True.
27 Cain and Abel.
28 King Arthur.
29 A corpse that has been reanimated by sorcery.
30 Germany.
31 Indiana Jones.
32 Greek.

33 Joan of Arc.
34 (a) Hebrew.
35 (b) Haneda.
36 The VW Beetle.
37 A tusk.
38 Tinkerbell.
39 The Republicans and the Democrats.
40 Gold.
41 A mound containing relics
42 Salt water.
43 It's false, though commonly believed.
44 He was the messenger of the gods.
45 Valhalla.
46 A one-humped camel.
47 No, but it has poor sight.
48 Soak it in vinegar to soften the shell.
49 Julius Caesar.
50 Twenty.

People (24-25)

1 Merlin.
2 Friar Tuck.
3 Peter Pan.
4 Christopher Robin.
5 George Washington.
6 Hercules.
7 The Statue of Liberty.
8 Mona Lisa.
9 Canute.
10 Charles I.
11 Hope and Charity.
12 Bilbo Baggins.
13 Adolph Hitler.
14 Doc Holliday.
15 King John.
16 Willy Wonka.
17 Fidel Castro.
18 Yuri Gagarin.
19 Neil Armstrong.
20 Richard I.
21 He was a highwayman.
22 Abel.
23 Cleopatra.
24 Zeus.
25 Scheherezade.
26 Sinbad.
27 Murdering his wife.
28 Saddam Hussein.
29 President Lincoln.
30 Rhett Butler in *Gone With the Wind*.
31 Mao Zedong.
32 Napoleon Bonaparte.
33 Oedipus.
34 She was beheaded.
35 Richard III.
36 Crookback Dick.
37 Tom Sawyer.
38 German
39 An American frontier character
40 Tennis
41 The Mexican Revolution
42 St George.
43 John F. Kennedy.
44 George Eastman.
45 Little Red Riding Hood.
46 They were giants.

47 King Arthur's.
48 Dorothy.
49 Esau.
50 Julius Caesar.

The Earth (26-27)

1 The crust.
2 Geology.
3 Fossils.
4 Geography.
5 No.
6 The core.
7 70%
8 Antarctica.
9 A volcano.
10 A crater.
11 A hole in the Earth's crust spouting fountains of boiling water.
12 An eruption.
13 The magnitude of an earthquake.
14 Tsunami.
15 A mountain.
16 Lines of latitude.
17 Lines of longitude.
18 Erosion.
19 Scree.
20 Up.
21 A swallow-hole.
22 The covering of the land by ice during an ice age.
23 A large 'river' of slowly moving ice.
24 A cold period in the Earth's history when the ice sheets are much larger than today.
25 A fjord.
26 A pile of debris left by moving ice.
27 Permanently frozen ground.
28 A narrow neck of land projecting into the sea.
29 A beach.
30 It has no tides.
31 A coral reef.
32 An island.
33 Tide.
34 An especially high or low tide.
35 The atmosphere.
36 Nitrogen.
37 The trapping of heat by gases in the atmosphere.
38 An instrument for measuring atmospheric pressure.
39 An instrument for measuring temperature.
40 Wind.
41 Pressure.
42 Fog (or mist).
43 The amount of water vapor in the air.
44 Hurricane.
45 No.
46 A dark, liquid fossil fuel formed from tiny plants and animals.
47 A solid fossil fuel made from the remains of plants.
48 Methane.
49 Green.
50 Gold, silver, and platinum.

Pot Luck (28-29)

1 Exactly the same amount.
2 Crab.
3 (c) Ceres.
4 Albino.
5 A dice game.
6 (d) patience.
7 The water lily.
8 (b) a painter.
9 (a) an opera.
10 The jumbo jet.
11 (b) Boeing.
12 Sails.
13 (c) Elvis Presley.
14 The north wind.
15 Switzerland.
16 Washington DC.
17 (c) Sweden.
18 Basketball.
19 The are both called kids.
20 Cygnets.
21 Goslings.
22 An artificial language.
23 The Quakers.
24 Lemmings.
25 (b) rhubarb.
26 True.
27 (c) a jellyfish.
28 (d) Scotland.
29 A fish.
30 Florida.
31 Peking.
32 (c) Korea.
33 The Pope.
34 In the roof.
35 A deep, narrow valley or gorge worn by running water.
36 Because light travels in straight lines.
37 Evens.
38 Egypt.
39 Seventy.
40 A semi-precious stone.
41 An allergic reaction to pollen.
42 China.
43 Five loaves and three fish.
44 Spain.
45 A horse.
46 Hieroglyphs.
47 A shade of blue.
48 A lucky accident.
49 Astrology is an attempt to predict events by observation of the stars. Astronomy is the scientific observation of all cosmic phenomena.
50 The Great Bear.

Synonyms (30-31)

1 (a) animated.
2 (b) gloomy.
3 (a) make.
4 (b) toil.
5 (a) keen.
6 (c) brotherly.
7 (b) bizarre.

8 (b) generous.
9 (a) memento.
10 (b) flawless.
11 (a) witty.
12 (b) understandable.
13 (b) mysterious.
14 (a) dark.
15 (a) handy.
16 (b) spoken.
17 (a) several.
18 (c) strong.
19 (a) delicate.
20 (b) contented.
21 (b) caught.
22 (b) improbable.
23 (a) bravery.
24 (b) require.
25 (a) change.
26 (b) crack.
27 (c) stroke.
28 (a) ask.
29 (c) part.
30 (b) make.
31 (b) honorable.
32 (a) arrange.
33 (c) continual.
34 (a) amount.
35 (c) inquiry.
36 (a) specimen.
37 (b) disloyalty.
38 (c) thankless.
39 (a) beat.
40 (b) crave.
41 (a) perfect.
42 (b) beastly.
43 (a) condense.
44 (b) hang.
45 (b) acquire.
46 (c) often.
47 (b) wrestle.
48 (a) listen.
49 (a) envy.
50 (a) depart.

Nature (32-33)

1 Moths move around at night, have hair-like or feathery antennae, stout bodies, and a frenulum that holds the front and back wings together.
2 Toads are more terrestrial and have a broader body and rougher, drier skin.
3 The cat family.
4 The dog.
5 In the Antarctic.
6 In the Arctic.
7 The potato.
8 Crows.
9 The Great White.
10 The science of classification.
11 Frog spawn is laid in a jelly-like mass, toad spawn is laid in strips like tape.
12 The cuckoo.
13 An Australian wild dog.
14 A domestic animal that has returned to the wild.
15 The emu.

16 The cat.
17 No. They are usually warning other birds to keep out of their territory or trying to attract a mate.
18 No. Fish extract oxygen from the water by the use of gills.
19 Yes, but only over short distances. The horse is fastest over long distances but, surprisingly, humans are faster over very long distances.
20 No. It's an animal.
21 Warm blooded.
22 Yes. Some species can, for example, use a thorn to pick grubs out of cracks.
23 They are arachnids.
24 They are crustaceans.
25 To warn other creatures to keep away.
26 The female.
27 A fish
28 The female.
29 Rats and the fleas which lived on them.
30 A fruit.
31 Flying south for the winter.
32 No. Seagulls have become skilled scavengers and many live inland almost permanently.
33 No. Its brain is actually very small.
34 The skunk.
35 Wolverine
36 They are all types of miniature orange.
37 A crane fly.
38 The poppy.
39 A fungus that grows symbiotically with algae.
40 The hyena.
41 In the USA or China.
42 Mainly, but they eat meat when they can get it.
43 A cygnet.
44 An elver.
45 Scarab
46 Yes.
47 Daisy.
48 Heather.
49 A small freshwater fish with spines along its back.
50 Porcupine fish.

Pot Luck (34-35)

1 Disney.
2 The Jackson Five.
3 Poland.
4 The one nearest the kerb.
5 Nelson Mandela.
6 The USA.
7 Cancer.
8 Telling fortunes.
9 Alpha.
10 Oysters.
11 Yes – it's difficult but possible.
12 The Nazis.
13 They were all concentration camps.
14 The FBI.
15 The CIA.
16 Great Britain.
17 Divine healing.

18 Cambodia.
19 Tennis.
20 Space travel.
21 France.
22 A circle of grass that grows longer than the surrounding grass.
23 Greece.
24 Greece and Turkey.
25 Approximately two thirds.
26 Sleeping for 20 years.
27 Japan.
28 Gladiators.
29 A lamp post.
30 Six.
31 John-Boy.
32 She is a lawyer.
33 Genesis.
34 Geranium. All the others are girls' names.
35 It is said that they had toes instead of hooves.
36 They were born from a mother who died in childbirth.
37 Native Americans.
38 Something of no use.
39 A drey.
40 An Inuit.
41 To keep them dry in the rainy season.
42 The Baltic States.
43 In Sherwood Forest.
44 The west coast.
45 A mouth organ.
46 Alexander.
47 By how many concentric rings it has.
48 A World-Wide Web site address (URL stands for Unique Resource Locator).
49 Zimbabwe.
50 Demons.

Opposites (36-37)

1 (c) disinterested.
2 (a) thankless.
3 (a) mean.
4 (b) free.
5 (b) superficial.
6 (c) industrious.
7 (a) imaginary.
8 (b) relaxed.
9 (a) extant.
10 (c) decrease.
11 (c) earnest.
12 (c) partial.
13 (b) delectation.
14 (b) vacuous.
15 (c) fascinating.
16 (a) barren.
17 (b) purchase.
18 (b) listless.
19 (b) advance.
20 (a) dull.
21 b) noisy
22 (c) cheerful.
23 c) disperse.
24 (b) clever.
25 a) promote
26 (c) sour.

27 (b) free.
28 (c) descend.
29 b) civilized
30 a) esteem
31 b) discreate
32 (b) pessimistic.
33 b) antagonist
34 a) dissonance
35 b) dismantle
36 c) dearth
37 a) extraneous
38 (b) friendly.
39 (a) blunt.
40 b) withdrawn
41 (b) shrink.
42 (b) awkward.
43 (c) flameproof.
44 (a) big.
45 (b) huge.
46 (a) order.
47 (b) wet.
48 (c) fed.
49 b) traditional
50 (a) bland.

Classical Music (38-39)

1 Wolfgang Amadeus Mozart.
2 Nine.
3 *Aida*.
4 Czech.
5 Georg Friedrich Handel.
6 Very fast.
7 Four.
8 The Berlin Philharmonic.
9 Peter Tchaikovsky.
10 One.
11 A woodwind instrument.
12 A ballet.
13 Edvard Grieg.
14 Poland.
15 In a slow tempo.
16 *Der Ring des Nibelungen*.
17 The libretto.
18 Tenor.
19 Gioacchino Rossini.
20 The music should be plucked rather than played with a bow.
21 A brass instrument.
22 *Peter and the Wolf*.
23 Johann Sebastian Bach.
24 It is unfinished.
25 The cello.
26 Finnish.
27 Ludwig van Beethoven.
28 A harpsichord.
29 Baroque.
30 An orchestra and one or more solo instruments.
31 A cycle of lyrical songs.
32 Georges Bizet.
33 A woodwind instrument.
34 Henry Purcell.
35 The piano.
36 Don Giovanni.
37 Maurice Ravel.
38 Haydn.

39 Deafness.
40 'Jupiter' Symphony.
41 The violin.
42 Antonio Vivaldi.
43 A dance.
44 Austrian.
45 Six.
46 Increasing volume gradually.
47 *The Nutcracker Suite.*
48 The piano.
49 Antonín Dvořák.
50 Very slowly.

Pot Luck (40-41)

1 Dana Scully.
2 Dirty Harry.
3 Sherlock Holmes.
4 It is the name sometimes given to the southern states of the USA.
5 A type of nut.
6 A Brazil.
7 Punch and Judy.
8 Russia.
9 Play it; it is a musical instrument.
10 Drums.
11 Basketball; it is the National Basketball Association.
12 Cricket; it stands for Marylebone Cricket Club.
13 Children's diseases.
14 Stuff dead animals.
15 German.
16 Yes; it's twice as long.
17 Uranium.
18 Da da da daah! Da da da daah!
19 It struck an iceberg.
20 *The Cosby Show.*
21 Jodie Foster.
22 Blossom.
23 Schroeder.
24 Pigpen.
25 Tiger Lily.
26 Loco weed.
27 Until we meet again.
28 Gesundheit.
29 A savoury roll.
30 Japan.
31 They are all types of dried grape.
32 A bullfight.
33 France.
34 Julie Andrews.
35 Dick van Dyke.
36 They are members of the Jackson family.
37 Mexico.
38 A Mexican spirit brewed from cactus.
39 A small dog.
40 Listen to the internal workings of someone's body.
41 Morla the Aged.
42 The original 13 colonies.
43 Strange disappearances of ships and aircraft.
44 The Outback.
45 Italian bread sticks.
46 Morocco.
47 Rice.

48 Japan.
49 Russia.
50 Israel.

Nature (42-43)

1 A horse and a donkey.
2 He rolls himself into a ball.
3 The chameleon.
4 They are made of ivory.
5 It sheds its needles in the winter.
6 Australia.
7 The female lion has no mane.
8 The giraffe.
9 None.
10 Nectar.
11 The tail.
12 A foal.
13 An acorn.
14 A rodent.
15 Eight.
16 Gills.
17 The blue whale.
18 A caterpillar.
19 None, they are deaf.
20 Leopard fur has black spots, while that of a tiger is stripy.
21 Their newborn babies.
22 The hyena.
23 Yellow.
24 No, it is a type of rodent.
25 Mongrels.
26 A turtle.
27 His ability to fly.
28 A drone.
29 A vixen.
30 Dead animals.
31 To find insects.
32 Ink.
33 In underground burrows.
34 A reptile.
35 A mushroom.
36 It can inflate it by expanding its skin.
37 Blood.
38 A rooster.
39 The ostrich.
40 Bamboo.
41 Packs.
42 Slugs have no shell; snails do.
43 The arachnids.
44 Near water, mainly rivers and lakes.
45 There are not caught as kippers, they are smoked herrings.
46 A bitch.
47 Dozing in warm muddy water; they feed by night.
48 It hibernates.
49 A freshwater fish with razor-sharp teeth, capable of killing human beings.
50 An amphibian.

Odd One Out (44-45)

1 (a) Magic Johnson: the others are actors.
2 (b) Yeltsin: he is a politician whereas the others were writers.
3 (d) Barbra Streisand: the others are

opera singers.
4 (b) Karl Marx: he was a philosopher whereas the others were comedians.
5 (d) Chaplin.
6 (b) grissini: they are bread sticks.
7 (b) stickleback they are too small to eat.
8 (c) Hungarian it is the only one not derived from Latin.
9 (b) whisky.
10 (a) lion: it is a big cat whereas the others are relatives of the dog.
11 (b) uranium: it is not used in jewellery.
12 (d) cedar: it is coniferous whereas the others are broad-leaved.
13 (b) a tabby: it is a mongrel whereas the others are pedigrees.
14 (c) Estonia: it is not a Scandinavian country.
15 (c) German: the flag is red, black, and gold, not red, white, and blue like the others.
16 (b) England.
17 (d) Grimaldi.
18 (c) Atlantis: it is a mythical continent.
19 (a) giggle: we say a gaggle of geese.
20 (c) garibaldi.
21 (c) the QE2 : all the others are sailing ships.
22 (d) Luxembourg: it is not an island.
23 (b) Gladstone: he was not a president of the USA.
24 (c) Charlemagne: he lived in a different period from the others.
25 (b) Russian.
26 (a) the nine of diamonds: it is the only one not to feature a person.
27 (b) arabica: it is a type of coffee.
28 (b) speculum.
29 (d) bloomers.
30 (a) Blue Mountain.
31 (b) Gabriela Sabatini: she is Argentinian.
32 (a) fibreglass.
33 (c) binnacle: it is part of a ship's compass.
34 (a) topi: it is a hat.
35 (d) long johns: they are underwear.
36 (d) periwinkle: it is a plant.
37 (a) barracuda: it is a fish.
38 (d) fruit bat.
39 (c) avuncular: it means 'having to do with uncles'.
40 (a) tumulus: it is a grave mound.
41 (c) lucifer: it is another name for the Devil.
42 (c) incunabula: they are old books.
43 (a) Prado.
44 (c) Greenwich Village : it is in New York, although Greenwich is in London.
45 (b) Leicester Square: it is in London.
46 (d) Ecuador.
47 (d) Leon Trotsky: he was a revolutionary.
48 (b) lepidoptera: it is an insect.
49 (d) Jewish.
50 (a) 13.

Pot Luck (46-47)

1. An acropolis.
2. A young tree.
3. A nectarine has a smooth, waxy skin, whereas peach skin is fuzzy.
4. Jupiter.
5. Leaves.
6. The dashboard.
7. Migration.
8. Elvis Presley.
9. A follicle
10. Gemini.
11. Ringo Starr.
12. Quartz.
13. Mexico.
14. Papyrus.
15. A cub.
16. Italy.
17. Extra Terrestrial.
18. Venison.
19. New York.
20. *Thriller* by Michael Jackson.
21. Robin Williams.
22. Spain.
23. SE Asia
24. Deciduous.
25. Lava.
26. Blind people.
27. White cabbage.
28. The koala's.
29. Brass instruments.
30. Very Important Person.
31. Tina Turner.
32. Mammals.
33. An antibiotic.
34. A mongrel.
35. Red and white.
36. A sickle.
37. Venus.
38. A wild dog.
39. The Rolling Stones.
40. Gold.
41. Hieroglyphics.
42. Daedalus.
43. Frescoes.
44. The Renaissance.
45. A pentagon.
46. A millennium.
47. Oscars.
48. Tentacles.
49. Native Americans.
50. They mummified them.

Books (48-49)

1. Louisa May Alcott.
2. The Hattifatteners.
3. *To Kill a Mockingbird.*
4. Charlotte Brontë.
5. Redwall.
6. *Lord of the Flies.*
7. Karlson on the Roof.
8. *Charlie and the Great Glass Elevator.*
9. The Wild Wood
10. J.R.R. Tolkien.
11. The Nomes.
12. Diggers.
13. *Wind in the Willows.*
14. *The Lost World.*
15. *King Solomon's Mines.*
16. Bacteria.
17. Ransom wrote *Swallows and Amazons.*
18. The Snowman.
19. The Psammead.
20. Jesus.
21. *The Lion, The Witch and the Wardrobe.*
22. They have furry feet with leathery soles.
23. Jupiter.
24. 'I'll thcream and thcream til I'm thick!'
25. Toto.
26. Injun Joe.
27. Mr Plod.
28. Lynn Reid Banks.
29. Pippi Longstocking.
30. King Arthur.
31. To solve a crime.
32. A hot air balloon.
33. Frank and Joe.
34. *A Tale of Two Cities.*
35. The Scarlet Pimpernel.
36. *The Eagle of the Ninth.*
37. Jerome K. Jerome.
38. Gulliver.
39. Joan Aiken.
40. Sherlock Holmes.
41. Jack London.
42. Kim's game.
43. *Tom Thumb.*
44. Long John Silver.
45. An otter.
46. Exmoor.
47. *Wuthering Heights.*
48. She wrote *The Railway Children.*
49. Russia.
50. The Brothers Grimm.

Places (50-51)

1. The Suez Canal.
2. Canberra.
3. Istanbul.
4. Denmark.
5. Paris.
6. Sweden and Finland.
7. Canada.
8. Fjords.
9. English and Afrikaans.
10. Athens.
11. Mont Blanc.
12. South Africa.
13. Boston.
14. Cape Horn.
15. Mississippi-Missouri.
16. Chicago.
17. French and Flemish.
18. Paris.
19. The Netherlands.
20. Venice.
21. Spain and Portugal.
22. Greece.
23. Mount Etna.
24. France.
25. c) Argentina.
26. Africa.
27. Rio de Janeiro.
28. None – it is an independent republic.
29. Paris.
30. Arabic.
31. Alaska.
32. Finland.
33. The Mormons.
34. Brazil.
35. Berlin.
36. Kilimanjaro.
37. Singapore.
38. Seine.
39. Canaries.
40. Lake Michigan.
41. Siam.
42. Sardinia.
43. In North Africa, between the Mediterranean and the Sahara desert.
44. Geneva.
45. Buenos Aires.
46. Crete.
47. Portuguese.
48. Saint Petersburg.
49. The Netherlands.
50. Great Britain.

Pot Luck (52-53)

1. The mammoth.
2. Libra.
3. A violin is played with a bow, while the guitar is plucked.
4. Freddie Mercury.
5. Dancing.
6. Ninety minutes.
7. A telescope.
8. The Vikings.
9. Sunny weather.
10. Snow White and the Seven Dwarfs.
11. Pharaoh.
12. The American Civil War.
13. The ozone layer.
14. China.
15. Spain.
16. That somebody has died.
17. Jurassic Park.
18. Fish.
19. Fairy tales.
20. It is the brightest star in the sky.
21. It sprays them with a bad-smelling liquid.
22. Poland.
23. France.
24. Gladiators.
25. It does not have the name of the country printed on it.
26. The Republic of Ireland.
27. An astronomer.
28. The mulberry tree.
29. Germany.
30. Paris.
31. Black, red, and gold.
32. France.

33 He has only one eye.
34 Sherwood Forest, England.
35 Faster than the speed of sound.
36 Cubic feet.
37 The goalkeeper.
38 A South American cowboy.
39 Italy.
40 A carnivore.
41 A meteorologist.
42 The denominator.
43 Condensation.
44 A warren.
45 Aphrodite.
46 Russia.
47 A total eclipse of the Sun.
48 An ape.
49 Leave the pitch.
50 A pride.

Synonyms (54-55)

1 (b) honorable.
2 (a) frightened.
3 (c) obese.
4 (a) happy.
5 (b) untrue.
6 (c) healthy.
7 (b) grasping.
8 (c) childish.
9 (a) indecent.
10 (b) thanks.
11 (a) polite.
12 (b) encounter.
13 (a) exclude.
14 (c) overcome.
15 (b) beg.
16 (b) progress.
17 (a) believe.
18 (c) argue.
19 (a) ease.
20 (b) upset.
21 (b) gain.
22 (c) follow.
23 (a) elegant.
24 (c) ferocious.
25 (a) risky.
26 (b) fuzzy.
27 (a) gloomy.
28 (c) agile.
29 (a) marvellous.
30 (b) vicious.
31 (a) overdue.
32 (c) absolute.
33 (b) sureness.
34 (a) lively.
35 (b) explain.
36 (a) turn.
37 (b) holy.
38 (b) charm.
39 (a) sadness.
40 (b) petty.
41 (c) merry.
42 (b) moan.
43 (a) juvenile.
44 (b) loudmouthed.
45 (a) flamboyant.
46 (b) elementary.

47 (b) bizarre.
48 (a) grim.
49 (a) lucky.
50 (b) usual.

Books (56-57)

1 The drink.
2 A top hat.
3 The Cheshire cat.
4 The Teenage Mutant Ninja Turtles.
5 James Bond.
6 Flash Gordon.
7 John the Baptist.
8 The Foreign Legion.
9 She.
10 Captain Good.
11 Bertie Wooster's butler.
12 *Budgie the Little Helicopter.*
13 *The Hitchhiker's Guide to the Galaxy.*
14 Terry Pratchett.
15 Mrs Haversham.
16 He was a blacksmith.
17 Bill Sykes.
18 *A Christmas Carol.*
19 Ebenezer.
20 Tin Tin.
21 Snowy.
22 The Moomin stories.
23 The Groke.
24 The Hobgoblin.
25 The Queen.
26 *The Last of the Mohicans.*
27 *To Kill a Mockingbird.*
28 ...*Steps.*
29 ...*Courage.*
30 ...*Mask.*
31 Green.
32 Dracula.
33 Science fiction.
34 Tarzan.
35 *What Katy Did Next.*
36 ...*Prairie.*
37 Universe.
38 Jane Austen.
39 Arthur C. Clarke.
40 A walking plant with a deadly sting.
41 In the depths of the ocean.
42 *The Chrysalids.*
43 Horror.
44 ...*Cristo.*
45 Russia.
46 Danny.
47 Because he had secret plans and clever tricks.
48 Trunky the elephant threw him up by his tail until he crashed into the sun and was sizzled up like a sausage.
49 The caterpillar eats his way through the book and leaves holes in the pages.
50 Dr Seuss.

Pot Luck (58-59)

1 The Union Jack.
2 The Republicans and the Democrats.
3 Paris.

4 Lower.
5 A brass instrument.
6 A compass.
7 Compact Disc.
8 A type of wrestling originating in Japan.
9 A hot air balloon.
10 The Milky Way.
11 (a) polyester.
12 In a cave.
13 Mars.
14 A glacier.
15 A pig.
16 One year.
17 Macaulay Culkin.
18 John Lennon.
19 A double bass.
20 France
21 A number that can be divided only by itself and 1 without leaving a remainder.
22 A sculptor.
23 The pollen.
24 A boomerang.
25 *Raiders of the Lost Ark.*
26 A shuttlecock.
27 Native Americans.
28 Victory in Europe.
29 Only in the Northen hemisphere. In the Southern Hemisphere it is reversed.
30 The Stars and Stripes.
31 Twenty-four hours.
32 James Bond.
33 A diamond.
34 The Olympic Games.
35 Iraq.
36 (d) a litre.
37 Round or oval.
38 The telegraphic code bearing his name.
39 It has a bull's head and a man's body.
40 A hexagon.
41 Six.
42 Beethoven.
43 China.
44 Hollywood, California.
45 Boris Becker.
46 Chess.
47 Personal Computer.
48 Denim, which is a type of cotton.
49 A hovercraft.
50 A moat.

Odd One Out (60-61)

1 (a) cauliflower: all the others are root vegetables.
2 (c) The *Living Daylights*: all the others are produced by Steven Spielberg.
3 (a) biceps: it is a muscle whereas all the others are bones.
4 (c) hyena: all the others belong to the cat family.
5 (b) flute: all the others are brass instruments.
6 (b) cumulus: it is a type of cloud whereas all the others are storms.
7 (d) backgammon: all the others are card games.
8 (d) slide projector: all the others are

devices for producing sound.

9 (a) tennis: all the others are team sports.
10 (d) mango: the others are citrus fruits.
11 (a) panda: the others are marsupials and are native to Australia.
12 (c) Hugh Grant: all the others played have James Bond.
13 (a) rose: all the others grow from bulbs.
14 (d) Galileo Galilei: he was a physicist whereas all the others were painters.
15 (d) Thames: all the others are on the American continent.
16 (b) Orion: it is a star whereas all the others are planets.
17 (a) Kensington: all the others are boroughs of New York.
18 (b) moussaka: all the others are made with pasta.
19 (d) Nick Faldo: he is a golf champion whereas all the others play tennis.
20 (b) Mickey Mouse: the others are *Loony Toons* characters.
21 (d) polenta: all the others are types of cheese.
22 (b) wolf spider: all the others are insects.
23 (c) Beverly Hills: all the others are airports.
24 (d) mustard: all the others are herbs.
25 (b) Elvis Presley: all the others were part of the Beatles.
26 (d) hovercraft: all the others are types of air travel.
27 (b) tendons: all the others are blood vessels.
28 (a) saltpeter: all the others are gems.
29 (c) bassoon: all the others are stringed instruments.
30 (a) Cairo: all the others are situated in Israel.
31 (b) Minotaur: all the others are Greek gods.
32 (a) albatross: all the others are types of dinosaurs.
33 (d) Bedouines: all the others are Native American tribes.
34 (c) Egypt: all the others are part of Europe.
35 (a) orange: all the others are primary colours.
36 (d) foal, all the others are female animals whereas a foal may be male or female.
37 (b) mansion: all the others are places of worship.
38 (c) Buenos Aires: all the others are situated in the USA.
39 (d) rhubarb: all the others grow on trees.
40 (a) Hook: all the others are about animals.
41 (d) Rembrandt van Rijn: all the others were composers.
42 (b) fox: all the others are rodents.
43 (d) Ringo Starr: all the others are lead singers of groups.
44 (a) Abraham Lincoln: all the others

were famous scientists.
45 (d) *Home Alone*: all the others are cartoons.
46 (c) sugar: all the others are spices.
47 (b) Scrabble: all the others are played with a dice.
48 (b) toad: it is an amphibian whereas all the others are reptiles.
49 (c) Winston Churchill: all the others were American presidents.
50 (d) coca cola: it is the only one that does not contain alcohol.

Places (62-63)

1 Spain.
2 London.
3 Brazil.
4 Austria.
5 Australia.
6 Egypt.
7 Scandinavia.
8 Asia.
9 Tokyo.
10 The Panama Canal.
11 South Africa.
12 Rome.
13 Moscow.
14 The Pacific.
15 The Himalayas.
16 Spanish.
17 There is one star for every one of the states.
18 The Leaning Tower.
19 Berlin.
20 New Zealand.
21 It is a national park created to preserve species of wild animal.
22 The world's largest desert.
23 Alaska.
24 Africa.
25 Hindu.
26 Moscow.
27 Spain.
28 Ireland.
29 Europe and Asia.
30 San Francisco.
31 None, it is an island.
32 Cairo.
33 The Alps.
34 Athens.
35 Brazil.
36 Because of its high level of salt there are no living creatures.
37 Australia.
38 The Atlantic Ocean.
39 St Petersburg.
40 Hawaii.
41 Canada.
42 New York City.
43 Bangkok. It is the capital of Thailand, and all the others are Indian cities.
44 The Tower of London.
45 Italy.
46 Beijing.
47 Cuba.
48 Paris.

49 Hebrew.
50 Australia.

Pot Luck (64-65)

1 A tiger.
2 An oak tree.
3 It is the timespan of World War II.
4 Charles I.
5 Cairo.
6 Eight.
7 H_2O.
8 Electricity.
9 Pluto.
10 Rain, snow, and hail.
11 Rickshaw.
12 A type of fruit.
13 No.
14 The depth of water.
15 Yugoslavia.
16 Spain.
17 Origami.
18 Africa.
19 No; they can only glide.
20 True; it was pressed into bricks and used as currency.
21 Yes; there is white gold.
22 No; they are a dirty pink and grey.
23 Twenty.
24 Thirteen.
25 The naked mole rat.
26 Tree people.
27 (c) the Camargue; the others are deserts.
28 They are pulled by the force of the Earth's gravity.
29 (a) granite.
30 (b) Tolstoy; the others are composers.
31 A leap year.
32 The chow chow.
33 A beagle.
34 Poland.
35 Frog spawn is a jellied mass; toad spawn comes in long strips.
36 Flash Gordon.
37 Pluto.
38 Snails.
39 A hundred.
40 A nest.
41 A fish.
42 A mosquito.
43 Bubonic plague.
44 The halves both live and become separate worms.
45 Plants.
46 The speed of sound.
47 Light.
48 In a cave.
49 Fear of open spaces.
50 Cat.

Pop Music (66-67)

1 Oasis.
2 Icelandic.
3 UB40.
4 *So Far So Good.*

5   'It Must Have Been Love'.
6   *Automatic For the People.*
7   The Bee Gees.
8   Mick Hucknall.
9   Blondie.
10 The Lightning Seeds.
11 *Glittering Prize.*
12 Canadian.
13 *We Can't Dance.*
14 *The Division Bell.*
15 The Communards.
16 Blur.
17 'Saving All My Love For You'.
18 'Papa Don't Preach'.
19 Chrissie Hynde.
20 The Live Aid Concert in 1985.
21 'Sultans of Swing'.
22 Queen.
23 Eternal.
24 *Crossroads.*
25 *Ten Summoners Tales.*
26 Bad.
27 Pulp.
28 Tina Turner.
29 Culture Club.
30 Sheryl Crow.
31 *Our Town.*
32 *Bat Out of Hell II.*
33 The Supremes.
34 Neil Diamond.
35 Blur.
36 M People.
37 Andrew Ridgeley.
38 Level 42.
39 Let Loose.
40 The Human League.
41 The Cranberries.
42 Erasure (or Depeche Mode or Yazoo).
43 Annie Lennox.
44 R.E.M.
45 *Carry on up the Charts.*
46 The Pogues.
47 Boyzone.
48 Bob Marley.
49 Nirvana.
50 Duran Duran.

Science (68-69)

1   They float.
2   A filament.
3   Because water expands when it turns
    into ice.
4   They repel each other.
5   Red, yellow, and blue.
6   A barometer.
7   Hot air always rises, and the difference
    in temperature is greater on a cold day.
8   A sound.
9   A conductor.
10 Whether a substance is acid or alkaline.
11 Ampere.
12 Heat enters the atmosphere from the
    sun and is trapped by gases such as
    carbon dioxide, methane, and water
    vapor. Therefore the heat of the
    atmosphere increases.

13 Copper and tin.
14 The Theory of Relativity.
15 (b) Gogol.
16 Germination.
17 Oxidation.
18 True.
19 Sun spots.
20 Like a lizard.
21 Plants.
22 No, though some objects, for example
    feathers, experience air resistance which
    makes them fall more slowly than a
    compact object of the same weight.
23 Anticlockwise.
24 Continental drift.
25 The tip.
26 Gravity.
27 The speed at which it must travel to
    escape Earth's gravity.
28 Graphite.
29 Fool's gold.
30 Diamond.
31 Steel.
32 Stainless steel.
33 In soil.
34 It prevents ultraviolet and other harmful
    radiation from penetrating the
    atmosphere.
35 The Northern Lights.
36 Megabytes.
37 Cathode ray tube.
38 Yes.
39 Rings.
40 It resembles glass.
41 There is no difference: they both mean
    'easily set on fire'.
42 Methane.
43 In cereal grains (especially corn and
    wheat).
44 Argon.
45 The atomic bomb.
46 Basic Input Output System.
47 Compact Disk – Read Only Memory.
48 Dry ice.
49 A dust particle.
50 Helium.

Pot Luck (70-71)

1   Theseus.
2   Germany.
3   Islam.
4   A herbivore.
5   A constellation.
6   Leonardo da Vinci.
7   Stamps.
8   A stethoscope.
9   Wood.
10 The Nobel Peace Prize.
11 Superman.
12 France's.
13 A geologist.
14 Capricorn.
15 Rabbi.
16 Incisors.
17 Belgium.
18 Hawaii.

19 Vatican City.
20 Roger Moore.
21 The bulk of the gold bullion reserves of
    the USA.
22 The White House.
23 Spiders.
24 Dogs.
25 Telly Savalas.
26 North.
27 London.
28 Monsoon.
29 *The Empire Strikes Back.*
30 Ninety.
31 Works of art: it's an art gallery.
32 Brussels.
33 A rodent.
34 A dead body.
35 Steven Spielberg.
36 Pinocchio's.
37 The central nervous system.
38 Australia.
39 A tributary.
40 Hearts, spades, diamonds, and clubs.
41 *Top Gun.*
42 Morning.
43 A hectare.
44 Holland.
45 China.
46 Red and green.
47 Marsupials.
48 Germany.
49 The back; they form the spinal column.
50 Canada.

Places (72-73)

1   Rome.
2   The Pacific.
3   Venice.
4   Arabic.
5   The Mediterranean.
6   Germany.
7   North America.
8   Washington DC.
9   London.
10 Mount Everest.
11 (c) Russia.
12 The USA.
13 England.
14 (d) Paris; all the others are American
    cities.
15 The English Channel.
16 California.
17 Europe.
18 Europe and Asia.
19 (e) Germany; all the others are island
    states.
20 Moscow.
21 North.
22 Scotland.
23 (b) Moscow.
24 Winter.
25 London.
26 Amsterdam.
27 The Atlantic.
28 Spain.
29 English and Welsh.

40 An Indian curry soup.
41 A cake made of thin layers of pastry, nuts, and honey.
42 Egg yolks, sugar, and wine.
43 The small end of the loin.
44 Ricotta.
45 The carrot family.
46 Kohlrabi.
47 A broth flavoured with thin strips of vegetables.
48 Turkish delight.
49 A thick soup containing vegetables, pasta, and broth.
50 Shaped pasta dumplings made from semolina or potato flour.

History (86-87)

1 Admiral Tirpitz.
2 The Domesday Book.
3 The Peninsular War.
4 He burned the cakes.
5 A chicken in every pot.
6 Alexander the Great.
7 Sukarno.
8 Lincoln, Garfield, McKinley, Kennedy.
9 Marie Antoinette.
10 Siam.
11 Zimbabwe.
12 Stinking Billy.
13 Japan.
14 1861.
15 Wounded Knee.
16 The Field of the Cloth of Gold.
17 Rorke's Drift.
18 Ireland.
19 The Rosetta Stone.
20 The Civil War.
21 Warfare.
22 The Ptolemies.
23 A form of writing.
24 People's Republic of China.
25 Cyrano de Bergerac.
26 The Dead Sea Scrolls.
27 Dracula.
28 The thugs.
29 Benjamin Franklin.
30 The Julian.
31 Atlanta.
32 Australia.
33 Incunabula.
34 Marco Polo.
35 The Quakers.
36 His news agency.
37 Paul Revere.
38 Amelia Earhart.
39 Ignatius Loyola.
40 The Inquisition.
41 Palaeolithic paintings.
42 David Lloyd George.
43 Messalina.
44 Hiroshima and Nagasaki.
45 Papyrus.
46 South Vietnam.
47 Ho Chi Minh City.
48 Robespierre.

49 Heinrich Himmler.
50 Sir Francis Drake.

Sport (88-89)

1 Germany and Argentina.
2 Martina Navratilova.
3 Mark Spitz.
4 100 meters.
5 Jayne Torvill and Christopher Dean.
6 New Zealand.
7 Sandy Lyle.
8 Carl Lewis.
9 Eighteen.
10 Five.
11 Fencing.
12 Swimming.
13 Eleven.
14 Olga Korbut.
15 Table tennis.
16 Baseball.
17 Florence Griffith Joyner.
18 Muhammad Ali.
19 The Netherlands.
20 Jesse Owens.
21 Stefan Edberg.
22 Squash.
23 Matt Biondi.
24 Golf.
25 Bob Beamon.
26 Boxing.
27 Monica Seles.
28 Eleven.
29 Bernhard Langer.
30 Rugby.
31 Mike Tyson.
32 Brazil.
33 Athens.
34 Nadia Comaneci.
35 Andre Agassi.
36 Golf.
37 The USA together with 57 other nations boycotted the games.
38 A motor race.
39 The Brown Bomber.
40 Seven.
41 Miguel Indurain.
42 John McEnroe.
43 Nick Faldo.
44 The zebra.
45 Tennis.
46 Seoul, Korea.
47 A 'cannon'.
48 Chris Evert.
49 The five continents.
50 Swimming, cross-country running, fencing, riding, and shooting.

The Arts (90-91)

1 The cast were all children.
2 *Pygmalion.*
3 *West Side Story.*
4 *To Kill a Mocking Bird.*
5 Stuart Sutcliffe and Pete Best.

6 Walt Disney.
7 *The Mousetrap.*
8 Cliff Richard.
9 Boris Karloff.
10 *The Elephant Man.*
11 *10 Rillington Place.*
12 'From Me to You', 'She Loves You', and 'I Wanna Hold Your Hand'.
13 Leonard Cohen.
14 Noel Coward.
15 The Sex Pistols.
16 James Taylor.
17 Bert Weedon.
18 Barbra Streisand.
19 Cecil B. DeMille.
20 *Stagecoach.*
21 Anthony Quinn.
22 Oscar Wilde.
23 *Who's Afraid of Virginia Woolf.*
24 Rudyard Kipling.
25 *The Great Plague.*
26 Al Jolson.
27 *Macbeth.*
28 Over an alleged homosexual relationship between characters in the film.
29 J.M.W. Turner.
30 *Oklahoma!*
31 George Gershwin.
32 Dave Brubeck.
33 Andrew Lloyd Webber.
34 Audrey Hepburn.
35 *Gone With the Wind.*
36 'The Charge of the Light Brigade'.
37 Frans Hals.
38 Genesis.
39 Cher.
40 Jimmy Durante.
41 'Spirit in the Sky'.
42 Australia.
43 Ethel Merman.
44 John Lennon and Yoko Ono.
45 Brian Jones.
46 Borodin.
47 The Globe.
48 The Jersey Lily.
49 The Buffalo Bill Wild West Show.
50 Works; from the Latin *opus*.

Seas (92-93)

1 South Atlantic.
2 Near Antarctica.
3 The Indian Ocean.
4 The North Atlantic.
5 The Red Sea.
6 The Aegean.
7 The Sea of Marmara.
8 The Mediterranean.
9 In the middle of the land.
10 The Irish Sea.
11 La Manche.
12 The Strait of Gibraltar.
13 The Yellow Sea.
14 The Bay of Bengal.
15 The Bering Sea.
16 Between India and Sri Lanka.

17 The Gulf of Oman.
18 The Tasman Sea.
19 The Caribbean.
20 The Pacific.
21 The Java Sea.
22 Bismarck Sea.
23 The Coral Sea.
24 The Indian Ocean.
25 The South China Sea.
26 The Banda Sea.
27 The Makassar Strait.
28 The Sulu Sea.
29 North Australia.
30 Indonesia.
31 New Zealand.
32 The Pacific Ocean.
33 The Peru Basin.
34 The Norwegian Basin.
35 Barents Sea.
36 The Black and the Caspian seas.
37 The Gulf of Tongkin.
38 The Gulf of Mexico.
39 Drake Passage.
40 Hudson Bay.
41 Baffin Bay, Foxe Basin, Hudson Strait, Davis Strait.
42 The North Sea.
43 The Gulf of St. Lawrence.
44 The Red Sea.
45 Salt Lake.
46 The Gulf of Mexico.
47 Just off the coast of California near Los Angeles.
48 Los Angeles and San Diego.
49 The Straits of Florida.
50 Long Island Sound.

History (94-95)

1   The Houses of York and Lancaster.
2   A group of workers who rioted in industrial areas between 1812 and 1818 for fear of losing their jobs due to introduction of machinery.
3   The Crimean War.
4   A prison, in particular for political prisoners.
5   Giuseppe Garibaldi.
6   Otto von Bismarck.
7   Prince Albert.
8   Catherine of Aragon.
9   Babylonia.
10 The Ku Klux Klan.
11 The Mason-Dixon Line.
12 The Nuremberg Trials.
13 Josef Stalin.
14 Napoleon.
15 The English Civil War.
16 Girondists.
17 The Boer War.
18 Thomas Jefferson.
19 A secret terrorist organization operating in Kenya during the 1950s.
20 People who took part in the 1949 Gold Rush in California.
21 They wanted to end slavery.

22 Thomas Jackson.
23 The Russian ruling dynasty that ended with the abdication of Nicholas II during the Russian Revolution.
24 The Weimar Republic.
25 The Zulu War.
26 The British Commonwealth.
27 The abduction of Helen of Troy by Paris.
28 115 years.
29 Spartacus.
30 Charles I.
31 ANZACs.
32 The Bronze Age.
33 Mary I.
34 Pompeii.
35 Ireland.
36 The Moors.
37 The Norman conquest.
38 Hermann Goering.
39 Botany Bay.
40 Joseph Goebbles.
41 Romulus and Remus.
42 Churchill, Roosevelt, and Stalin.
43 Caligula.
44 Crazy Horse and Gall.
45 Napoleon's victories.
46 Londinium.
47 The Bounty.
48 World War II.
49 Sir Francis Drake.
50 Agamemnon.

Cities (96-97)

1   São Paolo.
2   Moscow.
3   New York.
4   Phnom Penh.
5   False. The capital is Ankara.
6   Dublin.
7   Khrung Thep.
8   Estonia.
9   Mongolia.
10 Chicago.
11 Jerusalem.
12 Taiwan.
13 Paris.
14 London.
15 London and New York.
16 Nairobi.
17 Atlanta.
18 Miami.
19 Las Vegas.
20 Brotherly love.
21 Detroit.
22 South Dakota.
23 Petra.
24 Venice.
25 London.
26 New York.
27 Paris.
28 Madrid.
29 The Gate of Heavenly Peace.
30 Leningrad.
31 One is in Kansas and the other adjacent to it in Missouri.

32 Benjamin Disraeli.
33 New York.
34 Calcutta.
35 Kyoto.
36 Berlin.
37 Prague.
38 Canterbury.
39 They are both university towns.
40 Ely.
41 Megiddo.
42 It is situated on a delta like the Egyptian city after which it is named.
43 Venice.
44 Amsterdam.
45 Frankfurt.
46 Sydney.
47 Berlin.
48 Edinburgh.
49 Stockholm.
50 Cologne.

Events (98-99)

1   (b) 1963.
2   1972.
3   (c) 1948.
4   (b) 1952.
5   1963.
6   (c) 1937.
7   1944.
8   (c) 1906.
9   1929.
10 (a) 1980.
11 (c) 1903.
12 1953.
13 (a) 1982.
14 (b) 1985.
15 (c) 1949.
16 1972.
17 (c) 1963.
18 (b) 1869.
19 1970.
20 (a) 1900.
21 (c) 1924.
22 (b) 1959.
23 1961.
24 (b) 1967.
25 (c) 1974.
26 (c) 1911.
27 (a) 1912.
28 1973.
29 (a) 1955.
30 (b) 1969.
31 (b) 1940.
32 1968.
33 (c) 1948.
34 (b) 1956.
35 (a) 1960.
36 1976.
37 (b) 1960.
38 (a) 1934.
39 1933.
40 (b) 1938.
41 (a) 1975.
42 (c) 1978.
43 1980.

44	1920s.
45	1930s
46	(a) 1973.
47	(c) 1990.
48	1988.
49	(b) 1984.
50	(a) 1952.

The Arts (100-101)

1 Stan Laurel.
2 1949.
3 Ethel Merman.
4 'What's up, Doc?'
5 1931.
6 Amos 'n' Andy.
7 1967.
8 Toulouse Lautrec.
9 Tahiti.
10 Evita.
11 Deanna Durbin.
12 *Grand Hotel*.
13 Bette Davis.
14 Quentin Crisp.
15 Christopher Lee.
16 Robert Burns.
17 Mr Spock.
18 Dylan Thomas.
19 Bob Dylan.
20 Woodstock.
21 The violin.
22 Stradivari.
23 It is a corruption of 'jaws harp', the instrument being held between the teeth.
24 Napoleon Bonaparte.
25 Manet.
26 *The Wasteland* by T.S. Eliot.
27 Dylan Thomas.
28 Mervyn Peake.
29 *1984* by George Orwell.
30 Samuel Johnson.
31 Stephen Crane.
32 Alec Guinness.
33 *Four Weddings and a Funeral*.
34 *The Last of the Mohicans*.
35 Helena Bonham-Carter.
36 Moomins.
37 Gandalf.
38 Sauron.
39 Tom Sawyer and Huckleberry Finn.
40 Brobdingnag.
41 *A Clockwork Orange*.
42 A leopard.
43 Mark Twain (according to Huck Finn).
44 Peter Pan.
45 Tarzan of the Apes.
46 Sweeney Todd.
47 Pippi Longstocking.
48 Agatha Christie.
49 Marie.
50 Marvin Lee Aday.

Inventions (102-103)

1 Alexander Graham Bell.
2 Television.
3 It was an early lie-detector.
4 Sir Clive Sinclair.
5 The jukebox.
6 To raise water.
7 Charles Babbage.
8 The first safe, and reasonably fast, passenger lift.
9 It was a form of central heating.
10 The Earl of Sandwich.
11 Alexander the Great.
12 Thomas Edison.
13 The wheel.
14 The Chinese.
15 Scandinavia.
16 Wales.
17 The saddle.
18 The whip.
19 The pendulum clock.
20 The slide rule.
21 Porcelain false teeth.
22 The Spinning Jenny.
23 Copper plated with a thin layer of real silver.
24 The parachute.
25 Bifocal lenses.
26 The Montgolfiers (in 1783).
27 He invented the steel nib in 1780.
28 John McAdam.
29 The first single-purpose electronic computer.
30 Photography.
31 Singer.
32 Antoine Sax.
33 Nitroglycerine. It was a very unstable explosive.
34 He invented the photographic negative.
35 Samuel Morse.
36 The hypodermic syringe.
37 Color photography.
38 He invented a machine to make it.
39 Fixing the soles to the uppers of shoes.
40 It was a primitive horseshoe tied on with leather thongs.
41 Chewing gum.
42 Coca Cola.
43 Waterman invented an improved ink supply so that the pen neither dried up nor flooded.
44 The bark of the willow tree.
45 The sphygmomanometer.
46 For security reasons it was pretended that they were water-storage tanks.
47 Diabetes.
48 Toothbrush bristles.
49 The glass cats' eyes used as road markings.
50 DDT.

Current Affairs (104-105)

1 Yasir Arafat.
2 Nelson Mandela.
3 Chernobyl.
4 Mikhail Gorbachev.
5 The Iron Curtain.
6 He was, in 1996, the person who had survived longest (2 years) with an artifical heart.
7 Ytzak Rabin.
8 IRA (Irish Republican Army).
9 Ronald Reagan.
10 1996.
11 Israel.
12 The United Nations.
13 Helmut Kohl.
14 A heavy fall of snow (last seen in 1963).
15 Mao Tse-tung.
16 The USA.
17 Berlin.
18 Mahatma Gandhi.
19 She had burned the soup.
20 (c) Spain.
21 Italy.
22 He was the first non-Italian pope.
23 F.W. de Klerk.
24 Northern Ireland.
25 Los Angeles.
26 Serbia.
27 1952.
28 The Republican Party.
29 Boris Yeltsin.
30 Afghanistan.
31 The invasion of Kuwait by Iraqi troops.
32 John F. Kennedy.
33 George Bush.
34 Taiwan.
35 Poland.
36 Jordan.
37 Jawaharlal Nehru.
38 George Bush.
39 Soweto.
40 John F Kennedy.
41 Muammar Al-Qaddafi.
42 Governor of Arkansas.
43 1991.
44 The taking hostage of more than 50 US citizens by Muslim extremists in Tehran.
45 Jordan.
46 Hosni Mubarak.
47 European Economic Community.
48 Great Britain.
49 1973.
50 The Watergate affair.

People (106-107)

1 1963.
2 Samuel Goldwyn.
3 Popeye.
4 Helen of Troy's.
5 Allen. Bob Dylan was born Robert Allen Zimmerman and Woody Allen was Allen Stewart Konigsberg.
6 Grigori Yefimovich Rasputin.
7 Sergeant Pepper.
8 John Wayne.
9 Mark Twain.
10 Bonnie and Clyde.
11 Mohandas Karamchand Gandhi.
12 George Washington.
13 Robinson Crusoe.
14 Athos, Porthos, Aramis, and D'Artagnan.

15 Boo Radley.
16 Martin Luther King, Jr.
17 Muhammad Ali.
18 King Harold II.
19 Stalin.
20 Captain James Cook.
21 Tarzan.
22 The FBI.
23 Guy Fawkes.
24 Marie Curie.
25 Huckleberry Finn.
26 Lyndon Baines Johnson.
27 Santa Anna.
28 The typewriter.
29 Orenthal James.
30 General de Gaulle.
31 Allan Pinkerton.
32 A short-barrelled pistol that had a large bore and was small enough to be carried in a pocket.
33 He wrote Alice in Wonderland under the name of Lewis Carroll.
34 James Cagney.
35 Sitting Bull.
36 Blackbeard.
37 Billy the Kid.
38 The Starship Enterprise.
39 George Orwell.
40 Anne.
41 Gulliver.
42 Dr Samuel Johnson.
43 Nelson.
44 Joan of Arc.
45 Robert the Bruce.
46 Benito Mussolini.
47 Tenzing Norgay.
48 Superman.
49 Robin Hood.
50 Sir Isaac Newton.

Events (108-109)

1 c) 1974.
2 (b) 1914.
3 (c) 1889.
4 1971.
5 (a) 1923.
6 (b) 1962.
7 (c) 1922.
8 1956.
9 (b) 1967.
10 (c) 1973.
11 (c) 1943.
12 1985.
13 (b) 1953.
14 (a) 1916.
15 (b) 1847.
16 1977.
17 (c) 1886.
18 (b) 1975.
19 (a) 1948.
20 1960.
21 (b) 1972.
22 (a) 1945.
23 1979.
24 (b) 1969.

25 (b) 1961.
26 (a) 1896.
27 (c) 1848.
28 1966.
29 (b) 1989.
30 (c) 1993.
31 (a) 1981.
32 1988.
33 (c) 1837.
34 (b) 1949.
35 1964.
36 (b) 1990.
37 (c) 1919.
38 (b) 1990.
39 1983.
40 (a) 1918.
41 (c) 1975.
42 (b) 1941.
43 (c) 1989.
44 1987.
45 (c) 1981.
46 (b) 1969.
47 (b) 1940.
48 1978.
49 (c) 1937.
50 (c) 1989.

Nature (110-111)

1 Blueberry.
2 Caorifoliaceae.
3 Newfoundland.
4 Panther.
5 It is a fungus with a red cap with white patches.
6 Carnivorous.
7 In water.
8 They suck the blood from other fish.
9 A crocodile.
10 Virginia creeper.
11 Captive parrots can live to more than 80 years.
12 It has a long pointed snout and often no tail.
13 No trees: only stunted shrubs, mosses, and lichens can survive.
14 Resin.
15 35.
16 The Arctic.
17 They hang upside down from branches.
18 Alpine regions.
19 A wild goat.
20 To intimidate other animals.
21 The llama.
22 A bat.
23 In his cheek pouches, which are expandable.
24 In Central and South America and South-east Asia.
25 The white rhinoceros.
26 A wild reindeer.
27 Coniferous forests.
28 A type of butterfly.
29 The iris family.
30 The condor.
31 It trips it up.

32 On a vine.
33 Mock orange.
34 A small monkey.
35 By squeezing it.
36 Marsupials.
37 In the open savanna south of the Sahara.
38 An antilope.
39 Amphibians.
40 The anopheles mosquito.
41 The grizzly bear.
42 The mandrill.
43 Australia.
44 The sturgeon.
45 Eucalyptus leaves.
46 The tsetse fly.
47 Only young ones do: the spots disappear when they get older.
48 A small short-necked giraffe, but it has zebra-like stripes on his buttocks and legs.
49 Blood.
50 A South American rodent.

Costume (112-113)

1 The Inuit.
2 A yarmulke (or kippah).
3 A poncho.
4 A partial wig.
5 A dhoti.
6 Keffiyeh.
7 Sarong.
8 Batik.
9 Chador.
10 Saffron (orange).
11 Kimono.
12 Obi.
13 Chaps.
14 A cummerbund.
15 A turban.
16 A sporran.
17 The desire to ride bicycles.
18 A small frame worn by a women to make their skirt stand out at the rear.
19 Busbies.
20 Sari.
21 A tutu.
22 A toga.
23 He was a famous dandy and leader of fashion who spent huge sums of money on clothes. Whatever he wore was considered good taste.
24 The New Look.
25 Teddy boys.
26 The peplos which was gradually replaced by the chiton.
27 Sovereignty over both Upper and Lower Egypt.
28 Trousers.
29 The hair.
30 A laurel wreath.
31 A purple border.
32 Greece.
33 Hose.
34 The bowler.

35 A steeple hat.
36 A monocle.
37 Wooden clogs.
38 The Duke of Wellington.
39 He added copper rivets
40 White.
41 Yellow.
42 Hunting pink.
43 Moccasins.
44 A very short tight-fitting jacket.
45 An artificial paunch, originating in Spain, made from padding stuffed into the front of a doublet.
46 They were much cheaper and did not uncurl when they became wet.
47 From Bikini Atoll, where nuclear bombs were tested.
48 A frock coat.
49 They could be flattened for storage under one's seat.
50 Plus fours. Shorter versions were called plus twos.

Nature (114-115)

1 Hedgehogs.
2 No.
3 No; it is made from the rice paper plant.
4 Acorns.
5 A sea horse.
6 Birch.
7 The strawberry.
8 The poppy.
9 King cobra.
10 The viper or adder.
11 A kind of grebe.
12 Primrose.
13 It eats insects.
14 The hare.
15 African.
16 Because the males have an inflatable trunk-like proboscis.
17 No; it comes from an infestation of filarial worms.
18 Smallpox.
19 The ladybird or ladybug.
20 Bluebell.
21 Paraguay tea.
22 A mature male gorilla.
23 The orang-utan.
24 Primate.
25 Ape-man.
26 Canine.
27 Chow chow.
28 Alsatian.
29 Shih Tzu.
30 The garden snail.
31 The hippopotamus (average 41 years); the horse lives on average only 20 years.
32 Fifty years.
33 The elephant (African 660 days) as against the white rhinoceros (480 days).
34 Congealed hair.
35 River horse.

36 Pachyderm.
37 Ganesh.
38 The fuchsia.
39 Deadly nightshade.
40 The sparrow.
41 Goat-like.
42 Ape-like.
43 Lizard-like.
44 Sheep and goats.
45 Bovine Spongiform Encephalopathy.
46 Rabies.
47 They are vampires.
48 A small bat.
49 The bison.
50 A cross between the American buffalo, or bison, and beef cattle. It is typically ⅜ buffalo and ⅝ bovine.

Shakespeare (116-117)

1 *Julius Caesar.*
2 Julius Caesar.
3 Cassius.
4 Mark Antony.
5 The Ides of March.
6 Antony and Cleopatra.
7 *As You Like It.*
8 Denmark.
9 Hamlet.
10 Elsinore.
11 He was a court jester.
12 Forty thousand.
13 'May violets spring!'
14 His father's.
15 *Henry V.*
16 'The fewer men, the greater share of honour.'
17 St. Crispin's.
18 *King Lear.*
19 Cordelia.
20 'They kill us for their sport.'
21 *Macbeth.*
22 'In thunder, lightning, or in rain?'
23 'Nose-painting, sleep, and urine.'
24 'Something wicked this way comes.'
25 Lady Macbeth.
26 Because he was 'from his mother's womb untimely ripped.'
27 *The Merchant of Venice.*
28 Shylock.
29 Portia.
30 'It droppeth as the gentle rain from heaven.'
31 'So shines a good deed in a naughty world.'
32 *The Merry Wives of Windsor.*
33 Divinity.
34 Puck.
35 'proud Titania.'
36 'the wild thyme blows.'
37 'Come not near our fairy queen.'
38 Iago.
39 Desdemona.
40 He strangled his wife.
41 Romeo and Juliet.
42 Mercutio.

43 Paris.
44 Montagues and Capulets.
45 'Lest that they love prove likewise variable.'
46 The king in Romeo and Juliet.
47 Romeo.
48 *The Taming of the Shrew.*
49 Miranda.
50 Brave new world.

Places (118-119)

1 Morocco.
2 Switzerland and France.
3 Tasmania.
4 Arizona.
5 A prison.
6 India.
7 Namibia.
8 Roman Catholic.
9 Hammerfest.
10 Austria.
11 Lizard Point.
12 Brooklyn.
13 Germany.
14 Istanbul.
15 Kashmir.
16 Denmark.
17 The Black Sea.
18 Table Mountain.
19 New South Wales.
20 Lithuania, Latvia, and Estonia.
21 The Pyrenees.
22 Jakarta.
23 Tierra del Fuego.
24 Fujiyama.
25 Tiber.
26 Moscow.
27 Neither – they are both on the same latitude.
28 Shanghai.
29 Majorca, Minorca, Ibiza.
30 Copenhagen.
31 The Swiss-Austrian border.
32 The Inner Hebrides.
33 Bosphorus.
34 Rabat.
35 Tunisia.
36 Lake Superior.
37 Agra.
38 Quebec.
39 Wyoming.
40 Northumberland.
41 In the Alps, on the Italian-Swiss border.
42 Honshu.
43 Tanganyika and Zanzibar.
44 Madrid.
45 Denver.
46 The Greater Antilles.
47 Tuscany.
48 Zambia.
49 The Rhine.
50 Portugal.

Medicine (120-121)

1 Glaucoma.
2 The cold virus keeps changing and therefore the immune system cannot recognize it.
3 Haemophilia.
4 Public places.
5 The gums.
6 They consist of 47 instead of 46 chromosomes.
7 Skin cancer.
8 Red blood cells.
9 The creation of blood clots in the arteries.
10 Asthma.
11 Vitamin D.
12 Breast cancer.
13 The narrowing of the arteries, restricting the flow of blood.
14 Thinning and weakening of the bones.
15 Acquired Immune Deficiency Syndrome.
16 A kind of dermatitis.
17 A severe seizure in someone suffering from epilepsy.
18 Small pox.
19 The lungs.
20 Electrocardiograph.
21 Yellow fever.
22 White blood cells.
23 A concave lens.
24 The herpes zoster virus.
25 The liver.
26 Paralysis.
27 Muscle spasms.
28 The brain cells.
29 Peritonitis.
30 The salivary glands.
31 The intestines.
32 The lungs.
33 Rubella.
34 The herpes simplex virus.
35 Syphilis.
36 Gastric ulcer.
37 Glandular fever.
38 Parkinson's disease.
39 Whooping cough.
40 A fungal infection of the skin.
41 The big toe.
42 To reduce the acid secretion of the stomach.
43 The blood supply to the brain is disrupted.
44 Sinusitis.
45 Piles.
46 The inflammation of one or more sebaceous glands on the eyelid.
47 The vertebrae.
48 Jaundice.
49 Blood vessels in the form of X-rays.
50 The clouding of the lens in the eye, which can eventually lead to blindness.

Sport (122-123)

1 Lillehammer, Norway.
2 Ivan Lendl.
3 Boxing.
4 Gertrude Ederle.
5 The Chicago Bears.
6 The decathlon consists of ten events, the modern pentathlon of only five.
7 A Japanese art of self-defence.
8 Tony Jacklin.
9 In the Bois de Bologne in Paris.
10 Motor racing.
11 Figure skating.
12 Ice hockey.
13 Seve Ballesteros.
14 Swimming.
15 Pierre de Coubertin.
16 Roger Bannister.
17 Twenty-six miles.
18 England.
19 Nine.
20 The New York Cosmos.
21 Jackie Robinson.
22 Johnny Weissmuller.
23 Golf.
24 Daley Thompson.
25 Eric Heiden.
26 A combination of cross-country skiing and target shooting.
27 Diego Maradona.
28 The 1936 Games in Berlin.
29 Pittsburgh.
30 The Football World Cup.
31 Steffi Graf.
32 Yankee Stadium.
33 Boxing.
34 Because of New Zealand's sporting links with South Africa.
35 Uruguay, in 1930.
36 Vault and floor exercises.
37 The marathon.
38 Golf.
39 Pete Sampras.
40 Steve Davis.
41 Badminton.
42 Paavo Nurmi.
43 Horse racing.
44 The 400m hurdles.
45 Thirteen.
46 Skiing.
47 Mexico City.
48 Gabriela Sabatini.
49 The Lions.
50 Its annual 24-hour car race.

Places (124-125)

1 Oimyakon in Siberia.
2 (b) Brazil, where the spoken language is Portuguese. All the others are Spanish-speaking countries.
3 (d) Cairo.
4 Portugal.
5 Roman Catholic.
6 (c) Hungary.
7 Wellington.
8 Ireland.
9 Louisiana.
10 Shanghai.
11 (a) Manchuria, which is part of China. All the other states formed part of the USSR.
12 Boston.
13 Monaco.
14 The Galapagos Islands.
15 Mammoth Cave in Kentucky.
16 The Great Barrier Reef.
17 Harare.
18 Fleet Street.
19 India; all the others are predominantly Moslem, whereas India is predominantly Hindu.
20 (b) Mauna Loa on Hawaii.
21 New York.
22 Sicily.
23 Norway.
24 Rome.
25 Spain.
26 Ireland.
27 (c) Tennessee.
28 Lima.
29 Northern Ireland.
30 Chantilly.
31 Buenos Aires.
32 The Zambezi river.
33 Israel.
34 Queensland.
35 The Everglades.
36 (c) Saudi Arabia.
37 New York.
38 Tobago.
39 Cuba.
40 (a) Utah.
41 Quebec.
42 Washington D.C.
43 Manila.
44 (c) Poland.
45 Switzerland.
46 Rome.
47 Florence.
48 London.
49 Florida.
50 South Africa.

The Weather (126-127)

1 The troposphere.
2 Fronts.
3 The Kelvin scale.
4 An anemometer.
5 An anemometer that keeps a record of wind speeds.
6 A hurricane.
7 The doldrums.
8 A tornado.
9 A rotating column of air, similar to a tornado but smaller, that raises dust from the earth.
10 To measure atmospheric humidity.
11 One that measures very small variations in atmospheric pressure.
12 Mercury.
13 The stratosphere.
14 It is sometimes used in an attempt to

15 Snow that has melted and refrozen into a rough, angular surface.
16 The upper part of a glacier where the snow turns into ice.
17 A polar weather condition caused by heavy cloud over the snow, in which light coming from above is approximately equal to light reflected from below.
18 Rock debris transported downhill by rain.
19 A rain gauge.
20 2.5m (100 in) per annum.
21 Rain that contains high levels of sulphuric or nitric acids.
22 A line drawn on a map to indicate points of equal rainfall.
23 Balloons.
24 The overflowing of a stream resulting from sudden heavy rain or a thaw.
25 A wind from the south-west or south that brings heavy rain in summer.
26 That which is produced by, or pertains to, flooding.
27 A high wave caused by the surge of a flood tide upstream in a narrowing estuary or by colliding tidal currents.
28 A tropical forest that has constant cloud cover throughout the year.
29 Cumulonimbus.
30 Clouds that are luminous at night.
31 A photoelectric instrument for ascertaining cloud heights.
32 An extremely powerful downward air current from a cumulonimbus cloud.
33 A high-altitude, thin, hazy cloud, usually covering the sky and often producing a halo effect.
34 Wisps of precipitation streaming from a cloud but evaporating before reaching the ground.
35 An optical device designed to project images of atmospheric phenomena, such as clouds, onto the inside of a dome.
36 A sky covered with many small cirrocumulus or altocumulus clouds, giving an overall effect of the markings to be found on a mackerel.
37 A long, narrow cirrus cloud with a flowing appearance.
38 That which causes them to form lumpy or fluffy masses.
39 The first experimental weather satellite launched by the USA in 1960.
40 The ratio of the amount of water vapor in the air at a specific temperature to the maximum amount that the air could hold at that temperature, expressed as a percentage.
41 A layer in a large body of water, such as a lake, that sharply separates regions differing in temperature.
42 The temperature of windless air that would have the same effect on

exposed human skin as a given combination of wind speed and air temperature.
43 The rate of decrease of atmospheric temperature with increase in altitude.
44 The temperature at which air becomes saturated and produces dew.
45 An area, such as a city or an industrial site, having consistently higher temperatures than surrounding areas because of a greater retention of heat.
46 An instrument that records simultaneously several meteorological conditions, such as temperature, pressure, and humidity.
47 Climate is the average weather conditions in an area over a long time (often cited as 30 years).
48 25 cm (10 in).
49 72 km/h (45 mph).
50 The thermosphere.

Popular Music and Musicals (128-129)

1 Ennio Morricone.
2 Ringo Starr.
3 Irving Berlin.
4 *Human Touch* and *Lucky Town*.
5 Josephine Baker.
6 *Sweet Charity*.
7 'Sacrifice'.
8 *The Fine Art of Surfacing*.
9 Vangelis.
10 Led Zeppelin.
11 *Sergeant Pepper's Lonely Hearts Club Band*.
12 T.S. Eliot.
13 'Waterloo Sunset'.
14 *Kiss Me, Kate*.
15 *No Jacket Required*.
16 Kiki Dee.
17 Jerome Kern.
18 'Power to All Our Friends'.
19 Trombone.
20 *The Works*.
21 Central Park in New York.
22 Julio Iglesias.
23 Michael Jackson.
24 *West Side Story*.
25 'Let it Be'.
26 Elton John.
27 Rodgers and Hammerstein.
28 Saxophone.
29 Rainbow.
30 Gospel music.
31 'Startin' Over'.
32 In the Appalachian Mountains.
33 Chinn and Chapman.
34 'Oh no, this is the road to hell.'
35 Andrew Lloyd Webber.
36 Dixieland.
37 'Heartbreak Hotel'.
38 Elkie Brooks.
39 'We Don't Need Another Hero'.

40 Irving Berlin.
41 *Out of Time*.
42 The Beach Boys.
43 Chuck Berry.
44 David Bowie.
45 John Coltrane.
46 Aretha Franklin.
47 The Faces.
48 Motown.
49 'Imagine'.
50 *Cabaret*.

Costume (130-131)

1 A cravat.
2 A crinoline.
3 In North Africa and the Middle East.
4 Breeches.
5 The 1920s.
6 A bandana.
7 A pinafore.
8 A fez.
9 The wide-legged, baggy trousers which were first worn by Oxford undergraduates.
10 Long and straight with a belt lowered to the hip.
11 Long johns.
12 A corset.
13 A waterproof hat with a broad rim at the back to protect the neck.
14 A piupi.
15 A grass skirt.
16 It is short-sleeved and brightly coloured and usually has a motif such as palm-trees or parrots.
17 Leather shorts, often with suspenders.
18 Long drawers worn in the 19th century.
19 A tartan wool.
20 Culottes.
21 A dirndl.
22 It tried to extend the skirt horizontally from the waist.
23 A one-piece garment consisting of a blouse with trousers attached to it.
24 To raise one's height in order to keep the feet clean in muddy streets.
25 They could be folded up.
26 A garter.
27 They end slightly above the knee.
28 Nylon.
29 Platforms.
30 None.
31 A ruff.
32 The clergy.
33 A himation.
34 Purple.
35 A beret.
36 A soft felt hat with a creased crown.
37 The 1960s.
38 A dinner jacket.
39 A black bow tie.
40 The clergy.
41 Natural.
42 A galosh.
43 Fabric.

44 Russia.
45 A loose-fitting, straight-cut dress, sometimes worn with a belt.
46 A loose, brightly-coloured African garment.
47 A wet suit.
48 Straw.
49 A gauntlet.
50 A muff.

Mountains (132-133)

1   New Zealand.
2   Mount McKinley.
3   The Sierra Nevada.
4   Mount Elbrus.
5   Tibet and Nepal.
6   The Blue Mountains.
7   (c) Nebraska.
8   Tanzania.
9   The Great Dividing Range.
10 Scotland.
11 The Black Forest.
12 The Ardennes.
13 The Grossglockner.
14 Romania.
15 The Alps and the Balkans.
16 South Africa.
17 The Sahara.
18 (a) Czechoslovakia.
19 The Atlas Mountains.
20 The French–Swiss border.
21 The Vosges.
22 The Erzgebirge.
23 The Himalayas.
24 K2.
25 India (Kashmir).
26 Mount Logan.
27 India and Nepal.
28 The Alps.
29 Austria and Italy.
30 Wales.
31 Mount Kenya.
32 The Black Sea and the Caspian Sea.
33 (b) Afghanistan.
34 Ben Nevis.
35 The Carpathian Mountains.
36 The Alps and Jura Mountains.
37 Mount Ararat.
38 The Aconcagua.
39 Antarctica.
40 Mount Kosciusko.
41 The Appalachian Mountains.
42 Mexico.
43 The Sequoia National Park.
44 Italy and Switzerland.
45 The Pennine Alps.
46 Mouna Kea.
47 Java and Sumatra.
48 Fujiyama.
49 The Pyrenees.
50 The Apennines.

Pop Music (134-135)

1   *Bad.*
2   Rodgers and Hammerstein.
3   Phil Collins.
4   The Rolling Stones.
5   *Don't Bore Us – Get to the Chorus.*
6   Diamond Life.
7   Whitney Houston.
8   The Sound of Music.
9   Wet Wet Wet.
10 U2.
11 Tina Turner.
12 *Labour of Love II.*
13 Carly Simon.
14 Supertramp.
15 *Flashdance.*
16 Burt Bacharach.
17 The trumpet.
18 *Saturday Night Fever.*
19 Ennio Morricone.
20 *Tears Roll Down.*
21 Bruce Springsteen.
22 *Bridge Over Troubled Water.*
23 *Oliver!*
24 Randy Newman.
25 Sting.
26 *Stars.*
27 1965.
28 Panpipes.
29 Neil Diamond.
30 The Seekers.
31 Cole Porter.
32 Edith Piaf.
33 *Legend.*
34 Chaka Khan.
35 M People.
36 *Grease.*
37 *The Jungle Book.*
38 Runrig.
39 Jamiroquai.
40 Lionel Richie.
41 Alison Moyet.
42 Little Richard.
43 1985.
44 Cher.
45 *Slippery When Wet.*
46 *The Kick Inside.*
47 *A Kind of Magic.*
48 Soft Cell.
49 *Magical Mystery Tour.*
50 Tori Amos.

Science (136-137)

1   Nitrogen.
2   9.81 m/second (32 feet/second).
3   Displacement.
4   Aqua regia.
5   Trinitrotoluene.
6   Radio detecting and ranging.
7   Antoine Lavoisier.
8   An organic dye usually used as an indicator of acidity or alkalinity.
9   21%.
10 Copper.
11 Zinc.
12 Hydrogen sylphide.
13 Random Access Memory.
14 They can both be magnetized.
15 The crashing or booming sound produced by rapidly expanding air along the path of the electrical discharge of lightning.
16 Beetles.
17 Chlorophyll.
18 An alloy.
19 True.
20 Yes, the moon has the effect of causing movement in so-called 'solid' land.
21 The notion that life arrived on Earth from elsewhere in the universe.
22 An enzyme.
23 Polestar, North star, or polar star.
24 Andromeda.
25 Saturn.
26 Jupiter.
27 Mercury.
28 Water.
29 Jupiter.
30 Platinum.
31 A little over 297,600 km/sec (186,000 miles/sec).
32 148,800,000 km (93,000,000 miles).
33 3,456 km (2,160 miles).
34 A quantum leap.
35 Pasteurization.
36 An eclipse.
37 A vacuum.
38 The ball-point pen.
39 The Hoover vacuum cleaner.
40 A prosthesis.
41 Prevention of or protective treatment for disease.
42 Chaos theory.
43 Photosynthesis.
44 Etiolation.
45 Agar.
46 The Bunsen burner.
47 Horsepower.
48 0°C.
49 32°F.
50 Genetics.

Food & Drink (138-139)

1   Rice.
2   A small cake of minced food which is usually coated in breadcrumbs and fried.
3   The parsley family.
4   Sage.
5   Cornmeal.
6   Cucumbers, tomatoes, onions, and peppers.
7   Sangria.
8   Greece.
9   Lamb.
10 Paprika.
11 A slice of meat rolled around a filling.
12 Suet.
13 From the leg directly above the foot.
14 Sturgeon.
15 Chickpeas.
16 Cream.
17 Scotland.
18 Beer.

19 It is an Indian clay oven used for cooking meat and baking bread.
20 It is made of mayonnaise, chopped pickles, capers, and anchovies, and eaten cold.
21 Périgord.
22 A very dark, strong beer.
23 Vodka and orange juice.
24 Cannelloni.
25 A corn tortilla wrapped around a filling usually consisting of meat and cheese.
26 Jambalaya.
27 Cappuccino.
28 It is a cross between a grapefruit, an orange, and a tangerine.
29 Burgundy.
30 Vodka or gin and sweetened lime juice.
31 Ham.
32 The cabbage family.
33 Basil.
34 India.
35 A herring.
36 It is normally used for making salads.
37 An extract from soy beans.
38 Plums.
39 A sweetened bread which, after baking, is cut into slices and toasted.
40 Wine.
41 A type of Indian bread.
42 Spain.
43 Rye.
44 Spinach.
45 A type of bun.
46 A rich chocolate cake.
47 Almonds.
48 A soup.
49 The tenderloin.
50 Pieces of grilled meat on a skewer, often alternated with vegetables.

The Bible (140-141)

1   It is from the Greek word for books.
2   The Five Books of Moses.
3   Thirty-six.
4   Sixty-three.
5   The Apocrypha.
6   The Septuagint.
7   Because it was the work of 70 translators.
8   Those found among the Dead Sea Scrolls.
9   A codex.
10 The Torah.
11 The First and Second Books of Samuel.
12 MENE MENE TEKEL UPHARSIN.
13 Because they were suffering from famine.
14 Ishmael and Isaac.
15 Jericho.
16 Ham, Shem, and Japheth.
17 Jacob and Esau.
18 Daniel.
19 Solomon.
20 Delilah.
21 Goliath.

22 Judah.
23 The Sea of Galilee and the Dead Sea.
24 Nebuchadnezzar II.
25 The Essenes.
26 Moses.
27 The Canaanites.
28 Death of the first born.
29 The Queen of Sheba.
30 Assyria.
31 Cyrus.
32 Mesopotamia.
33 Herod the Great.
34 Lower Galilee.
35 The Sea of Tiberias.
36 St. Paul.
37 St. Stephen.
38 Matthew, Mark, Luke, John.
39 The Revelation of St. John the Divine.
40 It is the Number of the Beast.
41 Golgotha.
42 Caspar, Balthazar, Melchior.
43 John the Baptist.
44 Salome.
45 Conquest, War, Famine, Death.
46 The Synoptic Gospels.
47 Romans, Corinthians, Galtaians, Ephesians, Philippians, Colossians, Thessalonians, Timothy, Titus, Philemon.
48 There is no mention of it in Roman records.
49 Jude.
50 Matthias.

The USA (142-143)

1   Kentucky.
2   Rhode Island.
3   The Mississippi.
4   1787.
5   The Congress.
6   Thirteen.
7   California.
8   St. Augustine, Florida.
9   Andrew Jackson.
10 The Senate and The House of Representatives.
11 New York, Los Angeles and Chicago.
12 Tallahassee.
13 The Seminole War.
14 In the south-west, in particular New Mexico and Arizona.
15 The annexation of Texas by the USA in 1845.
16 The Confederacy.
17 The Republicans.
18 Two four-year terms.
19 Thirty-five.
20 Augusta.
21 Lyndon B. Johnson.
22 Washington.
23 Ross Perot.
24 New Deal.
25 The Potomac.
26 Mardi Gras.
27 The Star-spangled Banner.
28 Juneau.

29 The Apaches.
30 The Mississippi.
31 In the southern states, especially Louisiana.
32 Chicago.
33 The sale, manufacture and transportation of all alcoholic drinks.
34 Los Angeles.
35 The Rio Grande.
36 Long Island.
37 Ellis Island.
38 The Cheyennes and Sioux.
39 Little Rock.
40 The Erie Canal.
41 Columbus Day.
42 Franklin D. Roosevelt.
43 Death Valley, in California.
44 Harvard University.
45 San Francisco.
46 The Oregon Trail.
47 Texas.
48 Santa Fé.
49 The Hudson River.
50 The FBI (Federal Bureau of Investigation).

Recreation (144-145)

1   White.
2   Chinese chess.
3   Pontoon.
4   The shape of the ball.
5   Mohammad Ali.
6   Draughts or checkers.
7   Chess.
8   Billiards.
9   Poker.
10 Cricket.
11 Ten-pin bowling.
12 Baseball.
13 A gridiron.
14 Jai alai or pelota.
15 Judo.
16 40.
17 A scrum.
18 True.
19 Lacrosse.
20 Ice hockey.
21 The sin bin.
22 Basketball.
23 Seven.
24 Volleyball.
25 Baseball.
26 No, only wooden ones.
27 Toe and heel plates screwed to the soles of their boots.
28 An over.
29 Willow.
30 Real tennis.
31 Tennis.
32 The 19th century.
33 None.
34 Table tennis.
35 Yes.
36 The speed of the ball.
37 Golf.

38 Soccer.
39 Angling.
40 The Olympics.
41 Poker.
42 Roulette.
43 Boules.
44 Hurling.
45 Curling.
46 Mah jongg.
47 Gin rummy.
48 Scrabble.
49 The crossword.
50 Marathon.

Food and Drink (146-147)

1 Parmesan cheese.
2 A pepper.
3 Swede.
4 Seaweed.
5 A large shrimp.
6 Sicily.
7 A cheese.
8 A fool.
9 Fermented rice.
10 Pimento.
11 Sundae.
12 A ragout of meat or fish.
13 Egg yolk, oil, and lemon juice or vinegar.
14 A thick, sweetened and flavoured milk pudding.
15 A cream sauce with peppers and mushrooms.
16 Avocado.
17 Barley.
18 Chilli.
19 Brandy and gin.
20 Sour cream.
21 A mushroom, grown in eastern Asia.
22 Nutmeg.
23 Sausagemeat and breadcrumbs.
24 Egg whites and sugar.
25 Caraway seed
26 A cake.
27 Pâté and pastry.
28 Stewed fruit or cheese rolled up in a thin layer of pastry and baked.
29 You fry them lightly in an open pan, tossing them occasionally.
30 Avocado.
31 Orange peel.
32 A savoury pastry.
33 Béchamel sauce.
34 A sort of relish.
35 Rum, creamed coconut and pineapple juice.
36 Belgium.
37 The bouquet.
38 It contains spinach.
39 Tarragon and chervil.
40 A curry.
41 Chocolate.
42 Blackcurrants.
43 Japan.
44 Hollandaise sauce.
45 A roux.

46 A sherry.
47 The pancreas.
48 Chinese cooking.
49 Peanut sauce.
50 The small intestines.

The Human Body (148-149)

1 The iris.
2 The middle ear.
3 Arteries.
4 Nerve cells.
5 Meninges.
6 Corpus callosum.
7 The biceps.
8 It prevents the bones from rubbing and pressing against each other and thus wearing away.
9 Plasma.
10 The higher one is the systolic pressure (the peak of the contraction of the heart), the second for the diastolic pressure (the heart during relaxation).
11 Tendons.
12 Capillaries.
13 To fight infection.
14 The two pumps of the heart.
15 Insulin.
16 About 5 litres (10 pints).
17 At the base of the brain.
18 In the toes.
19 Bone marrow.
20 The femur, situated in the thigh.
21 The intercostal muscles in the ribs, and the diaphragm.
22 The pleura.
23 Trachea.
24 The hamstring.
25 Pepsin.
26 The gall bladder.
27 It emulsifies fat so that it can then enter the bloodstream.
28 The pancreas.
29 The duodenum, jejunum, and ileum.
30 The liver.
31 It has no function at all.
32 Chyme.
33 Amino acids.
34 The liver.
35 Mitochondria.
36 The kidneys.
37 Deoxyribonucleic acid.
38 Sebum.
39 Thirty-two.
40 Hair and nails.
41 The ureters.
42 Too much ultraviolet radiation in sunlight.
43 Eight pieces of bone that surround and protect the brain.
44 Sclera.
45 It is a part of the inner ear, responsible for hearing.
46 The two halves of the brain.
47 They show as freckles.
48 The heel.
49 The blood clotting mechanism.

50 The larynx.

Pot Luck (150-151)

1 Ian Fleming.
2 Leonardo da Vinci.
3 The Republicans.
4 The Spanish Steps.
5 Cricket.
6 Benazir Bhutto.
7 The Chinese Communist party.
8 The Middle Kingdom.
9 Queensland and Northern Territories Air Service.
10 Lake Victoria.
11 Sri Lanka.
12 Lion.
13 The Indian subcontinent.
14 Cambridge.
15 Multiple sclerosis.
16 Thomas Hardy.
17 The kidneys.
18 Bile.
19 The lawn mower.
20 The first monument of this kind was built at Halicarnassus to house the body of Mausolus.
21 Tsars and Tsarinas.
22 A surface-to-air-missile.
23 Japan.
24 Ezra Pound.
25 The Central Criminal Court.
26 Mark Chapman.
27 Lynette (Squeaky) Fromm.
28 Richard Nixon.
29 Someone who deputizes for a doctor or clergyman.
30 A dance.
31 Wallis Simpson.
32 Laos.
33 Republic of Ireland.
34 Scarlett O'Hara in Gone With the Wind.
35 Gaelic.
36 Joseph Heller.
37 1967.
38 West.
39 The Godfather.
40 Eeyore.
41 A funeral rite or ceremony.
42 Ruth Ellis.
43 1914.
44 Country and western.
45 Ernest Hemingway.
46 Breakfast at Tiffany's; Capote wrote the novel, Hepburn played the lead in the film.
47 Every four years.
48 Undertaker and mortician.
49 Cul is a vulgar word for buttocks.
50 Goolagong.

TOUGH

TOUGH

History (152-153)

1 1707.
2 Rutherford B. Hayes.
3 The Bastille.
4 Tarquin VII.
5 Anything pertaining to Charlemagne.
6 Hannibal.
7 There were four emperors.
8 Not at all. The military potential was realized very quickly.
9 They were descended from Vikings.
10 Sydney Harbour Bridge.
11 1767.
12 Ur of the Chaldees.
13 Visconti.
14 A dynasty of French kings.
15 The Colosseum.
16 The (Chiricahua) Apaches.
17 The Incas.
18 The guillotine.
19 Alfred Hitchcock's Blackmail (1929).
20 By the introduction of the Code Napoleon.
21 Jack the Ripper.
22 Alfred Dreyfus.
23 Leon Trotsky.
24 The Wright brothers make the first sustained, manned flights in a controlled, gasoline-powered aircraft.
25 El Cid (Ruy Diaz de Bivar).
26 Garibaldi.
27 Wolfe and Montcalm.
28 The wives of Henry VIII.
29 The Plantagenets.
30 Bucephalus (ox head).
31 David Rizzio.
32 Mardi Gras.
33 Georges Clemenceau.
34 It was the first modern cooperative society.
35 Pirates.
36 Prester John.
37 General Charles Gordon.
38 Bull Run.
39 Hannibal, Missouri.
40 Franklin D. Roosevelt.
41 Teddy Roosevelt (1903).
42 The Stone of Scone.
43 Oliver Cromwell.
44 They all held Geronimo prisoner at one time or another.
45 Robert E. Lee.
46 Martin Luther.
47 *Hoc est corpus* (*meum*).
48 Simon Bolivar.
49 Edo.
50 Lake Tanganyika.

Money (154-155)

1 Fort Knox in Kentucky.

2 Minting.
3 In the kingdom of Lydia, which is now known as Turkey.
4 The zloty.
5 Susan B. Anthony, a feminist leader.
6 Ten.
7 The thaler.
8 1971.
9 The dirham.
10 The Isle of Man, and the Channel Islands of Guernsey and Jersey.
11 Monte Carlo.
12 It was a silver coin used in Ancient Greece.
13 100 pfennig.
14 Numismatics.
15 Gold.
16 France.
17 The copper cent.
18 Twelve.
19 Tobacco leaves.
20 Sweden.
21 The forint.
22 The centime.
23 Intaglio plates.
24 China.
25 As dust.
26 The rupee.
27 Assignats.
28 The guinea.
29 Ten dollars.
30 The rand.
31 The Spanish conquerors of the Americas.
32 A female head representing the republic. It is popularly known as 'Marianne'.
33 The krona.
34 A farthing.
35 Japan.
36 Finland, which has a system that was introduced by the Russians.
37 The Ancient Greeks.
38 In Spain and Spanish America.
39 Copper plate money, from Sweden.
40 Venice.
41 A portrait of the emperor.
42 Copper, in the form of lumps.
43 In northern Italy.
44 There are two types of coin issued, one with French writing and one with Flemish writing.
45 Denmark, Sweden, and Norway.
46 The lira.
47 Telephone coins.
48 Cent.
49 Barter.
50 Krugerrands.

Transport (156-157)

1 It was the first one to fly around the world without needing to refuel.
2 TGV – *Trains à Grande Vitesse*.
3 London.

4 1976.
5 The Volkswagen 'Beetle'.
6 Flying, in the form of a hot-air balloon.
7 Spirit of St. Louis.
8 The explosion of the Hindenburg.
9 Steam locomotives used in the 1940s to haul freight trains across the Rocky Mountains.
10 Igor Sikorsky.
11 The de Havilland Comet 1, entering service in 1952.
12 The hovercraft.
13 The internal combustion engine.
14 The Model T, produced by the Ford Motor Company.
15 It is virtually invisible to radar.
16 A tandem.
17 It is a flat plate on the upper surface of the wing, which, when raised, increases drag and reduces lift.
18 The Savannah.
19 The hovercraft is lifted by a cushion of air, the hydrofoil by wings, similar to those of an aircraft.
20 Its framework, excluding the engine and masts.
21 Gliders.
22 Steam turbines.
23 The jet engine obtains the oxygen needed for burning fuel from the atmosphere whilst the rocket carries its own oxidant.
24 A sailing ship with a square rig and three masts, usually with two or more decks.
25 In a petrol engine the fuel-air mixture is ignited by a spark, but in a diesel engine by compression of the air in the cylinders.
26 Abraham Bower ran a 12-seater horse-drawn bus.
27 Captain Cook.
28 Kirkpatrick Macmillan.
29 Santa Maria.
30 Microlight.
31 Diesel engines.
32 Magellan's Vittoria.
33 A single-masted sailing ship.
34 Hackney.
35 That way they can maintain a safe air speed at a lower ground speed.
36 It had a large front wheel and a small rear wheel.
37 The Seikan tunnel between Honshu and Hokkaido.
38 Gottlieb Daimler.
39 They could not move off instantly as water had to boil first in order to produce steam.
40 England.
41 It had a steerable front wheel.
42 Usually by means of a drive chain, or in very expensive models by a driveshaft.
43 He built the first steam-powered

locomotive.
44 Paris and Istanbul.
45 Louis Bleriot.
46 A steam-powered automobile, the Stanley Steamer.
47 To produce an explosive fuel-air mixture.
48 The St. Gothard Tunnel.
49 The Pioneer Yelloway bus.
50 The Turtle, used in the American War of Independence.

Customs (158-159)

1 Hogmanay.
2 Trick or treat.
3 The maypole dance.
4 A festivity associated with much drinking.
5 The Jewish official who leads the musical part of a service.
6 (b) Christmas.
7 The Lord of Misrule.
8 Walpurgis Night (also called the Eve of Beltane).
9 Inuit.
10 Maoris.
11 New Year's Eve?
12 A religious service held on New Year's Eve.
13 The feast commemorating the exodus of the Jews from Egypt.
14 The Apaches.
15 The Kaaba
16 A rite of passage for Jewish girls.
17 They strangled them.
18 A scapegoat.
19 A boy formerly raised with a prince or other young nobleman and whipped for the latter's misdeeds.
20 Native Americans.
21 Irish or Scots.
22 Australian Aboriginals.
23 Walkabout.
24 Dreamtime.
25 The bull run.
26 People who had committed suicide.
27 After disembowelling himself, he was decapitated by a friend.
28 Smoking a pipe.
29 Mummify the dead.
30 He hears an owl say his name.
31 It supposedly cures the poisonous bite from a spider.
32 The Mafia.
33 His friends shave him with an axe.
34 A stake being driven through the heart (garlic in the mouth is optional).
35 The Indian custom, now outlawed, of burning a widow on the pyre of her husband.
36 Ramadan.
37 Holi.
38 Pancakes.
39 Ash Wednesday.
40 A haggis.
41 Black Rod.
42 The door is slammed in his face.
43 Guy Fawkes.
44 Thanskgiving.
45 The borders of a parish were established by beating the hedges which formed them.
46 Rum, sodomy, and the lash.
47 A pit with the bottom covered in pebbles and full of melted snow from the mountains. Walking barefoot in the icy water is supposed to be refreshing.
48 Infant baptism.
49 To the left.
50 Parsses.

The Arts (160-161)

1 Buster Keaton.
2 Charlie Chaplin.
3 Charles Vidor.
4 Prince Igor.
5 A gremlin.
6 Vaudeville.
7 Gary Cooper.
8 *Picnic at Hanging Rock*.
9 Edgar Allan Poe.
10 H.P. Lovecraft.
11 Marlene Dietrich.
12 Paul Scofield.
13 *Long Day's Journey into Night*.
14 Tennessee Williams.
15 Arthur Miller.
16 Jack Kerouac.
17 Walt Whitman.
18 *The Canterbury Tales*.
19 Louis Armstrong.
20 Melanie Safka.
21 Nick Park.
22 Emma Thompson.
23 Helena Bonham-Carter.
24 Jack Nicholson.
25 Master Blaster.
26 Nick Nolte.
27 China is invaded by Japan.
28 Goldfinger.
29 *Midnight Cowboy*.
30 Eddie Murphy and Dan Ackroyd in *Trading Places*.
31 'Twin Peaks'.
32 'The X Files'.
33 The third.
34 Marlon Brando.
35 *A Few Good Men*.
36 John Wayne.
37 *The Quest for Peace*.
38 Robert Shaw.
39 Barbara Vine.
40 Jarvis Cocker.
41 Sylvia Plath.
42 Roy Lichtenstein.
43 Simon & Garfunkel wrote the song 'So Long Frank Lloyd Wright', who designed the Guggenheim.
44 Don McLean.
45 *The Odd Couple*.
46 *Phantom of the Opera*.
47 *Walkabout*.
48 He is an obstetrician.
49 'The Addams Family'.
50 Lassie.

Foreign Phrases (162-163)

1 The USA.
2 A skull.
3 The Order of the Garter.
4 Julius Caesar of the invasion of Britain.
5 A healthy mind in a healthy body.
6 Acting beyond your lawful powers.
7 Borrowing makes sorrow.
8 Pleasure in the misfortunes of others.
9 The Royal Air Force.
10 Oh, the times! Oh, the manners!
11 Sic transit gloria mundi.
12 In a casino.
13 The more things change, the more they remain the same.
14 Carthage must be wiped out.
15 I think, therefore I am.
16 Divide and rule.
17 It is sweet and glorious to die for one's country.
18 Long time, no see.
19 'I have it!'
20 God with us.
21 The Prince of Wales'. It means 'I serve'.
22 Let there be light.
23 Seize the day.
24 All things are in flux.
25 What will be, will be.
26 Peace be upon you.
27 No answer is still an answer (silence gives consent).
28 Woman is changeable.
29 Children playing (always used ironically of adults).
30 Erin forever.
31 'Fortune favors fools' and 'Fortune favors the brave'.
32 It is a harmless thunderbolt.
33 A bolt of lightning.
34 A dramatic twist.
35 A punch.
36 People tell the truth when drunk.
37 While I breathe I hope.
38 It does move all the same.
39 Here I am and here I stay.
40 It does not please (a negative vote).
41 The will of God.
42 A grave (it means 'Here lies...').
43 No; it means 'Make haste slowly'.
44 Time flies.
45 No; it means 'I am willing but unable'.
46 Etc.
47 Yes; it means 'See Naples and die'.
48 O holy simplicity.
49 An unlikely and beneficial intervention (literally, God from the machine).
50 It is magnificent but it is not war.

Current Affairs (164-165)

1 Tamil separatists.
2 Sirimavo Bandaranaike of Sri Lanka.
3 George Papadopoulos.
4 Leopoldo Galtieri.

5 Egypt's membership was suspended because of its peace agreement with Israel.
6 Salvador Allende of Chile.
7 SWAPO.
8 Admiral John Poindexter and Lieutenant Colonel Oliver North.
9 Egypt.
10 The European Coal and Steel Community.
11 1980–88.
12 Olof Palme.
13 General Wojciech Jaruzelzki.
14 Spandau Prison in Berlin.
15 Ronald Reagan and Mikhail Gorbachev.
16 They tried to achieve status as political prisoners.
17 James Callaghan.
18 Louis Mountbatten.
19 Syria.
20 Felipe Gonzalez Marquez.
21 An East German spy was discovered in his administration.
22 Dan Quayle.
23 Manuel Noriega.
24 Enver Hoxha.
25 Great Britain, Ireland, and Denmark.
26 Apollo 11.
27 1966-9.
28 Javier Pérez de Cuellar.
29 Habib Bourguiba.
30 Papa Doc.
31 Adolf Eichmann.
32 1961.
33 Chou En-Lai.
34 King Farouk.
35 Sputnik I.
36 Alaska.
37 Jacques Chirac.
38 Azerbaijan.
39 Sheik Mujibar Rahmann.
40 His third wife, Maria Estela (Isabel) Martínez de Perón.
41 The kidnapping and beating of four young men, one of whom died.
42 1983.
43 Russia, Belorussia, and the Ukraine.
44 Governor of Georgia.
45 Sitiveni Rabuka.
46 Abel Muzorewa.
47 Fianna Fáil.
48 1979.
49 Gro Harlem Brundtland.
50 The People's Temple.

Odd One Out (166-167)

1 (c) python: it is a non-venomous constrictor.
2 (a) Schubert: all the others are Baroque composers.
3 (a) amaretto: it is a liqueur whereas all the others are fortified.
4 (d) ileum: it forms part of the small intestine.
5 (d) Paul Rubens, all the others were Impressionists.
6 (b) weeping willow.
7 (a) saxophone: it is a woodwind instrument.

9 (d) Oklahoma, all the others are situated along the east coast.
10 (a) calvados: it is a type of brandy whereas all the others are.
11 (a) Ceres: it is an asteroid.
12 (c) Claudio Arrau: who was a pianist whereas all the others are violinists.
13 (d) gazpacho: it is a type of soup whereas all the others are curries.
14 (a) lion: all the others are herbivores.
15 (d) Honduras: all the others are in Africa.
16 (c) Khrushchev: all the others were involved in the Russian Revolution.
17 (a) Massachusetts.
18 (c) podiatrist: all the others deal with children.
19 (c) snapdragon: all the others belong to the primrose family.
20 (a) The Bartered Bride: it is an opera whereas all the others are musicals.
21 (a) Mackerel: all the others are freshwater fish.
22 (d) patience: all the others are types of puzzle.
23 (a) Carl Lewis: all the others are swimmers.
24 (c) Casablanca: all the others are capital cities.
25 (d) John F. Kennedy.
26 (a) fly agaric.
27 (c) Frank Sinatra: all the others are rock 'n' roll singers.
28 (d) Madeira: all the others are in the West Indies.
29 (c) To Kill a Mockingbird: all the others star Audrey Hepburn.
30 (d) opera: all the others are forms of sacred music.
31 (a) Jacques Cousteau: he is an underwater explorer whereas the others are writers.
32 (c) amber: all the others are gemstones.
33 (d) salamander: it is an amphibian whereas all the others are reptiles.
34 (b) Corsica: all the others belong to Italy.
35 (a) Tunisia.
36 (c) coq au vin: none of the others contains meat.
37 (c) clavicle: all the others are types of muscle.
38 (b) Placido Domingo: he is a singer whereas all the others are composers.
39 (b) Normandy: all the others are in Italy.
40 (b) Tartarus.
41 (c) Egyptian: all the others were based on the American continent.
42 (a) Miami: all the others are US state capitals.
43 (a) Sir Isaac Newton: he was a scientist whereas all the others were inventors.
44 (c) cassis: all the others are types of brandy.
45 (c) Stewart Granger: all the others have been married to Elizabeth Taylor.
47 (a) Jimmy Carter: all the others were Republicans.
48 (c) Thailand.
49 (a) Battle of Verdun: it took place in World War I.
50 (d) retinol: it is a vitamin whereas all the

others are types of mineral.

Rivers (168-169)

1 South River.
2 The Missouri.
3 The Embarrass River.
4 The Thames.
5 The Missouri and Mississippi.
6 The Nile.
7 The Yellow River.
8 The Mekong.
9 The Jordan.
10 Baton Rouge, Louisiana.
11 The Danube.
12 Czechoslovakia and Germany.
13 Le Havre.
14 The Black Sea.
15 The Rhein.
16 Munich.
17 The Yukon.
18 The River Plate.
19 The Moskva.
20 The Volga.
21 The Ganges.
22 The Colorado.
23 The Hudson.
24 The Seine.
25 The Spree.
26 The River Kwai.
27 Bangkok.
28 The River Jordan.
29 The Congo.
30 Rio Grande and Rio Brave del Norte.
31 The St Lawrence.
32 The Amazon.
33 The Orinoco.
34 The Mersey.
35 The Douro and the Tagus.
36 The Donau.
37 Calcutta.
38 The Indus.
39 The Tennessee.
40 The Ohio.
41 The Mackenzie.
42 The Alabama.
43 The Susquehanna.
44 The Orange.
45 The San Joaquin.
46 The Missouri.
47 The Thames.
48 The Darling.
49 The Mekong.
50 The Charles.

Current Affairs (170-171)

1 Intifada.
2 The African National Congress.
3 Ronald Reagan.
4 Anwar Sadat.
5 Willy Brandt.
6 Nigeria.
7 Pinochet.
8 Algeria.
9 The nationalization of the Suez Canal.
10 Kenneth Kaunda.
11 Workers protested against the Soviet presence and the Russians moved into the capital with tanks.

12 The Viet Cong.
13 Jawaharlal Nehru.
14 Camp David Accords.
15 Memphis, Tennessee.
16 Uganda.
17 Challenger.
18 A terrorist bombing in a Berlin nightclub.
19 Maastricht.
20 In November 1989.
21 New York.
22 France, Germany, Italy, Belgium, The Netherlands, and Luxembourg.
23 Nicolae Ceaucescu.
24 Richard Nixon.
25 Bhopal in Central India.
26 Margaret Thatcher.
27 Organization of Petroleum Exporting Countries.
28 Nikita Khrushchev.
29 The Six Day War.
30 Slovenia and Croatia.
31 1949.
32 Mikhail Gorbachev.
33 The Khmer Rouge.
34 1979.
35 The Bay of Pigs.
36 Christiaan Barnard.
37 Cyprus.
38 To limit antiballistic missiles and nuclear missile systems in the USA and USSR.
39 Ayatollah Khomeini.
40 The policy of restructuring the Soviet economy and bureaucracy during the 1980s.
41 The United Nations.
42 Chinese Communist forces.
43 Lech Walesa.
44 Robert Mugabe.
45 Haile Selassie of Ethiopia.
46 François Mitterrand.
47 1973.
48 The Warsaw Pact.
49 The Prague Spring.
50 Archbishop Makarios III.

Quotations (172-173)

1 Dorothy Parker.
2 Abraham Lincoln.
3 A.L. Rowse.
4 Adam Smith.
5 Henry Ford.
6 Joseph Stalin.
7 Croesus.
8 Mickey Rooney.
9 John Knox.
10 Robert Louis Stevenson.
11 Winnie the Pooh.
12 F. Scott Fitzgerald.
13 Ernest Hemingway.
14 John F. Kennedy.
15 Charles Dickens.
16 Izaak Walton.
17 Judy Garland.
18 Katharine Hepburn.
19 Hermann Goering.
20 Albert Schweitzer.
21 Mother Teresa.
22 Louisa May Alcott.
23 McCarthyism.

24 Adolf Hitler.
25 Oliver Reed.
26 John F. Kennedy of Richard Nixon.
27 Robert E. Lee.
28 Robert Graves.
29 Peter Ustinov.
30 'You're not a star until they can spell your name in Karachi.'
31 Napoleon Bonaparte.
32 Bostonians.
33 When they finish it.
34 Mark Antony.
35 L.P. Hartley.
36 Lawrence Durrell.
37 Stephen Leacock.
38 Samuel Pepys.
39 'Thou Paradise of exiles, Italy!'
40 Philip Roth.
41 Phineas T. Barnum.
42 Theft.
43 Quentin Crisp.
44 Raymond Chandler.
45 Venice.
46 Gore Vidal.
47 Viscount Montgomery.
48 Virgil.
49 D.H. Lawrence.
50 Voltaire.

Space (174-175)

1 Mercury, Venus, Earth, Mars, Jupiter, Saturn, Uranus, Neptune, Pluto.
2 Phobos and Deimos.
3 Pluto.
4 A regular shower of meteors appearing to emanate from Eta Persei between July 25 and August 17.
5 On the Moon.
6 (b) Sea of Mysteries.
7 Unicorn.
8 1957.
9 Yuri Gagarin.
10 Valentina Tereshkova.
11 The first space walk was carried out.
12 It was the first international space mission with the USA.
13 It exploded on the launch pad but the crew were unharmed.
14 Helen Sharman.
15 It was a chimpanzee.
16 Alan Shepard.
17 Scott Glenn.
18 The Ring Nebula.
19 A reusable US space vehicle.
20 November 1982.
21 The Crab Nebula.
22 To fly by Halley's Comet.
23 Mariner 2.
24 Vikings 1 and 2.
25 There was a flaw in the light-gathering mirror.
26 Spiral.
27 3,476 km (2160 miles).
28 A faint band of light sometimes seen just after sunset or before sunrise, extending up from the horizon at the Sun's setting or rising point.
29 Carbon dioxide.
30 Quasars.

31 A stream of ionized hydrogen and helium that radiates outward from the Sun.
32 A luminous display of various forms and colours in the night sky.
33 The Aurora Borealis and the Aurora Australis.
34 It is when the Moon blocks the Sun's light from some area on the Earth.
35 It is the great circle on the celestial sphere that lies in the plane of the Earth's orbit.
36 A star that is abnormally faint for its white-hot temperature.
37 A star of great size and brightness that has a relatively low surface temperature.
38 A giant, red, double, and variable star.
39 Andromeda.
40 In the Northern Hemisphere, near Andromeda and Auriga.
41 Orion.
42 Any of various very large bright stars, such as Betelgeuse or Rigel, having a luminosity that is thousands of times greater than that of the Sun.
43 An immense body of highly rarified gas and dust in the interstellar spaces of galaxies.
44 An extremely small region of space-time with a gravitational field so intense that nothing can escape, not even light.
45 A hypothetical hole in outer space from which energy, stars, and other celestial matter emerge or explode.
46 Material that is believed to make up more than 90% of the mass of the universe but is not readily visible because it neither emits nor reflects electromegnetic radiation, such as light or radio signals.
47 A galaxy made up of antimatter.
48 The assemblage of all galaxies.
49 In the Northern Hemisphere, between Lacerta and Perseus and south of Cassiopeia.
50 Two irregular galaxies that are the nearest extragalactic objects.

Words (176-177)

1 (a) Eastern prince.
2 (c) sooty.
3 (b) defamation.
4 (c) gourd.
5 (a) pregnant.
6 (b) part of a church.
7 (c) sickness.
8 (a) opera text.
9 (b) howling.
10 (c) flower ovary.
11 (b) hat.
12 (b) hidden.
13 (c) humped.
14 (b) flash.
15 (b) temporary ban.
16 (a) blink.
17 (b) artificial body part.
18 (b) deputy.
19 (b) marsh.
20 (c) cell division.
21 (b) bombastic.

22	(c) scaly.	37	Yasir Arafat.
23	(a) gewgaw.	38	Cape Canaveral.
24	(b) tearful.	39	Tariq Aziz.
25	(c) describe.	40	The Christian Democratic Party.
26	(b) powerless.	41	Gdansk.
27	(a) ring-shaped.	42	1961.
28	(b) frenzied.	43	Rainbow Warrior.
29	(c) fabric.	44	Kurt Waldheim.
30	(a) fibre.	45	Pierre Trudeau.
31	(a) change shape.	46	Jacques Delors.
32	(c) dim.	47	Ytzhak Shamir.
33	(a) uninteresting.	48	Herald of Free Enterprise.
34	(b) imperfectly formed.	49	1973.
35	(b) yaws.	50	Strasbourg.
36	(a) spirochetes.		
37	(b) metallic element.		
38	(b) burn suddenly.		
39	(a) wandering.		
40	(b) tax.		
41	(a) style of music.		
42	(b) wheelbarrow.		
43	(a) piddock.		
44	(b) asking.		
45	(a) tallness.		
46	(a) heifer.		
47	(b) to constrain.		
48	(b) flower part.		
49	(a) everywhere.		
50	(a) canto.		

Current Affairs (178-179)

1 The Red Brigades.
2 Golda Meir.
3 Mother Teresa.
4 Joseph McCarthy.
5 Mujahedin.
6 Sharpeville, a suburb of Johannesburg.
7 F.W. de Klerk.
8 Jimmy Carter.
9 UNITA.
10 Sinai.
11 In a plane crash which was thought to be sabotage.
12 Aleksandr Solzhenitsyn.
13 COMECON.
14 Jean-Bedel Bokassa.
15 The Bader-Meinhof gang.
16 Ayatollah Khomeini.
17 Chaim Weizmann.
18 The Congress Party.
19 Eduard Shevardnadze.
20 Election fraud.
21 George VI.
22 Chief Mangosuthu Buthelezi.
23 Norman Schwarzkopf.
24 Chiang Kai-Shek.
25 Nicaragua.
26 A major oil-spill off the coast of Alaska in 1989.
27 1985.
28 BSE.
29 Jomo Kenyatta.
30 Georges Pompidou.
31 Internment.
32 The Basque Country in northern Spain.
33 The Likud Party.
34 1956.
35 Mohammed Ali Jinnah.
36 Dwight Eisenhower.

Islands (180-181)

1 Greenland.
2 Sardinia.
3 Madagascar.
4 The Isle of Wight.
5 The Isle of Man.
6 Formosa.
7 Corfu.
8 Sicily.
9 Hainan.
10 The Malvinas.
11 The Cyclades.
12 Sri Lanka.
13 Cyprus.
14 The Bahamas.
15 Manila.
16 Coney island.
17 Christmas Island.
18 Napoleon Bonaparte.
19 The Revelation of Saint John.
20 Cuba.
21 The Channel Islands.
22 Denmark. Copenhagen.
23 Sicily.
24 Corsica.
25 The Crimea.
26 Taiwan.
27 Borneo.
28 The Andaman Islands (and Nicobar Islands).
29 The Philippines.
30 Sri Lanka.
31 Cyprus.
32 The Seychelles.
33 South America.
34 Long Island.
35 Hawaii.
36 No, not quite.
37 Papua.
38 The Sandwich Islands.
39 An archipelago.
40 The Ryukyu islands.
41 The Gulf of Alaska.
42 Bahrain.
43 The Dominican Republic.
44 Port au Prince.
45 Hispaniola.
46 Haiti and Cuba.
47 It was used as a military base.
48 No. 8.
49 Fuerteventura.
50 The USA and the UK.

People (182-183)

1 Leda.
2 Achilles.
3 Taiwan.
4 Lawrence of Arabia.
5 Lord Palmerston.
6 Commissioner Nayland Smith.
7 The marathon.
8 John Milton.
9 Holden Caulfield.
10 Bismark.
11 Beria.
12 Boudicca.
13 Neptune.
14 Pontius Pilate.
15 Toulouse Lautrec.
16 Pablo Picasso.
17 A Perfect Day for Bananafish.
18 Franny.
19 Sanjay. All the others were assassinated. Sanjay died in a plane crash.
20 Polyphemus.
21 Loki.
22 Sita.
23 Dr Zhivago.
24 Horsa.
25 Napier.
26 Konrad Adenauer.
27 Elhanan.
28 He was the only person known from forensic evidence to have been crucified.
29 He was one of the great clowns of all time.
30 Cary Grant.
31 Fred Astaire and Ginger Rogers.
32 Bernardo Bertolucci.
33 Alfred Nobel.
34 Harvey Firestone.
35 Don Quixote.
36 Marco Polo.
37 Captain Webb.
38 The trap failed to work three times and in the end Lee's sentence was commuted to life imprisonment.
39 Ivan Denisovitch.
40 Confucius.
41 Mahatma Gandhi.
42 Akhenaton (Amenhotep IV).
43 Lord Byron.
44 Claudius.
45 Elizabeth I of England.
46 Prince Albert.
47 In a barrel of brandy.
48 Narcissus.
49 The gorgons.
50 Charlotte Corday.

Pot Luck (184-185)

1 A googol googols.
2 They are both called Eta.
3 The Earl of Shaftesbury.
4 It lies inside an enormous extinct volcanic crater.
5 The Euphrates.
6 South-west townships.
7 Singing in the Rain.
8 'I'm looking for loopholes.'

9   Lord Haw Haw.
10 The Common Market.
11 President Nasser.
12 The Knesset.
13 China.
14 A protein in fibrous connective tissue.
15 'Abandon all hope, you who enter here!'
16 Lao-tzu.
17 It was the world's first printed book.
18 They were the only British kings since William the Conqueror not to have been crowned.
19 Boudicca.
20 None. It is a story told of Caligula with no historical basis.
21 To make bricks without straw.
22 The mummification of corpses.
23 Seppuku.
24 The sackbut.
25 Bradford, Yorkshire.
26 Richard Dadd.
27 Evariste Galois.
28 Rastafarians.
29 No; it's a petrol bomb.
30 The tomb of Tutankhamen.
31 He set fire to the Reichstag.
32 Joseph Stalin.
33 Prosperous landed peasants in Czarist Russia.
34 The surrender of Robert E. Lee to Ulysses S. Grant.
35 Parsses.
36 The Spanish Armada.
37 He occupied the British Falkland Islands but was heavily defeated in the ensuing war.
38 Buddha.
39 *The Pillow Book of Sei Shonagon.*
40 Teddy Roosevelt.
41 Peru.
42 West Germany.
43 Octavian defeated Mark Antony.
44 John Wilkes.
45 Admiral Byng's.
46 They cannot bark.
47 Sepia.
48 A traditional Japanese poem having a fixed form of 5-7-5 syllables.
49 The ludicrous misuse of a word, especially by confusion with one of a similar sound.
50 Luigi Pirandello.

Classical Music (186-187)

1   Singspiel.
2   Four.
3   Maurice Ravel.
4   *Prince Igor.*
5   Ludwig van Beethoven.
6   Hungarian.
7   The violin.
8   Abdelazar by Henry Purcell.
9   *Sheherezade* by Rimsky-Korsakov.
10 Beethoven's Ninth Symphony.
11 Nine.
12 Felix Mendelssohn-Bartholdy.
13 Oratorio.
14 Viola da gamba.
15 Johannes Brahms.

16 *Peer Gynt Suite No.1.*
17 12.
18 Ludwig von Koechel.
19 Anton Schoenberg.
20 Bedrich Smetana.
21 The oboe family.
22 Four.
23 La Scala in Milan.
24 Joseph Haydn.
25 An interval is the simultaneous sounding of two pitches; a chord requires three or more pitches.
26 Felt hammers.
27 *Carmina Burana.*
28 *Fingal's Cave*
29 An octave.
30 The incidental music to *A Midsummer Night's Dream.*
31 Mikhail Glinka.
32 Claude Debussy.
33 The violin.
34 *Die Meistersinger von Nürnberg.*
35 The piano.
36 Aleksandr Borodin.
37 Soprano.
38 Very.
39 It has no slow movement.
40 Poland.
41 The guitar.
42 Richard Strauss.
43 Mezzo-soprano.
44 'Emperor'.
45 A stately court dance of the 17th and 18th centuries.
46 Jean Sibelius.
47 Falstaff, Otello, and Macbeth.
48 The 'Tragic'.
49 The violin.
50 A brass instrument similar in range to the tuba.

Wars & Battles (188-189)

1   France.
2   Austria.
3   The Austro-Russian army.
4   Lexington and Concord.
5   Russia and China.
6   The English Civil War.
7   The predominance of Protestantism and Catholicism.
8   The Unionists.
9   The English Channel and the North Sea.
10 Axis.
11 Germany, Austria-Hungary, and Turkey.
12 Bull Run, on the Potomac river.
13 1917.
14 Erwin Rommel.
15 The abdication of czar Nicholas II.
16 1954.
17 1961.
18 The Mensheviks.
19 George B. McClellan.
20 1805
21 Louis XVI.
22 The Treaty of Paris.
23 In Yorktown.
24 Gettysburg.
25 World War I.
26 Sinai.

27 Rolling Thunder.
28 The Tet Offensive.
29 The Boer War.
30 Albania.
31 Otto von Bismarck.
32 To drive the foreign community out of China.
33 The Second Punic War.
34 Ulysses S. Grant.
35 Britain, France, and Spain.
36 The Russians.
37 The Thirty Years' War.
38 Appomattox in Virginia.
39 John II.
40 Dunkirk.
41 The Yom Kippur War.
42 The Battle of the Somme in 1916.
43 Manchuria and Korea.
44 In 1905 The day became known as Bloody Sunday.
45 1899–1902.
46 To drive Turkey out of Europe.
47 Carthage.
48 The Hundred Years' War.
49 Gallipoli.
50 Agincourt

Books (190-191)

1   Jane Austen.
2   Alexander the Great.
3   It was the longest novel in the English language.
4   Flay the butler.
5   Bertie Wooster.
6   Thomas Pynchon.
7   It was named after a flamboyant character in *Barnaby Rudge.*
8   *The Misfortunes of Virtue.*
9   *Animal Farm.*
10 *A Passage to India.*
11 Aldous Huxley's.
12 Her diary.
13 The Bible.
14 H. Rider Haggard.
15 *The Iliad.*
16 *A la recherche du temps perdu.*
17 Robert Graves.
18 Israel.
19 *The Grapes of Wrath.*
20 Count Dracula.
21 Quasimodo.
22 Eric Blair (George Orwell).
23 C.P. Snow.
24 e e cummins.
25 *Scaramouche.*
26 *Foucault's Pendulum.*
27 Hal.
28 Anthony Burgess.
29 A giant.
30 Hans Christian Andersen.
31 Richard Hannay.
32 Dr Pangloss.
33 *A Vindication of the Rights of Woman.*
34 Earl Stanley Gardner.
35 Jeeves.
36 '...thy father lies; of his bones are coral made...'
37 Huckleberry Finn.
38 Simon Legree.

39 Mr Micawber.
40 The Billion Dollar Brain.
41 *A Midsummer Night's Dream*.
42 Mercutio in Romeo and Juliet.
43 Richard III.
44 'The owl, for all his feathers, was a-cold...'
45 Mrs Danvers.
46 *Ulysses*.
47 Johnny Vulcan.
48 Puddenhead Wilson.
49 Herman Hesse.
50 Tess of the D'Urbevilles.

Crime & Punishment (192-193)

1 Imprisoning people by their ankles.
2 The structure from which criminals were hanged.
3 They were sent overseas as a punishment, often to Australia.
4 An instrument of torture on which people were stretched.
5 He was hanged, drawn, and quartered.
6 Yes.
7 A human-shaped box with spikes on the inside. The victim was shut in it and impaled.
8 The cat o' nine tails was a type of whip. It was much used on ships and was kept in a sack when not in use.
9 She was beheaded.
10 They tried to hang him three times and the equipment would not work. His sentence was commuted to life imprisonment.
11 They were 'pressed' by being placed under a wooden board on which weights were piled.
12 Suspected witches were tied to it and ducked in water. If they sank they were regarded as innocent.
13 Witchfinder General.
14 Women who sat knitting beside the guillotine.
15 He was hanged.
16 The Inquisition.
17 A notoriously tough US prison.
18 The Richardsons.
19 Tax evasion.
20 Bonnie Parker and Clyde Barrow.
21 An instrument of torture for crushing the fingers.
22 He was shot by a Native American policeman.
23 Colonel Blood.
24 The murder of Sharon Tate.
25 The murder of her parents.
26 Dr Crippen.
27 Ian Brady and Myra Hindley.
28 A leather strap formerly used to punish Scottish schoolchildren.
29 Treason.
30 Sweeney Todd.
31 Prometheus.
32 Dragging a condemned man under the keel of a ship.
33 Walking the plank.

34 Sharia.
35 China.
36 Japan.
37 Russia.
38 His ear was cut off.
39 It involved financial ruin because they cost so much to keep.
40 By machine gun.
41 USA.
42 A system of prison camps used in the USSR mainly for the detention of political prisoners.
43 Only one.
44 Spartacus.
45 A punishment in which the victim was hung by the arms.
46 Beating the soles of the feet (especially done in Turkey).
47 Corrupting the youth of Athens.
48 Sisyphus.
49 Trial by ordeal.
50 It was a women's prison.

Classical Music (194-195)

1 The chromatic scale.
2 Felix Mendelssohn-Bartholdy.
3 Neumes.
4 Cello and orchestra.
5 *The Ruins of Athens*.
6 Zoltan Kodály.
7 His technical studies for the piano.
8 Aram Khachaturian; it is part of the ballet *Gayane*.
9 In Beethoven's *Pastoral Symphony*.
10 The cello.
11 'The Clock'.
12 Lohengrin, who was Parsifal's son.
13 Richard Addinsell.
14 B-flat or A.
15 Hungary.
16 Georges Bizet.
17 Sergei Prokofiev.
18 Fermata.
19 The organ.
20 Claudio Monteverdi.
21 A keyboard instrument, mainly the organ.
22 Baritone.
23 Violins.
24 To decrease in tempo.
25 Joaquin Rodrigo.
26 The oboe.
27 *Lulu*.
28 *Suite Bergamasque* by Debussy.
29 *The Sorcerer's Apprentice*.
30 'Little Russian'.
31 Soprano.
32 Brazilian.
33 Nicolai Rimsky-Korsakov.
34 *Turandot*.
35 Sir Thomas Beecham.
36 He developed a system of teaching music to children by the use of percussion instruments.
37 Pietro Mascagni.
38 Modulation.
39 Tenor.
40 Nicolai Rimsky-Korsakov and Aleksandr Glazunov.
41 Eugene Ormandy.

42 Frédéric Chopin.
43 Christoph Willibald von Gluck.
44 Tablature.
45 The piano.
46 Edvard Grieg.
47 An old French dance.
48 His masses, of which he wrote 105.
49 Franz Liszt.
50 Antonio Vivaldi.

Science (196-197)

1 It has no fixed shape.
2 Oestrogen.
3 The quark.
4 An electron.
5 Neon.
6 Gunpowder.
7 Nitroglycerine.
8 Angina pectoris.
9 The solar plexus.
10 The appendix.
11 Pollen.
12 It decreases.
13 An isobar.
14 Meteorology.
15 Stratocumulus.
16 The bends.
17 A bathysphere.
18 Lignin.
19 Sclerosis.
20 Symbiosis.
21 It represents absolute zero.
22 Entropy.
23 Sir Isaac Newton.
24 Edmund Halley.
25 Calculus.
26 A gastrolith.
27 Galileo Galilei.
28 Copernicus.
29 Ptolemy.
30 William Crookes.
31 Humphrey Davy.
32 Gatling.
33 The invention of photographic processes.
34 Thomas Edison.
35 Sir Joseph Swan.
36 Samuel Colt.
37 Charles Goodyear.
38 Two men, each called William Seward Burroughs, were responsible for them.
39 The Chinese.
40 AD 1278.
41 The thermos flask.
42 The production of explosives.
43 Proteins.
44 The sabre-toothed tiger.
45 Oxygen.
46 A deficiency in the amount of oxygen reaching body tissues.
47 An insecticide.
48 Ethyl alcohol containing no more than 1% water.
49 Heroin.
50 Ganglion.

World War II (198-199)

1 Poland.

2 Anschluss.
3 Joseph Stalin.
4 Lightning war.
5 Guderian.
6 Appeasement.
7 U-boats.
8 SS Athenia.
9 USSR.
10 September 3 1939.
11 Finland.
12 May 10 1940.
13 Dunkirk.
14 The Battle of Britain.
15 The USA.
16 About 300,000.
17 The USSR.
18 Georgi Zhukov.
19 Admiral Yamamoto.
20 Doodlebug.
21 Vichy.
22 General de Gaulle.
23 Benito Mussolini.
24 North Africa.
25 Werner von Braun.
26 It stood for Vergeltungswaffen (Vengeance Weapons).
27 It was an anti-tank weapon.
28 Katyusha (Katie).
29 A German multi-barreled rocket launcher.
30 The rocket traveled faster than sound so it was heard only after it had exploded.
31 ASDIC and SONAR.
32 Depth charges.
33 It prevented ships from setting off magnetic mines.
34 Operation Barbarossa.
35 Leningrad.
36 It was the main type of Russian battle tank.
37 The Russian winter.
38 No.
39 The bombing of Pearl Harbor by the Japanese.
40 Wolf packs.
41 Admiral Doenitz.
42 Goering.
43 The Afrikacorps.
44 A yellow Star of David.
45 The black market.
46 Extermination of the Jews.
47 Jean Moulin.
48 Paulus.
49 Surrender.
50 Operation Overlord.

Books (200-201)

1 Hawkeye and La Longe Carabine.
2 *The Golden Ass.*
3 *Watership Down.*
4 *Something Wicked This Way Comes.*
5 *Kingdom of the Wicked.*
6 Truman Capote.
7 *A Dance to the Music of Time.*
8 *The British Museum is Falling Down.*
9 *Elmer Gantry.*
10 *Les Liaisons Dangereuses.*
11 John le Carré.
12 Malcolm Bradbury wrote *Eating People is Wrong.*

13 *Brighton Rock.*
14 *The Great Gatsby.*
15 Sally Bowles.
16 Laurie Lee.
17 James Hogg.
18 Carrie.
19 Britain, Poland, and Germany.
20 Dorothy L. Sayers.
21 Ben Okri.
22 Joseph Campbell.
23 *The Black Arrow.*
24 *The Alexandria Quartet.*
25 The Indian Mutiny.
26 He was touring manager to the actor Henry Irving.
27 *A Brief History of Time.*
28 *The Black Cloud* by Fred Hoyle.
29 Milan Kundera.
30 *The Graduate* by Charles Webb.
31 *The Name of the Rose.*
32 With Love and Squalor.
33 *The Collector.*
34 *Project for a Revolution in New York* by Allain Robbe-Grillet.
35 Desmond Morris.
36 Jules Verne.
37 Spinoza.
38 Sir Thomas More.
39 *The Life of Benvenuto Cellini.*
40 Lake Woebegon.
41 *Flowers for Algernon.*
42 Eric Berne.
43 *I, Robot.*
44 Triffids.
45 Ancient Evenings.
46 *The King and I.*
47 *The Mandarins.*
48 *The Quiet American.*
49 Charles Darwin.
50 John Milton, *Paradise Lost.*

Pot Luck (202-203)

1 Orion.
2 The Pythian Games.
3 Indonesia's.
4 A scale-covered anteater.
5 The Battle of Poitiers.
6 The won.
7 Aaron Copland.
8 Vientiane.
9 Adolfo Suarez Gonsales.
10 Ferdinand Porsche.
11 The eardrum.
12 Aldosterone.
13 He was a philologist.
14 A branch of linguistics that investigates the origin and development of words.
15 New Year.
16 A large mongoose.
17 A verso.
18 Buttercup.
19 Alan Parker.
20 The cretaceous.
21 Chile.
22 Ulysses S. Grant.
23 Gioacchino Rossini.
24 The Carolingians.
25 *Pinocchio.*
26 Lech Walesa.

27 Carrara.
28 The stethoscope.
29 A mixture of water droplets and ice.
30 Polio.
31 Ken Boothe.
32 The Neckar.
33 Nikos Kazantzakis.
34 Friedrich Ebert.
35 Protons.
36 The decibel.
37 The kidneys.
38 In the Indian Ocean between the east African coast and Madagascar.
39 Jeremy Irons.
40 Gustave Courbet.
41 El Niño.
42 Angelo Badalamenti.
43 Nicaragua and Honduras.
44 Mainly dead skin cells.
45 Sirocco.
46 The Nevado del Ruiz in Colombia.
47 By eating raw or undercooked meat, especially pork.
48 Baku.
49 Robert Zemeckis.
50 The first Crusade.

Places (203-204)

1 Jaffa.
2 The Strait of Magellan.
3 Between Ireland and Wales.
4 The Arabian Sea.
5 Oder.
6 Ecuador.
7 The Denmark Strait.
8 Montevideo.
9 The St. Lawrence.
10 Hinduism.
11 Hungary.
12 Antarctica.
13 Peru.
14 The Andes.
15 The Vistula.
16 Sweden.
17 Somalia.
18 The Dodecanese.
19 The Tyrrhenian Sea.
20 Minnesota.
21 Oahu.
22 The Kalahari.
23 The Isles of Scilly.
24 The Caspian Sea.
25 Austria and Italy.
26 Luanda.
27 Crete.
28 The Dead Sea.
29 The Barents Sea, part of the Arctic Ocean.
30 New York.
31 Belgium.
32 Mongolia and north China.
33 The Garonne.
34 Denmark.
35 The Timor Sea.
36 Brasilia.
37 Minsk.
38 The Bering Strait.
39 In the Himalayas.
40 Porcelain.

41 Brazil, Bolivia, and Argentina.
42 Lake Ontario and Lake Erie.
43 Ohio.
44 The Aconcagua.
45 Ghana.
46 Botswana.
47 Cuba.
48 Vatican City.
49 Mozambique.
50 Marrakesh.

Quotations (206-207)

1 Linus in Peanuts.
2 Charles de Gaulle.
3 Abraham Lincoln.
4 'I will make a bargain with the Republicans. If they will stop telling lies about Democrats, we will stop telling the truth about them.'
5 Garrison Keillor.
6 Neville Chamberlain.
7 Cecil Rhodes.
8 Fidel Castro.
9 'You can't separate peace from freedom because no one can be at peace unless he has his freedom.'
10 Atticus Finch in To Kill a Mockingbird.
11 Fart and chew gum (later cleaned up by his aides to 'walk and chew gum').
12 Niccolo Machiavelli.
13 'It takes a lot of time to be a genius; you have to sit around so much doing nothing, really doing nothing.'
14 Sharon Stone.
15 'The most brutal, ugly, desperate, vicious form of expression it has been my misfortune to hear.'
16 George Bernard Shaw.
17 'A narcissist is someone better looking than you are.'
18 Ringo Starr.
19 Mae West.
20 Nelson Mandela.
21 Otto von Bismarck.
22 'Doctor Diet, Doctor Quiet, and Doctor Merryman.'
23 'Fidelity, perseverance, and to turn around three times before lying down.'
24 Kirk Douglas.
25 Alexander Dubcek.
26 The Duke of Wellington.
27 Alexandre Dumas.
28 Emily Brontë.
29 Eleanor Roosevelt.
30 Mary Queen of Scots.
31 Albert Einstein.
32 Robert Burns.
33 Dale Carnegie.
34 Oliver Hardy.
35 Stephen Sondheim.
36 'Me Tarzan, you Jane.'
37 On the playing fields of Eton.
38 Walt Whitman.
39 Bertie Wooster.
40 'J'accuse.'
41 Frank Zappa.
42 Frankenstein's monster.
43 John Keats.
44 Lord Alfred Douglas (intimate of Oscar Wilde).
45 Bob Dylan.
46 'Farewell my friends... I go to glory.'
47 John Wilkes Booth, having shot President Lincoln.
48 Rudyard Kipling.
49 Socrates.
50 Old age.

Popular Music & Musicals (208-209)

1 'Wuthering Heights'.
2 Jim Morrison.
3 Wings.
4 Leonard Bernstein.
5 'Penny Lane'.
6 'Waterloo'.
7 Glenn Miller.
8 A Night at the Opera.
9 Louis Armstrong.
10 'The Entertainer'.
11 'Mr Tambourine Man'.
12 Brothers in Arms.
13 Cats.
14 'Holiday'.
15 Tom Jones.
16 1977.
17 UB40 with Chrissie Hynde.
18 Andrew Lloyd Webber.
19 Annie Lennox.
20 'Mrs Robinson'.
21 Bob Dylan.
22 'What a Feeling'.
23 Oliver!
24 Rumours.
25 Gilbert and Sullivan.
26 Peter Gabriel.
27 'Love Me Do'.
28 Cole Porter.
29 'Bohemian Rhapsody'.
30 Woody Guthrie.
31 Annie Get Your Gun.
32 Sting.
33 Yul Brynner.
34 Buddy Holly.
35 'You Give Love a Bad Name'.
36 Shirley Bassey.
37 Reggae.
38 Mike Oldfield.
39 Harry Belafonte.
40 U2.
41 'The House of the Rising Sun'.
42 Marc Bolan.
43 Phantom of the Opera.
44 Edith Piaf.
45 'Your Song'.
46 Frederick Loewe.
47 Mick Jagger and David Bowie.
48 The Rocky Horror Picture Show.
49 Bono.
50 The Who.

World Religions (210-211)

1 Castes.
2 Mohammed.
3 The Torah.
4 Buddha.
5 Hinduism and Islam.
6 Christianity, Judaism, and Islam.
7 The Eucharist.
8 The Protestants.
9 The Talmud.
10 The Koran.
11 Kaddish.
12 The Holy Synod.
13 Buddhism.
14 Bahia.
15 A priest, assisted by a deacon and a choir.
16 Ramadan.
17 Buddha.
18 The deacon.
19 Yom Kippur.
20 Five times.
21 Brahman.
22 Zen Buddhism.
23 The Reformation.
24 Seven.
25 The Reverend John Wesley.
26 Ultimately to unify all Christian Churches.
27 Mecca.
28 Vishnu.
29 Passover, or Pesach.
30 A riddle in the form of a paradox, used as an aid for meditation.
31 Pork.
32 Taoism.
33 The Latin rite of Rome.
34 Veda.
35 Zionism.
36 Sayings and anecdotes by Mohammed.
37 Lent.
38 No; in the Eastern Orthodox Church the date is calculated differently and usually falls at least one, often several, weeks afterwards.
39 The Evangelical and the Reformed Churches.
40 The liberation from the cycle of rebirth.
41 Nirvana.
42 Sunni.
43 Yathrib, which was later renamed Medina.
44 Hegira.
45 Ascension Day.
46 The Untouchables.
47 Pentecost (or Whitsun).
48 Shavuot.
49 6 January.
50 Shiites.

Books (212-213)

1 The Grapes of Wrath.
2 William Faulkner.
3 Thomas Hardy.
4 Grendel's dam.
5 Beulah.
6 Rob Roy.
7 The Decameron.
8 Ernest Hemingway.
9 The Good Soldier Schweik.
10 Dashiell Hammett.
11 Raymond Chandler.
12 The Passing of the Third Floor Back.
13 Metamorphosis by Franz Kafka.
14 John Updike.

15 Trilby.
16 The stories are anonymous.
17 Plato.
18 Goethe.
19 Racine.
20 *The Tales of Genji.*
21 *The Pillow Book of Sei Shonagon.*
22 Joseph Conrad.
23 *Quo Vadis* by Henryk Sienkiewicz.
24 Gogol.
25 *The Brothers Karamazov.*
26 Charles Baudelaire.
27 Ngaio Marsh.
28 *Portnoy's Complaint.*
29 *The Hitchhiker's Guide to the Galaxy.*
30 World War I.
31 Katherine Mansfield.
32 Helen Keller.
33 Harriet Beecher Stowe.
34 *The Ramayana.*
35 *The Water Margin.*
36 Belgian.
37 Barnaby Rudge.
38 Robert Louis Stevenson.
39 George Bernard Shaw.
40 Barbara Cartland.
41 Sir Arthur Conan Doyle in *A Study in Scarlet.*
42 Sax Rohmer.
43 Captain Ahab in *Moby Dick.*
44 Joseph Conrad in *Lord Jim.*
45 *Northanger Abbey* and *Persuasion.*
46 Tom Jones.
47 Vladimir Nabokov in *Lolita.*
48 Woody Allen.
49 Oscar Wilde in *The Portrait of Dorian Gray.*
50 Lafcadio Hearn.

Botany (214-215)

1 Hemlock.
2 *Umbelliferae* (also called the parsley family).
3 Poppies.
4 Foxglove.
5 They are all deadly poisonous.
6 Fly agaric, used for killing flies.
7 Mistletoe.
8 The root.
9 Alkaloids.
10 Herb of Grace.
11 Caraway.
12 Hives or nettle rash.
13 Strawberry.
14 *Quercus robur* is the English oak; *Quercus coccinea* is the Red oak of North America.
15 Its longevity. Many yews live to an age of 1,000 years.
16 Monkey puzzle.
17 Willows.
18 Silver birch.
19 Magnolia.
20 Persimmon.
21 Mulberry.
22 Juniper.
23 Mountain ash.
24 The leaves.
25 The stamen.

26 A group of flowers on the same stem.
27 The stigma.
28 Nectar.
29 Because pollen grains stick to the bodies of insects and are passed to other flowers as part of the process of pollination.
30 It emits a cloud of spores.
31 Lichen.
32 Air pollution.
33 Their water-filled leaves and stems.
34 The bodies of captured insects.
35 Oxygen.
36 No.
37 Scorpion grass.
38 They have pairs of wings which act rather like helicopters.
39 Saffron.
40 They trap light energy.
41 Old World orchids.
42 It encourages rapid cell growth.
43 Tropism.
44 Etiolation.
45 The plant turns to face the light.
46 Its leaves fold up when touched.
47 They are burned to produce fertilizer.
48 Dead plant and animal material.
49 The Venus Fly Trap.
50 Grasses.

Sport & Games (216-217)

1 Go.
2 The playing of a card in a suit in which one holds a non-sequential higher card.
3 A Japanese board game resembling chess.
4 The Pythian games.
5 A series of games of which two out of three, or three out of five, must be won to terminate the play.
6 A reference book of rules for card games and other indoor games.
7 A card game similar to pinochle that is played with a deck of 64 cards.
8 A game in which one group of players leaves a trail of paper scraps for another group to follow.
9 A Chinese betting game in which the players lay wagers on the number of counters that will remain when a hidden pile of them has been divided by four.
10 A game in which disks are slid with a pronged cue along a smooth, level surface towards one of two usually triangular targets painted on the surface and divided into numbered scoring areas.
11 Chess.
12 To swap pieces of two colours from one side of the board to the other in the least number of 'knight' moves.
13 Knocking on someone's front door and running away.
14 Hallowe'en.
15 Richard Krajicek.
16 The Tour de France.
17 Basketball.
18 Eighteen.
19 The main difference is that in fives the

players use their hands, rather than a racquet, to hit the ball.
20 Hurling.
21 Scotland.
22 He invented basketball.
23 India.
24 By moving pegs along a board full of holes.
25 Billiards.
26 The game was always popular on passenger ships.
27 True; although the words, originally a trade name, were meant to represent the sound the ball makes and were adopted by the Chinese as being easy to say.
28 Royal flush.
29 Uruguay.
30 India.
31 Spinning tops.
32 The Diabolo.
33 Bowls.
34 Boules.
35 Russian roulette.
36 Draughts/checkers.
37 A game that involves hitting a ball on a long piece of elastic with a wooden bat.
38 An event (especially, though not exclusively, in skiing) where the contestants weave in and out of a series of posts.
39 Bobsleigh.
40 (c) Basho; he was a Japanese poet.
41 Germany.
42 Pachinko.
43 Golf; it is used to make balls.
44 You drive it away by hitting your own ball when the two are in contact.
45 It is to hit another player's ball in croquet.
46 A shepherd's crook.
47 Polo.
48 A violent Afghan game in which mounted players struggle for possession of a headless calf.
49 A Polish woman.
50 Pele.

Popular Music & Musicals (218-219)

1 David Gilmour.
2 Frank Loesser.
3 Chick Corea.
4 Paul Simon.
5 The Weavers.
6 Harold Melvin and The Blue Notes.
7 *Street Fighting Years.*
8 *Carousel.*
9 Steeleye Span.
10 Sting.
11 George Fenton.
12 Montserrat Caballe.
13 Michael Jackson and Lionel Richie.
14 Cole Porter.
15 Dire Straits.
16 Saxophone.
17 Bryan Ferry.
18 *Showboat.*

19 'Mary Had a Little Lamb'.
20 'Abracadabra'.
21 Spike Hughes.
22 *Walls and Bridges*.
23 Diana Ross and Lionel Richie.
24 Kris Kristofferson.
25 *Jesus Christ Superstar*.
26 Chris de Burgh.
27 Brian Eno.
28 *Double Vision*.
29 The Bay City Rollers.
30 Herbie Hancock.
31 The Attractions.
32 The Mindbenders.
33 Django Reinhardt.
34 'Let's Twist Again'.
35 Trumpet.
36 A-HA.
37 The Beatles.
38 Bert Kaempfert.
39 *Salad Days*.
40 'Silver Machine'.
41 The Nashville Sound.
42 Stevie Wonder.
43 John Lee Hooker.
44 *Rupert the Bear*.
45 Jeff Beck.
46 Barry Gibb.
47 *Promises Promises*.
48 *Holiday Inn*.
49 Culture Club.
50 Christopher Cross.

Pot Luck (220-221)

1 Never despair.
2 District of Columbia.
3 Tropic of Cancer.
4 Anticlockwise.
5 Grass.
6 Nine-tenths.
7 The Marianas Trench.
8 Red dust blown up from the Sahara by the sirocco.
9 True. The Kerosene fungus (*Amorpotheca resinae*) can extract carbon from fuel and turn it into carbohydrate.
10 The smallest amount needed to kill a guinea pig weighing 250g (9oz) within four days.
11 Longsightedness.
12 The touch receptors on the tongue are 100 times denser than those on the back.
13 20%.
14 True.
15 1924.
16 New Zealand, in 1893.
17 The Maid of Zaragoza.
18 Colonel Blood.
19 Using the same letter or syllable several times in rapid succession (e.g., 'He is bearded, balding, but basically benevolent').
20 Dentine.
21 A reading desk.
22 Bronze – a mixture of copper and tin.
23 Because helium is much lighter than air.
24 The smallest part of any substance that can exist and yet still exhibit all the chemical properties of the substance.
25 Because the container of the vacuum gives off tiny traces of vapour which destroy the vacuum.
26 Because it combines with the haemoglobin in blood thus eliminating oxygen.
27 The main source of ore in a region.
28 A shrub of north-west North America, having white flowers and a dark purple, edible fruit.
29 A Native American food prepared from dried strips of meat pounded into a paste, mixed with fat and berries, and pressed into small cakes.
30 The honey bear.
31 Old Glory.
32 Oliver Cromwell.
33 Nibelung.
34 Brunhild.
35 Troika.
36 A large bus.
37 A frame slung between trailing poles and pulled by a dog or horse, formerly used by Plains Indians as a conveyance for goods and belongings.
38 Adolf Hitler.
39 He was martyred.
40 Lambarene.
41 The Dalai Lama.
42 One of a pair of metal supports used for holding up logs in a fireplace.
43 A surgical instrument having circular, saw-like edges, used to cut out disks of bone, usually from the skull.
44 Above the troposphere and below the mesosphere.
45 A proof taken from composed type to allow for the correction of errors.
46 The last car on a freight train, having kitchen and sleeping facilities for the train crew.
47 John Calvin.
48 He advocated higher education for women and endowed Vassar College.
49 He was a candle maker.
50 Thomas Mann.

Gotcha! (222-223)

1 You thought Salome? No, she is not actually named in the Bible, the story comes from the ancient historian Josephus.
2 None of them was more than 5 ft tall.
3 Both members of a mating pair are hermaphrodite.
4 They did not rust.
5 Over 25,000.
6 It took place after he was dead.
7 Listening to 'The Lone Ranger' on the radio.
8 Joan of Arc.
9 The Boston Strangler.
10 Chattanooga, Tennessee.
11 Oregon.
12 Seventy.
13 Elhanan (II Samuel 21:19).
14 His body was stolen from the grave and held to ransom.
15 The Moon. Li Po was drunk and, while trying to kiss the reflection of the Moon, fell into the water and drowned.
16 They were all reported dead while still alive.
17 Nylon.
18 They all studied for holy orders.
19 An apple.
20 They were all believers in astrology.
21 They were Green, Berry, and Hill.
22 They all played American Football.
23 Every 12 days.
24 'Peccavi', which in Latin means 'I have sinned'.
25 Charlie Chaplin.
26 She was one of three very short actors who played ET in scenes when a puppet was not used.
27 A dislike of punctuation.
28 They all went bankrupt at some stage in their careers.
29 They each had a sexual relationship with Aristotle Onassis.
30 They all committed incest.
31 The first ever kiss in an Indian film.
32 They were all married.
34 They each wrote one novel.
35 An old Persian measure of length.
36 Wear it: it is a man's short cloak.
37 Probably spend it: it is a reward.
38 A rehoboam.
39 A stew of green indian corn, beans and, if you're lucky, pork.
40 Throw it: it is a stick for throwing.
41 Continual means 'continuing but with interruptions'; continuous means 'continuing without interruption'.
42 They both had affairs at a very early age.
43 They were both created by someone called Edgar.
44 They were all left-handed.
45 They all went over the Niagara Falls in a barrel.
46 A pretty girl.
47 They all started out as trademarks.
48 They were all noted cat lovers.
49 Abnormal sensitivity to pain.
50 An alloy of copper with tin or zinc, used to imitate gold.